# ALVA VANDERBILT BELMONT

# ALVA VANDERBILT BELMONT

*Unlikely Champion of Women's Rights*

SYLVIA D. HOFFERT

INDIANA UNIVERSITY PRESS
*Bloomington & Indianapolis*

This book is a publication of

Indiana University Press
601 North Morton Street
Bloomington, Indiana 47404-3797 USA

iupress.indiana.edu

*Telephone orders* 800-842-6796
*Fax orders* 812-855-7931



∞ The paper used in this publication meets the minimum requirements of the American National Standard for Information Sciences—Permanence of Paper for Printed Library Materials, ANSI Z39.48–1992.

Manufactured in the United States of America

Library of Congress Cataloging-in-Publication Data

Hoffert, Sylvia D.
Alva Vanderbilt Belmont : unlikely champion of women's rights / Sylvia D. Hoffert.
p. cm.
Includes bibliographical references and index.
ISBN 978-0-253-35661-1 (cloth : alk. paper) — ISBN 978-0-253-00560-1 (electronic book)
1. Belmont, Alva, 1853–1933. 2. Belmont, Alva, 1853–1933—Political and social views. 3. Feminists—United States—Biography. 4. Suffragists—United States—Biography. 5. Women political activists—United States—Biography. 6. Women—Suffrage—United States—History—20th century. 7. Women's rights—United States—History—20th century. 8. Socialites—New York (State)—New York—Biography. 9. Rich people—New York (State)—New York—Biography. I. Title.
HQ1413.B44H64 2012
305.42092—dc23
[B]

2011024056

1 2 3 4 5 17 16 15 14 13 12

# CONTENTS

# ACKNOWLEDGMENTS

IT IS A PLEASURE TO THANK those without whose help this book would never have been written and published. Like feminist reform movements, no book project can flourish without financial support. I would like to thank the College of Arts and Sciences at the University of North Carolina–Chapel Hill, the College of Liberal Arts at Texas A&M University, the Melbern G. Glasscock Center for Humanities Research at Texas A&M University, the History Department at Texas A&M University, and the Institute for Advanced Studies in the Humanities at the University of Edinburgh, Scotland, for theirs. Laura Micheletti Puaca and Art Lindeman provided invaluable help as my research assistants in the early stages of this project. I am deeply indebted to Sarah Hutcheon and the archivists at the Schlesinger Library at Harvard University for their assistance in accessing the documents in their collections. Paul Miller and John Tschirch of the Preservation Society of Newport County in Rhode Island and the archivists in the Special Collections Library at Duke University were both welcoming and helpful. My thanks also goes to Nancy Cott for inviting me to participate in the 2007 Schlesinger Library Summer Seminar in Gender History, "Writing Past Lives: Biography as History," and to the participants who provided thoughtful critiques of an early draft of one of my chapters. Peter Filene, my former colleague at UNC, read the entire manuscript in one of its earlier versions and provided invaluable help in revising it. Rebecca Schloss, Kate Engel, Cynthia Bouton, and April Hatfield read and commented upon all of my chapters. Ruth Crocker, Robyn Muncy, Laurie Maffly-Kipp, Kathleen McCarthy, Nancy Robertson, Wendy Gamber, and Theda Perdue offered me encouragement when I was much in need of it. Leon Fink, editor of *Labor,* graciously gave me permission to republish material taken from my article "Private Secretaries in Early Twentieth-Century America." The Huntington Library, the Schlesinger Library, the Regional Oral History Office at the Bancroft Library, the Rare Book, Manuscript and Special Collections Library at Duke, and the Preservation Society of Newport County gave me permission to quote from their documents. I am grateful to Bob Sloan, his staff, and the readers at Indiana University Press for their help. And finally, I thank my family, whose love and support have nurtured and sustained me for so many years.

*Sylvia D. Hoffert*
*Chapel Hill, North Carolina*

# INTRODUCTION

ALVA SMITH VANDERBILT BELMONT, a wealthy New York socialite and militant woman's rights advocate, was born in Mobile, Alabama, in 1853. But it took a lifetime for her to become what she was. The process of self-making that she engaged in was a complex and collaborative one that took place in constantly changing contexts. The stories she told about herself reflected that reality. As literary scholar John Paul Eakin has pointed out, such stories are a product of our ability to imaginatively use historical fact, memory, and circumstance to respond to our particular needs in a specific moment in time.[1] Thus, Belmont's understanding of herself was always fragmentary and to some degree fictive.

The story she told about herself and the stories others told about her are compelling and dramatic. Among other things, she married a millionaire, divorced him, and married a second. She forced her daughter to marry the most eligible aristocrat in Europe. After her second husband's death, she embraced the cause of woman's rights and then joined the National Woman's Party (NWP), which represented the most militant wing of the movement. It was largely her money that paid for both its suffrage and equal rights campaigns. She was not its only donor but she was certainly its most generous one.

The sources that document who she was and what she did provide the opportunity to explore the ways that lives are constructed and to relate that process of construction to the writing of autobiography and biography. Because self-making is rarely transparent, it presents a challenge to biographers, demanding that they work with layers of narrative texts created by a great number of people telling their stories in widely divergent contexts and at various periods in time.

Biographers must deal with what their subjects say about themselves as well as what others said of them. From those sources, biographers must shape their own narrative, one that arises not only from their research and life experiences but also from the personal relationships that they have formed with the people they are writing about.[2] In that sense, all biographies are in part autobiographies. Or as literary critic Paul Murray Kendall put it, "On the trail of another . . . the biographer must put up with finding himself at every turn."[3]

Belmont's financial support was crucial to the success of the suffrage and equal rights movements. But her contributions, like those of many philanthropists, came with strings attached. The result is that Belmont's story complicates our understanding of the interpersonal dynamics that characterized the American woman's rights movement in the early twentieth century and the strategic choices that militant feminists made as they carried out their various campaigns.

It was Belmont's financial support of the NWP that initially piqued my interest in her. Why, I asked, would a socially prominent, immensely wealthy woman in her mid-fifties, who had a vested interest in preserving the status quo and had shown no previous concern about the obvious social, economic, and political inequities that plagued the United States in the early twentieth century, suddenly become a feminist? Why did she donate money to the most militant wing of the woman's rights movement? And what were the consequences when she did?

Belmont was strong-willed, domineering, and determined to be the center of attention. What impact, I wondered, might identifying the tensions that resulted from her presence, how they manifested themselves, and the strategies that were used to resolve them have on our understanding and assessment of the woman's rights movement? And how might the master narrative of early twentieth-century feminism in America change if we placed at its center the story of someone who felt that she was bearing most of the burden for providing its leaders with enough financial support to carry out campaigns to promote suffrage and then equal rights?

In order to answer these questions, I structure my narrative of the life of Alva Belmont around an analysis of documents such as memoirs that are explicitly autobiographical as well as those with autobiographical dimensions such as court records, letters, and interviews written or dictated by those who, through their relationships with Belmont, participated in her self-making enterprise.[4] So this is as much a book about those who helped to "make" Belmont as it is about how Belmont made herself. Structuring my narrative in this manner allows me to highlight the complexity of her relationships with those who had the most influence on the way she portrayed herself. It also allows me to reflect upon the way in which the processes of self-making and the autobiographical documents describing those processes influence the writing of biography.

From the time she married in 1875, Belmont quite self-consciously attempted to position herself as a woman whose life was worthy of public notice. As Jo Burr Margadant has pointed out, "no one 'invents' a self apart from cultural notions available to them in a particular historical setting."[5] Alva defined her own womanhood and enhanced her newsworthiness by exploiting social, economic, and political fissures that allowed women ever-expanding opportunities for self-expression. In an effort to ensure that she received the attention that she craved, she solicited the cooperation of journalists who worked for large-circulation newspapers in New York City and elsewhere to turn herself into a social celebrity, thus guaranteeing that her name, that of her associates, and descriptions of their social and reform activities appeared regularly in the popular press.

What she discovered, of course, was that mercenary interest in selling newspapers often trumped truth telling (or telling the truth the way she wanted it told). She had no difficulty attracting the attention of the press, but she found it impossible to control what reporters had to say about her. One of her responses was to make an effort to tell her own story. So in 1917, she dictated a memoir to aspiring poet and social activist Sara Bard Field.[6] The manuscript that resulted described her life prior to her conversion to feminism and participation in the suffrage movement. Belmont must have found the process of remembering and self-revelation gratifying because two years later, she collaborated with Doris Stevens, a fellow suffragist acting as her secretary and companion, to produce an autobiographical account of her early involvement in the woman's rights movement. That short narrative took the form of an article.[7] Finally, sometime between 1928 and her death in 1933, she dictated yet another memoir to her then private secretary Mary Young. A much longer manuscript than the ones produced by either Field or Stevens, it expanded upon the topics she had previously decided would provide readers with an understanding of her character and an appreciation of her accomplishments.[8] It is clear that she originally intended to publish the first two manuscripts. Why she dictated the third is less obvious.

In each case, however, she tried to explain who she was, what she had done, and why she had done it. Belmont's conversion to feminism in 1909 had a profound impact on the content of her three memoirs. She apparently believed that her awareness of women's subordination was born in childhood. But it was not until she embraced the idea that something could actually be done to ensure that women had the same rights as men that she found a frame of reference for understanding the larger implications of women's inferior social, economic, legal, and social status. Expressing her feminist sympathies through political action first as a suffragist and then as an equal rights advocate served as an outlet for her pent-up anger and provided her with an opportunity to do something to challenge the control that men had over women's lives. Competitive to the core, she used the lens of feminism to convince herself that her life had more meaning than those of other rich women.

As her amanuenses listened to her reminisce, they took notes and then transcribed what they had written in order to produce a coherent narrative from their conversations with her. In doing so, each of them played an active role in shaping Belmont's story. Since it was up to them to interpret her words, Belmont gave them the opportunity to become something more than the ciphers she intended them to be. This is not to say that they consciously tried to distort her narrative. It is merely to suggest that they could not help but filter Belmont's testimony through their own values, political concerns, and personal experiences, thus making themselves a part of Belmont's story. Because they did so, the memoir manuscripts that they produced are both biographical in content and have unintended and unacknowledged autobiographical components. Field was more self-conscious and candid about her role as mediator than either Stevens or Young and, as we shall see, was quite frank about the ways in which she attempted to shape Belmont's reminiscences.[9] The result was that she framed the story she heard from Belmont into a narrative chronicling an emerging feminist awareness. Like Field, Stevens and Young actively shaped Belmont's story by telling it from their own perspectives. The difference is that we have to extrapolate from other evidence what their perspective was and how it influenced what they wrote. The challenge, then, is to untangle the complexities produced by the unwillingness or inability of Belmont to write her own memoir and to determine what the resulting manuscripts tell us about Belmont, her secretaries, and how their relationships shaped both her life story and the course of woman's rights activism.

After Belmont died, her ability to influence how her story was told ended, and others stepped into the breach. Shortly after Belmont's funeral, Stevens gave a deposition as the first step in her effort to file a claim against the Belmont estate. In it she described the time she spent with Alva, the work she did for her, and her feelings about the time they spent together. This 205-page document is as much a memoir as the three autobiographical essays dictated by Belmont.[10] Because its content is self-serving, it must be used with care. Nevertheless, its autobiographical component provides another perspective on how the interaction of two individuals helped to make both who they were and what they became.

Belmont's daughter, Consuelo Vanderbilt Balsan, the former Duchess of Marlborough, published her own memoir, *The Glitter and the Gold,* in 1952. In that book, Belmont emerged as the central figure in a domestic drama that was as tragic as it was compelling. When she published her autobiography, Consuelo was seventy-five years old and her mother had been dead for almost twenty years. But time had not diminished Consuelo's vivid memories of a childhood and adolescence spent under Alva's watchful eye. Incorporated into Consuelo's life story is a scathing diatribe against the woman who bore her, a dramatic depiction of their dysfunctional relationship, and a description of their eventual reconciliation.[11]

In the late 1950s, scholars working for the Regional Oral History Office at the University of California–Berkeley began producing an oral history of the woman's rights movement. The first person they interviewed was Field. By the early 1970s Alice Paul, the NWP's leader and a woman who worked closely with Alva for many years, had agreed to participate in the program. By granting interviews, both of these women engaged in autobiographical enterprises intended to preserve a permanent and public record of their accomplishments. Each had something to say about Belmont, but despite their dependence on her financial support, neither considered her an important figure in their lives or central to the work that they had been engaged in.[12]

Despite her efforts to leave a public record and thus guarantee that she would be remembered for her woman's rights activism, Alva remained invisible as a historical figure until 1976 when a graduate student at San Jose State University chose her as the subject for a master's thesis. For the next twenty-five years or so, historians-in-training outlined the story of her life, chronicled her many accomplishments, and tried to make a place for her in the annals of woman's rights history. Professional historians were not quick to follow their lead. Those who have written about the suffrage and equal rights movements have acknowledged her participation and financial contributions to both campaigns. But beyond that, they have not given her a central place in the movement that dominated her life and drained her purse for over twenty years.[13]

All of those involved in making Belmont available for public consumption had a stake in the process. Belmont's self-absorption compelled her to do whatever it took to draw attention to herself. Society editors exploited her social celebrity to fill their columns and thereby further their careers. By virtue of the expectation that Belmont's secretaries also serve as her companion, they too were deeply involved with her personally, benefited from the advantages and physical comfort that living with her provided them, and acquired the money that she paid them to support themselves. However they felt about her personally, feminist co-workers in the NWP needed to express a certain degree of deference toward her in order to ensure that she would continue to support their work. Consuelo presented her mother in such a way as to convince herself once and for all that she was free of her control. By diminishing Belmont's importance to the woman's rights movement, Field and Paul enhanced their own. And graduate students exploited Alva's story as a way to fulfill their degree requirements.

What is striking about the picture that they collectively produced of Belmont is how consistent it was. Belmont described herself as an imperious, energetic, and accomplished individual who craved the attention of others and always insisted on getting her own way. Those who wrote about her pictured her the same way. At the same time, however, the portraits they constructed were highly individualized. It is as if, through their collective efforts, Belmont was transformed into the brightly colored crystals inside a kaleidoscope. Those crystals at rest and refracted through the lens form a coherent pattern. But as the kaleidoscope is passed from one hand to another, the crystals are rearranged. And in their reordering, they form a familiar but entirely new design. It is my job as Alva Smith Vanderbilt Belmont's biographer to make sense of it all while at the same time acknowledging that once I begin constructing her story, she will yet again be transformed by my rearrangement of the crystals.

Belmont seemed to have intuitively understood that even as she engaged in the process of self-fashioning in order to explain herself to others, she was revealing only partial truths about herself. As Harvard psychologist Steven Pinker has put it, "None of us know what made us what we are, and when we have to say something [about the subject], we make up a good story."[14] For Belmont, engaging in an autobiographical project was not just a matter of self-awareness or even self-preservation; it was also an expression of her feminist sensibilities. It was within that frame of reference that she acknowledged her inability to be entirely forthcoming about herself. In a conversation with Field, she apparently said that she felt inhibited by the realization that men had traditionally used their patriarchal power to silence and distort women's voices. "So much that women say is not the truth of their souls. They say things men have taught them it is becoming and fitting a woman to say," she observed. She claimed to understand the importance of expressing what she really thought rather than saying what she assumed others expected her to think or say. But she was also aware that she was a product of her time and place. She was determined to challenge male power and privilege, but in 1917 she was still experimenting with the methods that seemed best suited to fulfill her goals. She was outraged at having been publicly humiliated by her first husband's extramarital affairs. But she was just as upset about the snubbing she received from her friends and acquaintances when she had the gumption to divorce him. It made her painfully aware that women did not always support each other even when it would have appeared in their interest to do so. She took away from that experience a sense of the way that her gender and social background inhibited her ability to say what she wanted to say, particularly when it concerned relationships between men and women. "I know I am not now in these pages revealing all that is essentially myself," she said. "I know I am consciously holding back much and probably unconsciously distorting the truth of much that is written. The world is not ready for the whole truth not even from man and much less from woman, and we women are new at the business of self revellation [*sic*]," she confessed.[15] What she had to say, she warned her potential readers, could not be considered true but rather a somewhat tarnished representation of the truth.[16] So, just as Pinker suggested, she made up a good story full of what she believed to be true combined with lies, exaggerations, misrememberings, and imaginings. The same can be said of those who wrote about her and their relationship with her. They all filtered her story through their memories and experiences to produce a version of the past that they hoped would be remembered as they, rather than others, told it.

So let us proceed to the representations of the truth that Belmont and her contemporaries left for us. Let us see how Belmont made herself and how they contributed to that process. What follows is a story of Belmont's life that begins with her birth, chronicles her role in the woman's rights movement, and ends with a discussion of how others constructed her life story after she died. Imbedded in the chronicle are layered narrative texts in which the boundaries between memoir, autobiography, biography, and oral history blur and the authority of the storytellers is contested, negotiated, and renegotiated as they go about the process of presenting their versions of the truth.[17]

# ALVA VANDERBILT BELMONT

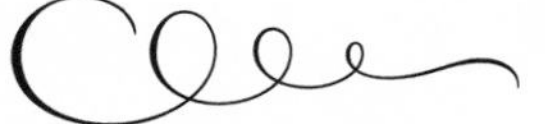

# 1 An Impossible Child

ALVA DESCRIBED HERSELF AS "an impossible child" when she dictated her memoir to her private secretary, Sara Bard Field, in the summer of 1917.[1] Some fifteen years later, she claimed that she "was probably the worst child that ever lived" in yet another attempt to tell the story of her life.[2] Those who wish to leave a portrait of themselves for posterity are not usually so self-critical, but there was nothing typical about Alva. Given the evidence she provided to illustrate her point, it seems clear that she was proud of her unwillingness to behave herself and her determination to do as she pleased despite the predictable consequences. Her reputation as a holy terror meant that she got a great deal of attention. But that attention was not necessarily accompanied by the affection she craved. She spent her whole life searching for some way to reconcile her willfulness with her desire for love and friendship.

The middle child in a family of five children, Alva was born into an affluent slaveholding family in the seaport town of Mobile, Alabama, on January 17, 1853.[3] Her father, Murray Forbes Smith, grew up in Virginia and trained as a lawyer. Born in 1823, her mother, Phoebe Ann, was the daughter of Robert Desha, a cotton planter and politician whose family was originally from Kentucky.[4] He served as a member of the Tennessee delegation to the U.S. House of Representatives from 1827 to 1831. During that time, he became involved in the political controversy surrounding the virtue of Margaret Timberlake Eaton, the wife of Andrew Jackson's secretary of war. The experience must have soured him on politics. He decided not to run for reelection in 1830, left Washington, and moved his family to Mobile, Alabama, where he established a business buying and selling cotton.[5]

Mobile was a boomtown by the 1850s. Located thirty miles from the Gulf of Mexico on the shimmering waters of Mobile Bay, it served as a commercial outlet for Alabama planters.[6] It was, said Hiram Fuller, "a pleasant city of some thirty-thousand inhabitants—where people live in cotton houses and ride in cotton carriages. They buy cotton, sell cotton, eat cotton, drink cotton, and dream cotton. They marry cotton wives, and unto them are born cotton children. In enumerating the charms of a fair widow, they begin by saying she makes so many bales of cotton."[7] A foreign visitor fascinated by what he saw, Fuller could not resist the temptation to engage in a bit of hyperbole. But he was essentially correct. Most of the inhabitants of Mobile were in one way or another associated with commercial services needed to sell and transport cotton.

When her parents married in 1840, Alva's father gave up his law practice in Virginia and moved to Mobile where he joined his father-in-law in the cotton business.[8] His success in selling and transporting cotton enabled him to live in a two-story, stone house with a crenulated roof and substantial-looking Tudor arches over the front porch. Located on the corner of Government and Conception Streets, it stood in the most fashionable part of the city.[9] Its spacious rooms were bright and airy, with big windows and high ceilings. Its lawn, dotted with magnolia trees and well-tended flower gardens, provided the space for his children to play. Attached to the back of the house were screened-in porches, one on each floor, designed to protect the home's inhabitants from Mobile's bothersome insect population and the sweltering heat of the summer sun. A luxurious bathhouse tiled in marble sat in the backyard. Alva lived in this home until she was about six.[10]

Alva explained her rebelliousness and refusal to conform to the expectations of others as a result of having been born into a family populated by individuals who, in her words, "would stand neither for oppression nor even dictation."[11] She claimed that her mother's forebears had been French Huguenots from La Rochelle who fled religious persecution after the revocation of the Edict of Nantes in 1685. They eventually found safe haven in Pennsylvania and then in the slave-holding South.[12]

Her paternal great-grandmother, Margaret Stirling, was equally determined to thwart efforts to dictate how she lived her life. Her aunt, Jean Stirling, the wife of James Erskine, Lord Alva and Barjarg, reared Margaret after her mother died. Much to the consternation of her guardians, Margaret met and fell in love with Dr. Murray Forbes of Edinburgh, a respectable man but certainly not the sort they expected her to marry. When she refused to give him up, her family disowned her. The couple fled Scotland and eventually settled in Virginia.[13] It was from the likes of these that Alva claimed to have learned to appreciate the value of personal liberty and the costs of claiming it.

If, as she alleged, stories of her forebears encouraged her to insist on doing as she pleased, experiences in her childhood sensitized her to the subordination of women and convinced her that misbehaving was an effective way to get what she wanted. One of her earliest memories was the death of her thirteen-year-old brother, Murray Forbes Jr., in November 1857.[14] Apparently, he had been their father's favorite. When friends came to offer their condolences, she heard them say to her mother, "Your husband will never recover from this blow. No one can take this child's place with him." Alva, who was four at the time, remembered being filled with "hot resentment" at the thought of her father's indifference to her. She simply could not believe that "a dead son [was] worth more than a live daughter."[15] That incident served as her introduction to male privilege and the patriarchal social system that supported it. She, quite literally, never got over it.

She clearly believed that the story was important. She included it in her first autobiography written in 1917 and again years later in the memoir she dictated to her private secretary before her death. Indeed, the story had both profound implications and extraordinary explanatory power in the sense that it provided her audience with a partial but plausible explanation for why the campaign for woman's rights had such appeal to her. Who could quarrel with the idea that a little girl's heart was broken when she realized that her gender denied her the love of her father?

What is striking about Alva's account of her brother's death is that it is in spirit, if not in the exact words, the same story that Elizabeth Cady Stanton told in her memoir published in 1898. When Stanton was eleven, her elder brother died. He was, as she put it, "the pride of my father's heart." Her father was inconsolable. "Pale and immovable" as he grieved at his son's bier, he seemed oblivious to her desire to provide him comfort. She stood for a long time watching him and then climbed into his lap. "He mechanically put his arm about me and, with my head resting against his beating heart, we both sat in silence," Stanton wrote. "At length he heaved a deep sigh and said: 'Oh daughter, I wish you were a boy!'" Stanton could not become the boy her father wished for, but she was determined to become as much like a boy as possible. She learned to ride horses and excelled in her schoolwork. But her father's only response to her academic and athletic accomplishments was to add insult to injury by observing again that she should have been born a boy. She admitted that thereafter her "sorrow" over her discovery "that a girl weighed less in the scale of being than a boy" was always on her mind.[16]

It seems inconceivable that Belmont and Stanton responded to virtually the same childhood experience in exactly the same way. It is more likely that Alva read Stanton's memoir or heard some version of the story once she began associating with women who had been involved in the early woman's rights movement. But there is absolutely no evidence to suggest that she was even aware of Stanton's story let alone that she used it to frame her own narrative. What is important here is that, like Stanton, Alva used the tale to give credibility to her claim that she was predisposed to sympathize with those who were concerned about the gender inequities that characterized American society and that she needed only to find herself in circumstances that would encourage her to act upon those sympathies before she became a woman's rights convert.

Alva claimed that following the death of her brother, she became extremely sensitive about the devaluation of girls. Indeed, once she discovered that boys had more freedom to express themselves than girls, she refused to have anything to do with the daughters of her mother's friends and did what she could to avoid participating in their activities.[17] She resented the fact that her swimming suit, which had long sleeves and covered her from neck to ankles, weighed her down and inhibited her movements and that she was forbidden to ride horses around the stable yard because it was considered too dangerous.[18] It soon became obvious to her, as she put it, that women and girls were expected to "play the part of spectators in the theatre of life while men and boys have the vivid action." "There was a static quality to a girl's life, a monotony and restriction in it from which I rebelled from the very first," she said.[19]

Rejecting what she called a girl's "hot house" existence, she claimed to have played only with boys so that she could enjoy the physical activities and independence that characterized their lives.[20] She rode her pony Dobin wherever she chose, sometimes to the beach, sometimes to the woods.[21] And with childish oblivion to the danger that was involved, she and her playmates rolled down the steep grassy slopes that led to the rocky beach in Newport, Rhode Island. As an adult she acknowledged that only "the inscrutable law of Chance" prevented them from dashing their brains out.[22]

Determined to do anything that was necessary in order to preserve the prerogative of enjoying the "freedom from excessive restraint" with which she felt that boys were blessed, she asked for no special treatment from them.[23] "I met them on their own ground," she said. "I gave blow for blow. I accepted any challenge. I stopped at nothing attempted."[24] But she sometimes had to defend her right to participate in their activities. Take the case of Pepe del Vallay, who came to visit her playmate Fernando Yznaga in Newport one summer. When Pepe expressed distaste for playing with a girl, he infuriated her but she took no action. One day, however, after she had scrambled up an apple tree, Pepe removed the ladder that she had used to reach its high branches. And when she began to climb down, he pelted her with apples. Dodging the fruit, she claims to have come "down that tree like a monkey." By the time she was on the ground, she was livid. Oblivious to her bleeding hands and skinned knees, she ran after the fleeing Pepe, threw him down, choked him, and stomped on him, all the while screaming, "'I'll show you what girls can do.'" She recalled that spectators stopped the fight and that she was temporarily excommunicated from polite society for her efforts. But well into her sixties, she continued to be proud of having defended her right to play with the boys.[25]

Not surprisingly, Alva was the bane of her mother's existence. "The combination of rebellion and daring were difficult for her to meet," she admitted.[26] As the mistress of a house filled with slaves and children, Phoebe was in charge of discipline. According to Alva, she relied on "wise and simple reasoning" when it was possible but resorted to corporeal punishment when she thought her children or servants deserved it. Alva maintained that while her mother found it necessary to punish her often, the whippings she administered were always "delivered in love not anger."[27] Family lore maintained that one year she received a whipping every day. But neither corporeal punishment nor the threat of it proved an effective deterrent. "I knew it would be the inevitable consequence of my actions just as death is the inevitable result of life," she confessed. She considered the punishment she received both deserved and unavoidable but found that the joy she experienced doing what she wished more than made up for the whippings, unpleasant and painful as they must have been.[28] So anticipating and accepting "the storm and chastisement" that were the inevitable consequences of her willfulness, she simply wore her mother down. Behavior, once proscribed and often repeated, eventually went unnoticed.[29] In retrospect she came to believe that "there was a force in me that seemed to compel me to do what I wanted to do regardless of what might happen afterwards."[30] As an adult, the conviction that rebellion and victimization were inextricably intertwined prepared her to accept the consequences of rejecting or thwarting social convention when it suited her interests to do so. Her mantra seems to have been "I will do what I please, I will be punished, I will persevere, I will triumph."

Alva's determination to dominate those around her also exhibited itself at an early age. The fact that she was living in a slave-owning society only encouraged her in that regard. On Sundays in Mobile, for example, she remembered watching out the library window in great anticipation for her godmother to drive up to the house to pick her up for dinner. When the liveried coachman pulled the barouche up to her godmother's house, Alva found a small group of slave children waiting for her in the drive. She remembered spending the rest of the day "tyrannizing" them. She denied that she physically harmed them, but she recalled being very "conscious of [her] superiority" and contemptuous of their apparent willingness to submit to her mistreatment. That being the case, she "lost no chance to assert [her] masterful position."[31]

When Alva was about six, her family moved to New York City.[32] It is unclear why her father abandoned his business and stately home in Alabama to move north. The panic of 1857 may have undermined his credit. Increasing sectional tensions may have forced him to choose between regional loyalty and commercial opportunity. There is also evidence to suggest that her mother was unhappy living in Mobile. Phoebe reputedly had social ambitions and spent vast amounts of money regularly hosting lavish entertainments. But for some reason those whom she hoped to impress remained aloof. According to one gossip, "Some people ate Mrs. Smith's suppers, many did not. There was needless and ungracious comment, and one swift writer pasquinaded her social ambition in a pamphlet for 'private' circulation."[33] Subjected to public humiliation, Phoebe may have been more than willing to find another milieu for her efforts to establish herself as a leader of society.

Whatever the couple's motivation for moving, Murray Smith's choice of New York was a calculated one. New York had long provided southern cotton merchants with credit, insurance, transportation, and marketing services. But the nature of the trade between New York and Mobile had gradually changed over the years. Originally cotton traders had sent their heavy, burlap-wrapped cotton bales to New York for transshipment to markets in New England, Liverpool, or Le Havre. By 1859, they had begun to cut costs by shipping their cotton directly to their customers. Still dependent on New York for financial services, however, they shipped samples of their cotton and bills of lading to agents in New York.[34] Alva's father had every reason to believe that his knowledge, experience, and connections would help to ensure his success in this lucrative business.

The change of scene may have improved her parents' prospects, but it did nothing to improve Alva's behavior. When it became clear to Phoebe that the nursemaids could not handle Alva, she assigned one of the family slaves to entertain her daughter and keep her out of trouble. His strategy for getting her to do what she was supposed to do was to bribe her by treating her to a trip to the market and then to the stables before he escorted her to school. He was, Alva recalled, "the first one who ever tried through any other means than the rod to direct my imperious rebellions." She claimed, however, that his success in controlling her depended upon her willingness to obey. In essence, she pictured herself as managing him instead of the other way around. When she was with Monroe, she said, she got what she wanted. "I bossed him," she confessed. "It was a case of absolute control on my part."[35]

When she could not stop someone from restricting her activities, she simply devised strategies to neutralize their efforts. Take the case of one of her governesses. As far as Alva was concerned, the woman's chief purpose in life was "to thwart the things I most wanted to do." For example, the governess was willing to allow her to play on the beach, but she would not let her swim in the ocean. "One day [the governess] was sitting on a wooden bench in a new silk dress the folds of which were spread out all about her," Alva remembered. Determined to jump into the waves as they crashed ashore, Alva persuaded some of her friends to distract the governess by dancing and whooping loudly while she and the others went behind the unsuspecting woman. With tacks in hand, they attached the skirt of the governess's dress to the bench so that she would be in no position to stop them when it became apparent that they were headed for the water. "The governess tried to rise and detain us but she was held fast and every move she made endangered the precious new silk dress. These were the lawless ways in which I got results," she confessed.[36]

Contempt for authority also manifested itself in her relations with her piano teacher. While she loved to draw, she claims to have loathed her music lessons. She remembered having an Italian music teacher who took umbrage at her unwillingness to practice. One day, in complete frustration, he took her fingers in his hands and pressed them onto the correct keys. She turned around and without hesitation slapped him in the face and then rushed out of the room declaring that she would never take another music lesson. Her embarrassed mother no doubt punished her. But her piano lessons stopped.[37]

And then there came the day when Alva decided that she no longer wanted to sleep in the nursery. When through "argument, persuasion, and attempted arbitration" she failed to convince her mother to allow her a room of her own, she decided to be so "hateful and disagreeable" that the nursemaid and governess would eventually insist that she be removed. She took a bath towel and "with awful deliberateness" smashed all of the little china figurines on the mantel of the nursery. Then with "cool but vicious strength," she attacked the framed picture above them. She may have received a memorable whipping for her destructiveness. But she emerged triumphant. Just as she had anticipated, she was banished from the nursery and allowed to sleep by herself.[38]

All of these childhood experiences fed Alva's sense of power and entitlement. By the time she was an adult, she had a reputation for being bossy and domineering, characteristics that did not endear her to friends and associates. But she claimed that her willingness to deal with the consequences of thwarting social convention gave her the courage to do so.

Despite their southern background, the Smith family remained in New York during the Civil War. It must have been difficult for them. Alva's father had no compunction about slaveholding.[39] In 1850 he owned nine slaves—three women, two men, and four children, whose ages ranged from one to fifty-five.[40] It is unclear how many of them he took with him to New York City or exactly what their status was when they got there. While New Yorkers were implicated in slavery by virtue of their economic interests, they did not condone the system. The legislature of New York abolished slavery in 1827. In 1841, it repealed a law that had allowed southerners visiting the state to keep their slaves for a period of nine months.[41] When the U.S. Supreme Court issued its decision in the Dred Scott case in 1857, New Yorkers were outraged at the suggestion that slaves' residence in free territory did not constitute the grounds for claiming their freedom and citizenship.[42] So as he made plans to move north, Alva's father must have realized that he could not reside in the state and treat those who had been his slaves in Alabama as if they were still in bondage. Apparently he accommodated New York law by keeping them as unpaid servants and providing them with room, board, clothing, and pin money. According to Alva, "Everything was given them, and if they by chance wanted something more, or any cash, they asked for it, and got it."[43]

Alva remembered hearing slavery discussed at the dinner table. Her father apparently sensed that the South's "peculiar institution" was doomed. If that proved to be the case, he believed that a gradual approach to emancipation was necessary in order to give slave owners time to adjust to a free labor system so they could maintain the productiveness of their land. Alva found it painful, she said, to see her father "torn between his convictions and his emotions."[44]

It was one thing to debate the issue of slavery in the privacy of one's home. It was something else altogether to be subjected to the moral judgment of one's minister every Sunday morning. The Smiths were Episcopalians and members of the Church of the Ascension in New

York City, which stood next door to their house. Their minister, the Rev. John Cotton Smith, apparently felt duty bound to give sermons berating the slaveholders in his congregation about the sin they were committing by owning and exploiting the labor of other human beings. Rather than sit in silence listening to his criticism, the Smiths joined other southern families in his congregation by withdrawing their membership in protest.[45]

Such behavior made them suspect. During the war they had to be careful not to attract attention to themselves, but there was little reason for them to be concerned about their safety. New Yorkers had strong commercial and financial ties to the South. Before the war began, the sale and shipment of southern cotton brought close to two hundred million dollars' worth of business into the city. Southern planters and cotton factors owed New York financial institutions about the same amount of money. New York newspapers had large subscription bases in the South. The city was a center for the illegal slave trade. And southern planters also had strong personal ties with New Yorkers. They vacationed with them in Saratoga Springs, and their daughters and sons married each other.[46] Moreover, as the war progressed, New York City became a refuge of sorts for southerners trying to escape the devastation of their homes and the problem of dealing with an increasingly unreliable labor force.[47]

Ambivalent about Abraham Lincoln, the Smiths became reluctant mourners when he was assassinated on April 15, 1865. Lincoln and his war effort did not have strong support among New Yorkers, but they were determined to pay him tribute. Out of respect, they lowered their flags to half-mast, closed their businesses, and placed black rosettes on the curtains of their windows. When his body arrived in the city, church bells tolled and military bands played funeral dirges.[48] So when the Smith family took no immediate public action to demonstrate their grief, Alva remembered that someone threatened to throw ink through their front windows. Phoebe responded sensibly by hanging three black bombazine bows on the front of their house.[49]

Realizing that it would be some time before he and other New Yorkers could establish normal trade and financial arrangements with their former southern customers, Alva's father began to feel that his position in New York was untenable. So he sold their Fifth Avenue house to Chicago entrepreneur Cyrus McCormick and moved his business to Liverpool and his family to Paris. Alva, her mother, and her sisters Armide, Jenny (Mary Virginia), and Julia lived in an apartment on the Champs-Élysées off and on for the next three years.[50]

When they arrived, they found a whole community of American expatriates living in Paris. The city attracted many visitors, some of whom stayed longer than they had originally intended. During the early years of the Second Empire, Louis Napoleon had begun transforming the city into a modern metropolis with wide boulevards and tree-lined avenues. New parks provided Paris's citizens with space for relaxation and entertainment.[51] The court of Napoleon III and Empress Eugenie was gay and inclusive. At court festivities that could include as many as five thousand guests, titled aristocrats hobnobbed with self-made men and foreigners, especially those with money and marriageable daughters. Eugenie spoke English and enjoyed Americans.[52] So Phoebe and her eldest daughter, Armide, were invited to receptions and parties where they met members of the French nobility as well as such notables as John Slidell, the former Confederate diplomat, and Marion Sims, the American gynecologist.[53] Alva was only twelve or thirteen when they arrived in Paris, so she had to watch from the sidelines while her elegantly dressed mother and older sister enjoyed themselves.

During their sojourn in Paris, Alva's mother absorbed the principles of French interior design and fashion established by the empress. Eugenie's approach to decorating was innovative. She upholstered her walls in silk and filled her private salon with bouquets of flowers. The living quarters of her palaces were elegant, as was befitting royalty, yet designed with comfort in mind.[54] She also established herself as a trendsetter in the area of women's fashion by introducing the cage crinoline in 1856. From then on, whatever Eugenie wore became popular among Parisian women who could afford to pay enormous sums for the elaborate Worth dresses that became her hallmark. Wealthy women in London and New York began ordering their clothes from Paris, thereby making adherence to French fashion one of the criteria for judging each other's social acceptability.[55]

Before her arrival in France, Alva had resisted attempts on the part of her parents to educate her. She was inquisitive and intelligent. Indeed, she claims that she was "crazy for knowledge."[56] But she found books too full of theories and abstractions to be of any interest, and she rebelled against the pedagogy of the day which demanded vast amounts of memorization.[57] She resented the fact that no one was willing to accommodate her individual learning style. "Education, instead of being fluid and poured into the mould of each individual was itself a mould into which all individuals were poured—especially in the case of girls—to be turned out exactly alike," she complained years later.[58] She found that interacting with real people was preferable to sitting at home doing her lessons and that what stimulated her intellect was "contact of mind with mind" and the "friction of thought" that conversation encouraged.[59] Adult dinnertime discussions engaged her imagination, and she thoroughly enjoyed taking notes on sermons delivered by Rev. Dr. Coahrelle, the minister at the French Protestant Church she attended. "The minister was a brilliant man," she noted, "and it gave me a particular thrill to feel myself getting his thoughts and recording them in orderly sequence."[60] Trips to Germany, Austria, France, and Italy made the world her school because it put her in contact with interesting people.[61] Travel seems to have satisfied both her hunger for knowledge and her appreciation of art, history, and geography.[62]

Sometime after her arrival in France, she asked her parents to send her to an expensive boarding school run by Mademoiselle Coulon located in a chateau with a beautiful garden surrounded by a high wall on the outskirts of Paris. Schools tend to be regimented institutions, and submitting to discipline was not Alva's strong suit. Most of the students at Coulon's school were French with a few English and American girls thrown in for good measure.[63] So Alva leveraged her Americanness into a license to behave as she wished. While other students were forced to eat whatever was put in front of them, she was allowed to leave her vegetables on her plate.[64] And while her classmates "lived by routine and rule; clock and bell," she made sure the rules did not apply to her. She remembered spending "hours in the top of a tree so high that none of the others could climb into it. The old gardener would stand below and plead with me to come down which I only did when I was self-persuaded."[65]

When she could not get attention by breaking the rules, she got it by causing a sensation. One evening a week, the students, carefully coiffed and dressed in their best clothes, appeared in the headmistress's drawing room to learn how to behave in polite society. Bored to tears by such exercises in deportment, Alva decided to do something to liven them up. She was the proud possessor of a head full of heavy, luxurious, dark-red hair. So one evening before she entered the room, she arranged it loosely. And when she appeared in the doorway of the headmistress's salon, she dramatically "let the whole great mass down and came in looking like the wife of the wild man from Borneo." Mademoiselle Coulon was not amused.[66]

It is not clear what the other students thought of her. She apparently made few attempts to befriend anyone other than two other American students, Minnie Stevens and Jessie Duncan.[67] Indeed, she was quite capable of making the lives of other students miserable. One day, for example, she found a fellow student from England crying because she had been assigned to present a report on Mary Queen of Scots and did not know how to do the research. Alva offered to help her. "Her misery ought to have nipped in the bud the practical joke which was forming in my mind, but it didn't," Alva later remembered. "As fast as the poor little English girl could write, I dictated the following amazing essay." The story that she dictated was as imaginative as it was ahistorical. And when her classmate read the essay before the other students and the headmistress the next day, they were astounded to hear that after Mary had embarked from France to claim her throne in Scotland "with a retinue of royal people in a galley decorated with flags and royal regalia," her ship sank in the fog off the coast of France and nothing further was heard of her. Alva remembered that when Mademoiselle Coulon heard that Mary had drowned before she had the opportunity to lose her head at the hand of her cousin Elizabeth I, an unforgettable "look of shocked dismay" spread over her face. Whereupon the headmistress stopped the recitation and lectured the poor English girl "for not reading history before she attempted to write it."[68]

Alva enjoyed her time at Coulon's school. Predictably she performed badly, so her teachers recommended that her parents remove her. She willingly admitted that she was learning nothing but French and that her parents were wasting a great deal of money by keeping her there. But she did not want to leave. After all, as she put it, "I had had my own way all the time. I was a law unto myself." So tearfully she returned home.[69]

Having rejected conventional attempts to educate her, she simply devised her own way of engaging in intellectual activity and eventually developed an approach to learning that depended as much upon lived experience as it did on reading books. Indeed, she maintained that her approach to educating herself had a profound impact on what she called her "inner life," setting the stage for her eventual emergence as a social reformer.[70]

By 1869, life in Paris, which had been so exciting and pleasant for most foreigners, was becoming increasingly difficult. Phoebe and her daughters had to have been aware that the cost of living was rising and the political situation was becoming more and more unstable. Those who opposed Louis Napoleon's regime had begun rioting in Bordeaux and Toulouse in 1868, and by 1869 political unrest had spread to the capital city. By June of that year, troops filled the streets of Paris in order to prevent working-class mobs from attacking the city's well-dressed, influential citizens. As the atmosphere became more and more menacing, foreigners began deserting the city in droves.[71] The Smiths were among them.

When the family returned to New York, Alva's father rented a house on 33rd Street, which her mother furnished tastefully in the Parisian style with furniture she had shipped from France.[72] Phoebe lived in that house for only two years. She died of inflammatory rheumatism on August 18, 1871, at the age of forty-eight.[73]

Alva was devastated by her mother's death. Having been dismissed by her father as inconsequential at the age of four, she spent her entire childhood and adolescence in perverse attempts to guarantee that she received the attention she thought she deserved from the only parent who seemed to care enough about her to discipline her. Despite the whippings she received on a regular basis from Phoebe, she claims to have cared for her mother deeply.[74] She was, she said, "the governing and controlling influence in my rebellious life."[75]

When she dictated her first memoir more than forty years after her mother's death, Alva still found it hard to describe her sense of loss. "When I try to tell what her death meant to me," she said, "I come up against a great blank wall of feeling for which there is no adequate expression.[76] She remembered thinking that she had lost her "best and truest friend."[77] But rather than succumbing to tears of grief, she claimed to have compensated for her sense of loss by writing daily missives "to some Great Person," an "Invisible Being" who took the form of her mother. She also decided to honor her mother's memory by taking up where her mother "left off" in order to "become what she would have me be." Toward that end, she initiated a campaign of self-improvement intended to instill in herself the sort of self-discipline that her mother had tried to teach her through entreaty, example, and, when necessary, punishment.[78]

Her mother's death may have been a personal tragedy for Alva, but it also had social implications that would affect her future. Just before her mother died, Alva's parents began the process of introducing her to society. But a death in the family meant that she could not attend parties until a year of mourning had been observed. So it was not until the fall of 1872 that Alva was free to attend theater and skating parties with other young people whose families, while not necessarily a part of the most exclusive social circles in the city, were certainly upwardly mobile and socially ambitious. Her closest friends were those she had met during summers in Newport or at school: Consuelo Yznaga, Minnie Stevens, and Jessie Duncan. But she also associated with young people from old New York families with names such as Cooper, Livingston, and Jay, all of whom had impeccable social credentials. Together they modeled their social activities on those of their parents. For the older crowd there was the Patriarchs Ball, sponsored by a prominent group of men who drew up a guest list that included members of the social elite. For the younger crowd, there was the New and Notables Ball held at Delmonico's restaurant.[79]

It was after her mother's death that she got to know William Kissam Vanderbilt, grandson of the fabulously wealthy Cornelius Vanderbilt.[80] The Vanderbilts had made their money in transportation. Cornelius, known as the Commodore, began his climb to fame and fortune by initiating a ferry service from Staten Island to Manhattan. He invested his profits from this venture in steamships and then in railroads. In 1869 he consolidated his holdings by forming the New York Central Railroad. Like Carnegie and Rockefeller, his business practices were often ethically questionable and sometimes dishonest. A brilliant businessman, he lived to make money and accumulated an immense fortune. By the time Alva met his grandson, the Commodore was worth an estimated $100 million.

It was a good thing that the Commodore took no interest in what people thought of him. Vulgar, uncharitable, and barely literate, he was not the sort to seek a position in New York society. He associated with whom he pleased without regard to their social position. Among those who sat at his dinner table were the disreputable Victoria Woodhull and her sister, Tennessee Claffin, a spiritualist whom Vanderbilt found charming and entertaining.[81] His children, of course, had their own social aspirations. And his grandchildren, properly schooled and well mannered, were a part of the fashionable set with whom Alva associated.

Born on Staten Island in 1849 and educated in the United States and Switzerland, William Kissam Vanderbilt began working for his grandfather's railroad when he was nineteen.[82] It is unclear where he met Alva or how much free time he had to spend with her. She invited him to her home for an informal reception on at least one occasion, but entertaining and maintaining the illusion of affluence became more and more difficult as her father's business began to fail.

According to Alva, Murray Smith was a man of the old school who believed "that no man was considered worthy to deal with who could not show credentials from his Business Career proving his integrity and trustworthiness."[83] He believed that a man's word was his bond and that a contract could be signed with a handshake. The result was that he was unable to adapt to the impersonal and ruthless business methods that laid the foundation for the accumulation of post–Civil War fortunes. He found himself living in a world where business was no longer conducted between men who knew and trusted each other. A world in which entrepreneurial businessmen watered the stock in their companies, reneged on their agreements, lied to their business partners, exploited their laborers, and cheated their customers was not a world he understood or had much sympathy with.

Those who, like Smith, refused to master what Alva called the art of "clever manipulation" found themselves unwilling or unable to compete.[84] Their businesses no longer flourished. It did not help, of course, that overspeculation in the construction of railroads and stock speculation at home and abroad plunged the country into a severe depression when on September 18, 1873, the investment bank run by Jay Cooke declared bankruptcy. What followed was a financial disaster. Railroad stocks plummeted, the New York Stock Exchange closed, and people crowded into banks to withdraw their deposits. When the government refused to intervene, the panic spread across the country. By midwinter in New York, hundreds of businesses had failed, the value of real estate had plummeted, and 25 percent of all workers had lost their jobs. Those who remained in the workforce saw their salaries decline and their prospects disappear.[85]

In the midst of such economic chaos, there was little Alva's father could do to protect himself from the financial embarrassment that would result in what appeared to be his impending business failure. The prospects of borrowing money to tide him over until the economy recovered were dim. So he moved his family to a cheaper house on 44th Street, encouraged them to economize, and joked about having to open a boarding house to make ends meet. He faced a grim future. He had four daughters with no marketable skills. Even if there were jobs to be had, they were in no position to contribute to the family's income or support themselves. It is not surprising that the stress of trying to keep up appearances began to affect his health.[86]

Murray Smith was from a generation who personalized the prospect of business failure. A man whose enterprising spirit and business success provided him with self-confidence, social status, and personal autonomy as well as the ability to provide for his family, he enjoyed the esteem of his contemporaries and assurance that he was fulfilling his manly responsibilities. Like other men of his day, he seems to have considered the prospect of insolvency to be the result of some personal inadequacy on his part rather than the result of economic factors beyond his control. His sense of impending failure and the loss of confidence in his manhood that typically accompanied it made it difficult for him to carry on.[87]

Whether to relieve himself of the need to feed his children for a few months or, as Alva remembered, because he wanted them to get to know their Virginia relatives, he sent them south in the summer of 1874 to visit his sister who lived near Culpepper, Virginia, located on the edge of the Blue Ridge Mountains halfway between Charlottesville and Washington, D.C. Before the Civil War, the Smiths of Virginia had prospered by growing long-staple cotton on the Sea Islands off the coast of Georgia. But the war and the loss of their slaves left them living in what can only be described as genteel poverty. Alva remembered that their spacious house looked shabby, the buildings on their property were in need of repair, and they seemed to have trouble convincing former slaves to engage in productive labor. Despite their reduced circumstances, they were determined to be as hospitable as their circumstances allowed and lavished their cousins with attention and vast amounts of food, which they apparently had in abundance.[88]

After spending time with her relatives, Alva traveled on to White Sulphur Springs, West Virginia, a resort community where southern families had built cottages before the Civil War so that they could enjoy the cool temperatures that the mountains provided. There she joined Lucy Oelrichs and Minnie Coster, friends from New York. Chaperoned by Lucy's mother who had southern connections, they stayed in what were by then quite dilapidated cabins and danced with young but clearly impoverished southern men at the Greenbrier Hotel. Lucy's beau, with William Kissam Vanderbilt in tow, came down to see them.[89]

Willie K., as he was known, proposed to Alva before they all returned to New York. The couple announced their engagement in the fall. On April 20, 1875, they married in Calvary Episcopal Church in New York City and then moved into a house on 44th Street given to them by William's father.[90]

There is no evidence that Alva married for love. But there is certainly reason to believe she married for money and social status. Her family may not have secured their claim to membership in the highest echelons of New York society, but they were on its periphery and ambitious.[91] And while Alva may not have appreciated precisely how bankruptcy might affect her material well-being and her family's future, it is clear that her father's anxiety about his declining fortunes made an impression on her and that she had no enthusiasm for living in poverty.

Alva may have been willing to admit that she was headstrong and domineering, but she was not willing to admit that she was a fortune hunter. When she told the story of her courtship and marriage, she preferred to assume the role of a self-sacrificing heroine. She claimed that her motive for marrying when she did was to save her family from the embarrassment and discomfort that was certain to accompany what they believed to be their impending destitution. Marrying into the Vanderbilt family, she said, was the only "practical" thing she could do under the circumstances.[92] Not only would it ensure that she would be able to take care of her as yet unmarried sisters, but it also would give her father, whose health was deteriorating rapidly, some peace of mind.[93]

As it turned out, she never had to assume responsibility for supporting the rest of her family. Two weeks after her wedding, her father died of a heart attack.[94] Whatever concern he may have had about the fate of his business, Murray Forbes Smith died a man of property who left his only son, Desha, $20,000 in cash and his four daughters the remaining proceeds from 1000 shares of Toledo, Peoria, and Warsaw Railroad stock estimated to have been worth $81 a share.[95] That sum invested wisely should have provided Alva and her sisters with an adequate income at least until they married. As it turned out, the only one who did not find a husband to support her was Armide. Jenny married Fernando Yznaga and then William Tiffany. Julia married the Comte de Fontenilliat.[96]

In an offhand remark made years later, Alva suggested that had her father died sooner, her whole life would have been different.[97] It is unclear what she meant by that statement. One possibility is that she came to believe that if she and her siblings had known of their inheritance before her wedding, she would not have married William Kissam Vanderbilt. But of course, by the time she made the comment, her first marriage had failed, she had divorced the father of her children, and she was still bitterly resentful of the punishment she was subjected to for having done so.

However she felt about her father's death, it smoothed the way for her integration into the Vanderbilt family. William H. Vanderbilt, her new father-in-law, used the occasion to assure her that he was willing to act as father surrogate should she feel the need of his support. And the old Commodore, always one to take an interest in a pretty lady in distress, offered her the use of his old homestead on Staten Island for a summer holiday when she mentioned that she enjoyed spending time in the country. She not only took him up on his offer but renovated the place.[98]

# 2 Every Inch a General

BECOMING A VANDERBILT provided Alva the opportunity to engage both literally and figuratively in a wide variety of construction projects. The most tangible of them were the houses that the fortune she now had access to made it possible for her to build on Long Island, in New York City, and in Newport, Rhode Island.[1] But she also defined motherhood as a kind of "constructive work" that demanded that she devote herself to building her children's characters and providing them with the "equipment" she thought they would need to succeed in the life she planned for them.[2] She spent an astonishing amount of time quite self-consciously exploiting the press in an effort to make herself into a social celebrity. And she attributed her desire to build a strong woman's rights movement both at home and abroad to her constructive instincts.[3]

Alva traced her passion for architecture and engineering to her childhood. She claimed that one of her first memories was of lying on the floor of her father's library building houses out of his books. "I can remember the sustained absorption with which I planned the passage ways, doors, windows and rooms of my book houses," she said.[4] During her sojourn in Paris in the 1860s, she recalled the pleasure she derived from sitting on park benches sketching the outlines of the buildings she saw before her.[5] And during a summer spent in Newport, she remembered recruiting her friends to help build a stone bridge from the shoreline of the Yzanga house to a small rock island jutting out from the shallow water nearby. She had fond memories of patiently tugging and pulling huge boulders so that they could serve as the building materials for the structure. She and her construction team did not just line up the stones to serve as a pathway across the water. Instead, they took what they knew of engineering into account so that their bridge "had a base and was built up with supports." When they were finished, they could easily make their way across to the island without getting wet. She was immensely proud of that bridge and credited its construction with teaching her to appreciate the value of good workmanship. She was heartbroken when, as a summer storm lashed the coastline, she had to watch the stone structure give way before the fury of the thundering waves.[6]

After Alva married, she and Willie K. lived comfortably in the 44th Street brownstone his father had given them. But they were wealthy only by association. All of that changed when the Commodore died in January 1877 and left Alva's husband $3 million.[7]

With part of the money, they purchased 900 acres on Long Island near the town of Islip and hired Richard Morris Hunt to design and supervise the building of an English Tudor-style country house intended to serve as a hunting lodge. They named it Idlehour.[8] It was Alva's first opportunity to indulge her passion for construction to build something permanent.

Desperate to find an outlet for her creative instincts, Alva found in Hunt a perfect partner. Living and traveling in Europe had provided her with an appreciation of art and architecture. And an adventuresome spirit and desire for attention encouraged her to experiment with both architectural style and interior design. She now had the money to pay for the very best materials and workmanship. And Hunt had both the technical training to take her ideas and give them physical form as well as the patience to put up with her volatile temperament.

As they worked together, Alva developed enormous respect for Hunt, who became both her teacher and her friend. They did not always get along. Their "word battles," as she called them, were legendary. They argued over both design and construction. But her affection and respect for him never wavered. The hours they spent together in his office pouring over house plans were some of the most enjoyable in her life. In Hunt, she found a creative mind, a gifted technician, an engaging companion, and an intellectual equal.[9]

Hunt had barely turned over the keys to Idlehour when Alva began planning a new city residence to be built on Fifth Avenue.[10] She was unhappy living in a brownstone. Familiar with the sparkling white town homes built along London's crescents and the mansard-roofed mansions that lined the fashionable streets of Paris, she claims to have been dismayed by the crude uniformity and ugliness of the houses in New York.[11]

She maintained that she put her "whole soul" into building her grand new home. She wanted to build an edifice that would stand as a public "expression in outward and visible terms of the importance of the Vanderbilt family." At the same time, she wanted to establish her reputation as an arbiter of beauty and good taste by patronizing talented architects and interior designers. It was their responsibility, she believed, to represent "not only wealth but knowledge and culture" in their building projects. Her new house was to be more than just a residence. It was to be a public building, privately owned, that would provide all New Yorkers with the opportunity to expand their appreciation of architecture, art history, and interior décor.[12]

The key component of her vision was innovation. With Hunt's help, she designed a magnificent home built of Indiana limestone on the model of a French chateau, a dramatic contrast to the drab brownstones owned by her friends. Once she had approved the preliminary design, she left Hunt in charge of the construction and went to Europe to complete plans for the building's interior.

Friends and acquaintances wrote to her of their dismay as the structure began to take form in her absence. They did not quite know what to make of the unconventional building material that she had chosen. And some of them apparently considered the figures of naked children that appeared on the façade of the building a disgrace. Predictably, Alva dismissed their objections out of hand, concluding that New Yorkers were not just unsophisticated and provincial but "fatally tainted by Puritanism." That being the case, she was not surprised that they were incapable of appreciating "the exquisite beauty of the human form and . . . its significance in connection with the special period" that she and Hunt were trying to represent.[13] Despite their criticism, she reveled in the attention that her innovations bestowed upon her. Such notice was a crucial component of her campaign to turn herself into a social celebrity.

In late nineteenth- and early twentieth-century America, a wide variety of factors encouraged the growth of celebrity culture. Notions about the importance of the individual and his or her potential for greatness found expression in urban environments such as New York City, which were characterized by anonymity and socioeconomic mobility. It was in such settings that opportunities for the sort of performative self-representation typical of those who courted celebrity flourished. The rise in literacy, the availability of leisure time, and the expansion of the entertainment industry combined with the growth of the mass media with its focus on human interest stories, the rise of consumer culture with its emphasis on the value of commodities, advances in communication technology, and systematic image management by public relations firms and advertising executives all encouraged public interest in celebrities.[14]

When Alva arrived on the social scene, seeking celebrity was a relatively new phenomenon among the members of New York's upper crust. Before the Civil War, New York's wealthiest citizens typically socialized in the privacy of their homes. They intentionally kept their number of intimate associates small and tended to shun the notice of the press.[15] Only occasionally did they allow newspaper reporters to attend and publish descriptions of their social functions.[16] By the 1880s, however, those who claimed or hoped to claim a prominent place for themselves in society expanded the number and variety of people they were willing to entertain and accept invitations from. They began, quite self-consciously, to use public spaces to display their wealth and social connections by entertaining their guests in hotels, restaurants, and clubs. They not only made themselves accessible to journalists but also hired social secretaries and press agents whose job it was to cultivate the attention of reporters so their celebrity could be established.[17] By nurturing what historian Thomas Baker has called the "commercialization of intimacy," they turned their lives into public spectacles and themselves into commodities.[18]

As a number of scholars have pointed out, the exploitation of the culture of celebrity functions as more than just a strategy for getting attention or making money. They argue that in the late nineteenth and early twentieth centuries, celebrities provided a mechanism that could be used to embody and personalize social, political, aesthetic, and moral issues. Moreover, fascination with celebrities provided the general public with a way to cope with a wide variety of concerns, including alarm over the increasing influence of large corporations on the economy and government; anxieties about race, gender, and class; unease about the shift toward the glorification of leisure, consumption, and self-gratification in a society built upon hard work and self-sacrifice; and the need to preserve a sense of individuality in an increasingly complex, anonymous, and impersonal world.[19] They maintain that because celebrities were acknowledged to be public figures, they were in a position to shape social values and serve as agents of social change.[20]

The culture of celebrity allowed ordinary Americans to construct their own fantasies about who they were and what they aspired to be by providing them with frames of reference for those fantasies. Alva provided such a frame of reference for those who read about her in the newspapers. She embodied the ambitious woman determined to use her family's economic resources to make a place for herself and her family among the social elite. It was the scale of her efforts to consolidate her family's social position and then to use it to promote social and political reform that was exceptional. Millions of Americans aspired to make enough money to allow them to move up the social ladder, to become arbiters of taste and influential members of their communities. The whole concept of "self-making" was based on the belief that such mobility was possible. Those without vast economic resources could at least imitate her strategies albeit on a more modest scale. They could, for example, entertain those whom they considered to be the right sort of people and engage in public acts of philanthropy and advocacy that might merit the attention of the local press.

Businessmen and newspaper editors collaborated in the production of celebrity culture. Hotel and restaurants managers, whose establishments served as sites for events hosted by members of the smart set, hired public relations specialists whose job it was to ensure as much publicity for themselves and their patrons as possible.[21] Newspaper editors, determined to mine any source of news that might increase circulation, employed reporters whose sense of fashion, understanding of the intricacies of social etiquette and protocol, and familiarity with the names and lineage of socially prominent families allowed them to infiltrate the world of the rich by remaining as inconspicuous as possible while reporting on their activities. Knowing how to dress appropriately and which fork to use at dinner was critical for their success. Part guest, part journalist, they nurtured relationships with social leaders, their servants, and their friends to secure information in order to write society columns and feature stories describing the homes, social activities, and philanthropic endeavors of the social elite both in New York City and the resort communities that they frequented. Doing so helped to sell papers by promoting what one scholar has called an "invasive familiarity" that allowed those outside New York society to trespass vicariously on social territory to which they had no claim.[22]

The *New York World* was one such newspaper. After purchasing the *World* in May 1883, Joseph Pulitzer turned it into a high-circulation daily that privileged the publication of human interest stories written in clear, colorful, but simple language designed to appeal to the masses. Grudgingly respectful of those who made their fortunes in the rough-and-tumble world of big business, he was ambivalent about the nouveaux riches and critical of their extravagant lifestyles. He, like the editor before him, regularly published a gossip column entitled "The World of Society." He considered the rich fair game for satire and ridicule and did not hesitate to sensationalize news about their private lives and social activities.[23] In doing so, he was as likely as not to use stories about them to comment upon the social tensions that resulted from the economic chasm that separated the rich from the working class.[24]

By comparison, social news in the *New York Times* was relatively tame. A sober, dignified organ of the Republican Party, the *Times* was noted for its campaigns against corruption and waste during the 1870s and 1880s. At the same time, however, it, like its competitors, regularly chronicled the marriages, deaths, parties, philanthropic gestures, travels, and polo matches of the rich.[25] After Adolph Ochs purchased the *Times* in August 1896, he turned it into a newspaper intended for businessmen. Featuring government, financial, and market news as well as commentary on New York social life, the *Times* developed a reputation for trustworthiness, impartiality, and respectability.[26]

Despite the differences in their content, tone, and readers, both papers were well run, widely read, and financially successful. Together with others throughout the country who used the same business model, they present a fairly representative impression of the amount, range, and quality of press exposure that Alva was able to garner for herself and the causes that she eventually championed.

When Alva married in 1875, newspaper editors had only just begun to capitalize on the social elites' activities as a way of expanding their circulation. Her wedding received only passing notice in the *Times*.[27] The *World* carried no notice at all. Enterprising and socially ambitious, she immediately began her campaign to establish a place for herself and her new family in the highest echelons of New York City's society. Toward that end she did what she could to make sure her name, listed as Mrs. W. K. Vanderbilt, regularly appeared in society columns. But it was not until her Manhattan mansion was finished that she was able to exploit the vicarious interest of the public in activities of the very rich to become front-page news in newspapers across the country.

By announcing that she was about to give a costume ball for 1200 guests, she guaranteed the attention she craved. Organizing an event of such magnitude was a complicated matter. Mastering the art of choosing whom to include; arranging for the printing, addressing, and delivery of invitations; selecting caterers, musicians, and florists; making security arrangements; and then orchestrating the evening's entertainment was no easy task. She certainly had the means to hire help to deal with such matters, but in the end she was the one who was ultimately responsible for the success of any social event that she sponsored. She would spend the next forty years refining her skills in event planning and nurturing a mutually exploitive relationship with the press. In the process, she developed administrative expertise that would establish her reputation as an accomplished and successful society hostess, a reputation that would eventually help provide the entrée she needed to establish a place for herself as one of the most widely recognized leaders of the woman suffrage movement.

The Vanderbilt ball, held on March 26, 1883, was first- and second-page, multi-columned news in the *New York Times*. Alva Vanderbilt or someone on her staff stage-managed the lead article by inviting a *Times* reporter to view the interior of her new mansion prior to the event and by providing the journalist with such raw material as the name of her florist; the precise dimensions of the grand hall, gymnasium, and dining room; and the types of stone and wood paneling used in the interior as well as the names that appeared on her guest list. She even allowed a reporter to mingle with what he described as a "motley crowd of princes, monks, cavaliers, highlanders, queens, kings, dairy-maids, bull-fighters, knights, brigands, and nobles" during the evening's festivities.[28]

The *New York World* gave the event more extensive coverage than Alva could have hoped for. Unfortunately, not all of it was entirely positive or congratulatory. Two days before the costume ball, the *World* ran a headline on page one that read: "Social Dynamite: A Conspiracy of Wall Flowers, Bores, and 'Dudes' against the Vanderbilt Ball." Satirizing the pettiness of the socially ambitious, the story alleged that a "tremendous conspiracy" had been formed by "disappointed 'dudes' and uninvited damsels to frighten away from [Vanderbilt's] entertainment all the expected guests." According to the article, "Easter eggs" were to be delivered to everyone on the Vanderbilt guest list warning them not to attend the ball if they wanted to avoid "the fate designed by Guy Fawkes for the British Parliament." The *World* assured its readers that there was little reason to believe that the Vanderbilts' guests would really be blown to smithereens. It seems, it reported, that New York's milliners, tailors, hairdressers, drivers, and florists were determined to turn themselves into "a vigilant corps of independent and unpaid detectives" in order to prevent the festivities from being interrupted. Their willingness to do so, the article suggested, was not so much the result of their sense of civic responsibility as it was a reflection of their economic interest. As the *World* pointed out, the livelihoods of New York's service providers were dependent upon the patronage of the rich. Therefore, self-interest demanded that they protect their portion of the projected $250,000 (almost $6 million in today's currency) that was likely to be spent to make the ball a success.[29] Not willing to drop the matter, the paper ran a sequel to the article the next day titled "The Dudes' Little Plot Exploded by 'The World' to Their Consternation and Dismay," an example of journalistic self-promotion intended to assure the paper's readers of its ability to provide them with the latest, in-depth, inclusive coverage of social affairs in New York.[30]

Such melodrama provided an opportunity for the *World* to comment on both the social and economic consequences of class divisions and the pursuit of self-interest. Besides providing the Vanderbilts with free public exposure, the conspiracy story allowed the *World* to exploit the publicity value of the Vanderbilt name in order to sell newspapers beyond what would have been possible had they confined themselves, like the *Times,* to a mere description of the ball. The *World*'s pre-party commentary on the Vanderbilt gala also gave the paper an opportunity not only to express its ambivalence about the rich, their values, and their activities but also to accuse the working class of being complicit in supporting a level of extravagance that allowed members of the social elite to spend absurd amounts of money in order to entertain themselves as a way of distributing the wealth of the rich to the city's service providers and those who were employed by them. The *World* made the case that many of New York City's independent small business owners and their employees benefited from upper-crust profligacy and hedonism. By suggesting that such interdependence served the interests of both the upper class and the working class, the *World* presented its readers with a provocative commentary on the accumulation of wealth and its influence on class relations. The *World*'s story also served as a parody on class warfare that humanized the Vanderbilts and their guests by exposing the vulnerability that accompanied the status and publicity they so valued. It empowered working-class service providers by portraying them as mediators in the competitive struggle that characterized upper-class life.

Having had its fun, the *World* ultimately treated the ball as a news event. Under a headline that read "An Event Never Equaled in the Social Annals of the Metropolis," it published a first- and second-page, four-column postmortem on the ball, describing in detail the guests' costumes, the Vanderbilt mansion, and the decorations that festooned its walls.[31] The *World*'s final comment on the event appeared on its society page four days after the fact. Describing the ball as unmatched in its "magnificence," "stateliness," and "sumptuousness," the *World* lampooned the Vanderbilts' guests by teasing them about the physical discomfort they endured when they willingly chose to wear the expensive and elaborate costumes produced by New York's milliners and tailors. And it ridiculed them for engaging in a secret and competitive effort to outdo each other that resulted in what it described as the appearance of too many "Mary Stuarts."[32] The culture of one-upmanship that characterized the lives of the newly rich, the columnist suggested, had wreaked a just vengeance on them by exposing their lack of imagination, superficiality, and exaggerated sense of self-importance.

Alva also got her fair share of attention from papers in Boston, Atlanta, Baltimore, St. Louis, and Los Angeles, which, like their New York counterparts, featured news of the Vanderbilt ball on their first page.[33] The *Chicago Daily Tribune* alone published six stories describing the costume ball, including reference to the *World's* dude" story.[34] While most editors confined their commentary to descriptions of the Vanderbilt mansion, its splendid decor, and its elaborately costumed guests, some, like the *St. Louis Post-Dispatch,* criticized the Vanderbilts' ostentatious display of what it dubbed "insolent wealth and offensive luxury." While the social elite of New York dance, eat, and drink the night away in luxurious surroundings, "tens and hundreds of thousands of the poor of New York will huddle and shiver in frail and rickety tenements, with their lean bodies unfed from their last meal," its editor pointed out, suggesting that such an unequal distribution of wealth could only evoke "deep rumblings of a great discontent and the mutterings of a wide uprising."[35]

Alva considered the ball a social triumph. She died believing that "it was the most brilliant ball ever given in New York" and that it "marked an epoch" in the city's social history.[36] What she thought of the national press coverage she received in her first attempt to orchestrate her public image we have no way of knowing. But what must have been clear to her as she reflected on it was that managing the press was no easy task and that however much a society hostess tried to control the information available to eager reporters, dictating what appeared in the newspapers was next to impossible. It turned out that it was easier to get attention than it was to control the sort of attention one received.

On December 8, 1885, Alva's father-in-law died, leaving her husband $65 million.[37] Now with access to a staggering amount of money, Alva, again in collaboration with Hunt, began constructing a home on Bellevue Avenue in Newport, Rhode Island. Inspired by the Parthenon in Athens and the Petit Trianon in Versailles, she hired European craftsmen to build the house of marble, some domestic but most imported from Italy and Africa. Once it was completed, she decorated the entire house with art, tapestries, and antiques shipped from abroad.

Marble House may have been extravagantly sumptuous but it was not as large as some of the other mansions on Bellevue Avenue. There were only four rooms on the main floor off the grand entrance hall—a reception room gilded from floor to ceiling in twenty-two-karat gold; a dark, gloomy repository called the Gothic Room intended to display the most impressive of Alva's newly purchased antiques, sculpture, and paintings; a dining room encased in rose-colored marble; and a small sitting-room library whose floor-to-ceiling windows looked out to the sea. A gallery ran along the back of the house on the main floor. Halfway up the stairs at each end of the mezzanine were sitting rooms, one for Alva and one for Willie K. And on the second floor was a bedroom for each member of the family plus a two-room guest suite. The servants slept on the third floor under the eaves of the house and did much of their work in the basement. Alva considered the structure a "triumph." It stood, she said, as testimony to the imagination, creativity, and skill of both herself and her architect.[38]

Alva liked to think that, during the early years of her marriage, she devoted at least as much time to rearing her children as she did to building houses.[39] Just as she traced her interest in architecture to her childhood, so too did she trace her interest in parenting to her youthful obsession with dolls. She claims to have thought of her dolls as extensions of herself. Indeed, she remembered having put "into their china or sawdust bodies all" of her "own feelings." She imagined that they could be happy or sad, angry or content. Determined to ensure their comfort, she recalled feeding them when she thought they might be hungry and letting them rest when she thought they were tired. Before she went to bed, she remembered carefully undressing both her own dolls and those of her sister in preparation for their night's sleep.[40]

Alva claimed that the joy she experienced when she learned she was to be a mother, the happiness she felt when her first child, Consuelo, was born, and the seriousness with which she carried out her maternal responsibilities served as clear evidence of her deeply embedded maternalism.[41] She professed to have believed that rearing children was as much a "sacred trust" as it was an opportunity to engage in what she called "constructive" work. Her children were, like her homes, not only of her creation but also her link to the future.[42] The product of a generation raised with the idea that a woman could find fulfillment as a mother through suffering and selfless devotion to her children, she believed herself to have been more conscientious and self-sacrificing than many of her upper-class contemporaries, whom she considered neglectful.[43] In retrospect, she found mothering a fulfilling, satisfying experience.

She credited her own mother with being her role model. Despite both convention and the financial resources that would have allowed her to do so, Phoebe refused to relegate her children to the nursery. Alva remembered eating with her parents, sleeping within earshot of their bedroom, and attending their levees and dinner parties.[44] Phoebe was especially insistent that her children travel abroad with her. "There are very few parents of the present day who would encumber themselves by four children, a dog and a bird" when it would have been so much easier to have left them all at home, Alva remarked in retrospect. Her mother considered travel an important part of their education, and Alva believed that she and her sisters "profited by her desire to broaden our minds and teach us to observe."[45]

Convinced that her mother "had given the very best of herself for her children's welfare," Alva was determined to do the same.[46] She bore three children in seven years: Consuelo in March 1877, William Kissam Jr. about eighteen months later in 1878, and Harold Stirling in July 1884.[47] She claimed that during their childhood she was more concerned about their welfare than her own. In an amazing feat of selective memory (considering the time she spent engaged in building projects and social activities), she credited herself with having spent her children's impressionable years entertaining them, nurturing their individuality, lunching with them regularly, closely supervising their education, and teaching them to accept their responsibilities toward those less fortunate than themselves.[48] She claimed to have devoted the same energy in shaping her children's minds, bodies, and characters as she did in constructing her beautiful homes. From her point of view, the two projects were analogous.[49]

"Having insisted in my own childhood on my individual liberty, I tried to give it to my children," she confessed years after her children were grown. Believing, as she put it, that "if you want a thing well done you must do it yourself," she was proud of her efforts to help her children function in the world she knew awaited them. She attempted to teach them the principles of capitalist economics as well as the importance of fulfilling their philanthropic obligations by supervising a garden project at Idlehour. After the children harvested the vegetables they had planted, she purchased the produce. With children in tow, she delivered their bounty to the Trinity Seaside Home, a convalescent facility for children that she had built on the grounds of the estate.[50]

She also remembered their sailing adventures on a pond at Idlehour as opportunities to teach them geography. Some days, she said, they sailed from Dover to Calais. On others, they traveled from New York to Liverpool, while her eldest son provided the sensation of rough seas by rocking the small boat.[51]

In a desire to encourage the development of her children's conversational and debating skills, she instituted a "children's dining table" where she joined her children, their governesses, tutors, and friends during their midday meal so that they could participate in discussions of whatever topics appealed to them. In retrospect, she insisted that "no persuasion of friend or occasion could draw me from this reunion time with the family." And in order to nurture her children's self-confidence and train them in public speaking, she regularly scheduled a "recitation hour" on Saturday nights when the three of them were expected to recite a poem of their choice before their parents and their guests.[52]

At the same time, however, she claims to have gone to great lengths to indulge their "various inclinations and preferences" by ensuring that their educations were individualized.[53] So her youngest son, who was an excellent student, had a different course of instruction than his elder brother, who had no interest whatever in books. Tutors were in charge when they were young. She eventually sent the two boys to boarding school at St. Mark's in Southborough, Massachusetts, and then on to Harvard.[54]

Alva's ambitions for her children were straightforward and class specific. She wanted her sons to become gentlemen, to understand their obligations toward those less fortunate than themselves, and to take their place in the international world of business, wealth, and social privilege.[55] Because of their father's wealth and her reputation as a society hostess, their economic and social futures were secure. As adults, they could work or not as they pleased. But she was determined that they not "squander the fortunes" that they were destined to inherit.[56]

Willie K. Jr. and Harold fulfilled the expectations she had for them. Both worked for the New York Central Railroad, served in the U.S. Navy in World War I, and became accomplished yachtsmen. Her elder son had a less-distinguished public service career than his younger brother, who received honors for his work as a member of the British War Relief effort during World War II and served as president of the Board of Trustees of Vanderbilt University from 1954 until his death in 1970.[57]

Alva's goal for her daughter was to prepare her for marriage and a life dedicated to philanthropy and public service. It never occurred to her that Consuelo might find fulfillment and a place for herself in public life as a single woman of means. Oblivious to the possibilities for independent action that were increasingly available to women who could support themselves, she was determined to live vicariously through her oldest child whose fate she had decided was to marry a man whose social position would allow her to pursue the goals her mother set for her. "Consuelo's marriage was of scarcely less importance to me than it was to her," she confessed. "In her future my own was in a sense wrapped."[58] Toward that end, she completely controlled her daughter's early life.

We learn of the forms that domination took and the influence that it had on their relationship through Consuelo's memoir, published in 1952 almost twenty years after her mother's death.[59] In her autobiography, Consuelo shaped Alva's image to suit her own purposes. The story that Consuelo told, a tragic and melodramatic tale of her own and her mother's making, served as the interpretive device she used to explain her life's trajectory—her transformation from a timid, retiring child into an outgoing, sophisticated, socially responsible woman of the world. In the process of formulating that story, Consuelo constructed a counter text to the one that Alva so carefully and self-consciously created in her memoirs.

Consuelo's memory of her mother bore little resemblance to the woman Alva remembered being. The product of a generation who came of age when definitions of good mothering were changing and when conflicts between mothers and daughters were as inevitable as they had always been, Consuelo, focusing on her mother's inadequacies, indulged in an unrestrained and remarkable display of mother blaming.[60] From her point of view, the maternal attentiveness that

Alva took such pride in was merely an example of her self-centeredness. As such, it was hardly constructive and certainly not benign.

Consuelo claimed to remember very little about her childhood and by extension her mother.[61] But the first fifty-four pages of her text belie that claim and testify to the bond of blood and class interests that bound them together in a clash of wills. Consuelo's description of her childhood reads like a variation on the story of Cinderella complete with a young, beautiful, but passive heroine who lived in a castle; an overbearing, terrifying, and malevolent mother figure; a loving and generous but weak-willed, largely absent father; stepsisters in the form of servants, tutors, and governesses; and a prince or two in shining armor. The only figure that is conspicuously missing is a fairy godmother.[62]

Consuelo began her memoir by providing her readers with a visual framework for appreciating her powerlessness in relation to her mother. During her youth, she told her readers, she sat for two portraits, both commissioned by her mother from the same artist, Carolus-Duran. The first, she said, portrayed her as a "vital" little girl dressed in red velvet with a "cloud of dark hair," a "small, oval face," large eyes, "a pert little nose," and dimples accentuating a "mischievous smile." Standing before an innocuous drape, she had no context besides that of the obvious affluence of her family and, by extension, no will of her own.

The second portrait was quite a different matter. Painted when she was seventeen, a debutante, and about to go on the marriage market, it served as an advertisement of sorts, a testimony to her mother's social ambitions. In that portrait, Consuelo described herself as a "remote," "disdainful," yet elegant figure dressed all in white, descending a staircase placed against a "classic landscape in the English eighteenth-century style" meant to represent her future as the wife of an aristocrat. It was, she told her readers, a portrait modeled after those painted by Thomas Gainsborough and Sir Joshua Reynolds intended to hang in the public rooms of a great country house.[63] Those two portraits appear to have served as a visual reminder to Consuelo of the impact that her mother had on her life.

Consuelo claimed that she adored her father. He had, she said, "a generous and unselfish nature." She remembered him as a gentle, sweet, funny man—a dashing cavalier who always seemed to take pleasure in having fun and seeing people happy.[64]

Fun-loving he may have been, but as a parent William Kissam Vanderbilt was absent and ineffectual. It was her mother, Consuelo told her readers, who controlled her life—her education, her recreation, her choice of friends, even her thoughts.[65] Not one to mince words where her mother was concerned, Consuelo described Alva as "a born dictator" who "dominated events about her as thoroughly as she eventually dominated her husband and her children." From the perspective of old age, Consuelo saw herself as nothing more than one of her mother's "projects," an individual who, denied the right to her own will or opinions, was merely a "pawn" to be moved about as her mother wished.[66] Even the space of her bedroom at Marble House, which she described as gloomy and "austere," was her mother's space rather than her own. Alva, she reported, chose every piece of furniture and every ornament to suit her own taste. There was no evidence that the room was inhabited by a young girl because Alva forbade "the intrusion" of Consuelo's "personal possessions." Consuelo concluded that "there was in her love of me something of the creative spirit of the artist." Placing her daughter in such a room, Consuelo believed, resulted from her mother's "wish to produce me as a finished specimen framed in a perfect setting." The result of her mother's efforts was to make Consuelo feel as if she were as much an ornament as the elaborate grooming set laid out on her dressing table. "My person was dedicated to whatever final disposal she had in mind," she said.[67]

Consuelo's litany of complaints against her mother dated from her birth in 1877, which she noted no one bothered to register, an oversight which she claimed caused her no end of trouble when she reached adulthood.[68] The chronicle she presents of her childhood and adolescence is filled with incidents that destroyed her self-confidence and undermined her self-esteem. At her mother's hands, she claims to have suffered the embarrassment of wearing period costumes that both distinguished and, by implication, alienated her from other children.[69] When she was old enough to have an opinion about the matter of her clothes, her mother told her that she "had no taste" and continued to dictate what she could and could not wear.[70] Then there was the humiliation of having to listen to her mother discuss the unfortunate shape of her nose.[71] Alva habitually dismissed her daughter's opinions out of hand. "She brooked no contradiction," Consuelo remembered. "When once I replied, 'I thought I was doing right,' she stated, 'I don't ask *you* to think, *I* do the thinking, you do as you are told,' which reduced me to imbecility."[72]

Consuelo found her mother's emotional volatility terrifying. Alva's violent temper was "the bane of her life and those who shared it," she wrote. There was no way of escaping it. Her tantrums were, Consuelo confessed, "like a tempest that at times engulfed us all."[73] Consuelo's response to them appears to have been to develop an exaggerated sense of responsibility for helping to maintain some sort of emotional equilibrium in the household. Take, for example, the evening she and her brother were permitted to enter their mother's bedroom to watch her dress for a party. As Alva went to take her jewels out of the safe, she discovered that it would not open. Consuelo remembered feeling an overwhelming sense of panic. It is not clear whether she thought that she was about to have to endure another of her mother's temper tantrums or whether, for some reason, she thought she might be held responsible for her mother's inability to work the combination on the lock. Whatever the case, she remembered running to her room and praying "fervently that a miracle would open the safe." When she eventually worked up the courage to return, whatever drama had been played out in her absence was over, and her mother was wearing her pearls.[74] All was well, and nothing more was said about the matter.

Added to the emotional pain she experienced during her childhood was the physical pain her mother subjected her to. Alva, like Phoebe, was a harsh disciplinarian who did not hesitate to use whatever was at hand, including her riding whip, to punish her children for what Consuelo felt were "minor delinquencies." Consuelo had vivid memories of the "last such lashing" her legs received "as I stood while my mother wielded her crop." She and one of her brothers had been enjoying a sail on the pond at Idlehour when their governess called them in. When they reluctantly neared the shore, the woman caught the boat and placed one of her legs on board while leaving the other on the bank in order to guarantee that the children did not put out again. They found the temptation to do so overwhelming, and the governess ended up in the water. "It seemed very funny at the time," Consuelo remembered, but as they trekked home accompanied by a furious and bedraggled governess, "the incident lost its charm." Consuelo endured her punishment stoically but claimed that such treatment bred "inhibitions" from which she suffered for the rest of her life.[75]

She remembered eating at the children's dining table that her mother was so proud of as an unpleasant experience that provided Alva rather than her children with the opportunity to engage in conversation. Typically, Consuelo wrote, her mother presided over the dining table set for six or eight guests who were more likely to be adults than children. Indeed, Consuelo distinctly remembered feeling that her mother had no interest in allowing her to express her views on whatever subject was being discussed.[76]

Consuelo attributed her childhood anxieties and exaggerated sense of responsibility to having been denied the love and attention that she craved. Despite the constant presence of servants, she characterized her childhood as a lonely and "solitary one," constrained by the "artificial" prohibitions that her mother placed on her.[77] Unlike her middle-class sisters who grew to adulthood as members of a community of schoolgirls, she was rarely subjected to peer pressure, did not imbibe strategies for achieving success outside marriage, and had little opportunity to free herself from the scrutiny of adults.[78] Educated at home, often separated from her brothers, and "profoundly unhappy" with her life, particularly as her parents became more and more estranged, she turned to books for company and to religion for solace and developed into what she describes as an intuitive, sensitive, inhibited, and introspective young woman with an "inferiority complex" that expressed itself in "hypersensitiveness and a quick temper."[79]

By the time she reached adulthood, Consuelo was exactly the sort of person in appearance, intellect, and temperament that her mother wished her to be: Five foot six inches tall, she was a slender young woman with "raven black hair" and dark brown eyes. She had, according to her mother, a "good mind," a love of learning, and "high moral sense of service" as well as the "mentality to direct it." Unlike Alva, she never made an effort to establish her independence or flagrantly flaunt the rules set up for her. She was, in her mother's eyes, a quite "docile and tractable" young woman who was "rather conservative in her attitude toward life." Consuelo seemed determined to please, willing to defer to her mother's wishes and conform to her expectations.

Anxious "to see such an equipment given the widest possible field for serious activity," Alva began efforts to arrange Consuelo's marriage to a man whose situation would allow her daughter to use her social position to engage in useful work.[80] By the time Consuelo reached adulthood, Alva had developed a sincere contempt for most society women. In her opinion, they lived in passive contentment as the playthings of men rather than doing something worthwhile with their lives.[81] She wanted something more for her daughter.

But just when she should have been planning Consuelo's debut and arranging her introduction to suitable young men, Alva found herself faced with a personal crisis of her own. Her marriage was about to end.

There is no way to know what expectations Alva originally brought to her union with Willie K. Reared in a fairly insular environment, she met only those individuals carefully chosen by her parents. And when she began to participate in social activities after her mother's death, she was always accompanied by a chaperone.[82] There is little reason to think that when she married she knew much about sex or was very much aware of the double standard of morality that allowed, and in some circles even encouraged, married men to seek sexual gratification from women who were not their wives.

Once wed, however, Alva concluded that upper-class men expected very little from the women they married except that they be good-looking, well groomed, and ready to serve their husband's sexual needs when asked to do so. She also observed that the men she knew did not look to their wives for intellectual stimulation, wisdom, or companionship. She watched as the men around her tired of their wives and then relegated them to what she deemed "a stupid domestic sphere" where they were expected to fill their lives with "children, housekeeping, and perfunctory social duties." And she came to resent the fact that it was the responsibility of these "idle, useless, lonely" women to maintain the respectability of their families by suffering in silence the humiliation that their husbands subjected them to.[83]

She believed that men colluded in efforts to perpetuate this code of conduct.[84] Wealthy men seemed to think, she said, that "they could do anything they liked; have anything, or any woman, they, for the moment wanted." There were no penalties for someone like John Jacob Astor, whose yachting parties, she claimed, "were public scandals. He would take women of every class and kind, even chamber maids out of the hotels of the coastwise cities where the yacht put in, to amuse himself and the men of his party."[85]

Given the circumstances, she could not have been surprised when her husband began to spend more time at his club, the racetrack, and the gaming table than he did at home. Experience had shown her that, like many of his friends, he was a man easily flattered by women who wished to benefit from a relationship with him.[86] It was only a matter of time before he rejected her for someone younger and more attractive.

It is not clear when Alva discovered that her husband was unfaithful. But when she found out about his affair with a woman in Paris, she filed for divorce. According to a reporter from the *New York Tribune,* Willie K. was excessively indiscreet where his extramarital love life was concerned. He "persisted in public devotion to [his paramour] despite all attempts at dissuasion on the part of his friends." It was impossible not to notice that when he attended the theater or went driving through the boulevards of Paris, he did so in her company. And it "was common report that he had been so utterly regardless of appearances as to fit out in the Vanderbilt livery the servants for the expensive establishment he maintained in Paris for this woman."[87]

Alva was not prepared to play second fiddle to anyone, let alone her husband's mistresses. And she certainly was not willing to suffer public humiliation at his hands. The final split came in 1894, as they were sailing on their yacht. When they stopped speaking to each other, they used Consuelo as their intermediary, demanding that she carry angry messages back and forth between them, a job their daughter understandably found painful.[88] Once the cruise ended, Alva left her husband and took Consuelo to Paris and then to England. After they returned to the United States in September, she filed for divorce on the grounds of adultery.[89]

The family spent Christmas in Newport. Willie K. arrived from France on December 12 and came to Marble House the next morning to see the children. When Alva was not conferring with her lawyers, she distracted herself by going to social events with Consuelo and a few of her male friends. Negotiations concerning the terms of the divorce continued throughout the holidays. Willie K. left for Europe a month after he had arrived. And Alva took Consuelo back to the Continent in March after assuring herself that the boys were settled at school.[90]

Alva usually courted the attention of the press, but news of her divorce was not likely to produce the sort of publicity that she was interested in. It was concern over this issue that prompted one of her lawyers, Joseph Choate, to try to dissuade her from pursuing her suit in the first place.[91] Arguing that the social authority of the upper class was a fragile commodity that could be sustained only if they were able to convince their social inferiors that they were committed to stable family life and social responsibility, he pleaded with her to sacrifice herself in the interest of self-preservation and class solidarity. "No member of [the upper class] must expose another member to criticism lest the whole foundation of wealth be undermined," he told her.[92]

Undeterred by his arguments, Alva proceeded with her case. She had no difficulty persuading the court to give her a divorce. Behind closed doors, witnesses brought over from France provided convincing testimony that Willie K. had, indeed, been unfaithful to her. She received her decree on March 5, 1895, along with custody of her children, the right to remarry, and a generous financial settlement.[93]

As might have been expected, the *Times* ran a story focusing on the legal settlement while the *World* published a frank and lengthy discussion of William K. Vanderbilt's alleged adultery with a woman identified as the fortune-hunting Nellie Neustretter.[94] A few months before the divorce was announced, the *World* had published a front-page story announcing the birth of a child to Neustretter.[95] Once it became clear that the Vanderbilt marriage was over, it focused on the class implications of Willie K's affair. People from every social class should be concerned with the Vanderbilt divorce, it told its readers. It had particular importance for the thousands of railroad workers employed by Vanderbilt's New York Central Railroad. After all, it pointed out, profits from "the fares which they collect, the freight money that they earn, and any trifling reduction that be made in their number" were being diverted to provide the "notorious" Nellie Neustretter of Paris with such comforts as her position as William K.'s mistress demanded.[96]

With her name conspicuously displayed in front-page headlines from New York and Atlanta to Chicago and Los Angeles, Alva now prepared to suffer the consequences of having publicly exposed the moral failings of New York City's social elite.[97] "I got my divorce and just a[s] in childhood days [when] I accepted the whipping my mother gave me for taking the forbidden liberty, so I bared my back to the whipping of Society for taking a freedom which would eventually better them as well as myself," she said.[98] "Women were not supposed to divorce their husbands in those days, whatever their provocation, and social ostracism threatened anyone daring enough, or self respecting enough, to do it." She got what she expected: "Society was by turns stunned, horrified, and then savage in its opposition and criticism."[99] What was particularly troubling to her was that those who were most likely to condemn her were the very women whose marriages were the most unhappy.[100] By divorcing her husband, she exposed a reality that women in her social set preferred to keep hidden, if only to preserve their own self-respect. Alva condemned them as cowards.

The repercussions were swift in coming and extremely painful. Two days after her divorce, she attended the theater in New York with twelve of her friends.[101] It took great courage for her to do so. Predictably many of her old associates refused to speak to her in an effort to render her invisible. "When I walked into Trinity Church in Newport on a Sunday soon after obtaining my divorce, not a single one of my old friends would recognize me," she remembered years later. "Having done homage to Christ who taught brotherly love, they walked by me with cold stares or insolent looks. They gathered in little groups and made it evident they were speaking of their disapprobation of my conduct." When she went to a dinner party given by one of the few friends who remained loyal and supportive, she found that the only woman who would talk to her was the hostess. Her memories of her discomfort were vivid: "When the men were left in the dining room, the women would sweep away from me, leaving me standing alone so that the hostess was forced to come to the rescue." She was somewhat surprised that her male acquaintances seemed perfectly at ease with her. She concluded that as long as their wives and daughters did not follow her example, they had no intention of denying themselves the pleasure of conversing with a "rebel who had dared to be different from the rest."[102]

Once it became clear that many of her former associates considered her a social pariah, it would have been understandable if Alva had withdrawn from society for a while. But she was not one to give up without a fight. Moreover, she had a marriageable daughter whose future was at stake. Afraid that Consuelo would be forced to endure the same sort of snubbing that she was experiencing, Alva hosted a series of small, informal receptions to introduce Consuelo to New York society rather than host a debutante ball in her honor.[103] She then turned her energies to presenting her daughter to French society and arranging her marriage.

Given the fact that Consuelo was an eligible young heiress, the process of finding a suitable husband for her was fraught with potential difficulties. Since Alva had never allowed Consuelo to associate freely with her peers, she had no way to gauge the depth of Consuelo's emotional vulnerability to romantic fantasies. And she knew that presenting her daughter to society meant thrusting Consuelo into the company of charming, handsome fortune-hunters.

Alva's unfortunate experience with male infidelity made her contemptuous of youthful infatuation and romantic attachment as the basis for an enduring relationship between husband and wife. By the time she was beginning to give serious thought to her daughter's marriage prospects, she was cynical about marriage and had come to believe that it was inevitable that whatever affection Consuelo might have for the man she married would diminish as time passed. So she convinced herself that unless she placed her daughter in a position to transfer her energy from trying to please her husband to serving others, Consuelo was destined to find herself, as Sara Bard Field put it in Alva's memoir, a "mere amusement" to her husband and a "domestic slave" to her children.[104] The result was that Alva did what she could to shield her daughter from any man "for whom she might have a youthful and passing fancy that would lead her into a marriage where there was no opportunity for self growth through public ministry" and tried to instill in Consuelo the skills and social sensibilities that would allow her to have a meaningful life beyond that of wife and mother.[105]

Alva looked to Europe as the place most likely to provide Consuelo with an opportunity to dedicate her life to public service. "Title and wealth in Europe mean that men and women are tied to the established obligations that go with titles and wealth," she said. If nothing else, she pointed out, fear of public censure was enough to compel both aristocrats and their wives to fulfill their philanthropic responsibilities.[106] She was well aware, for example, that women who married into landowning families in England were expected to assume responsibility for the welfare of those who lived on their estates both because their rank demanded it and because benevolence was seen as the special provenance of women. Toward that end, they acted as "ladies bountiful," distributing food, clothing, bedding, medicine, and Christmas presents to servants and tenants alike. They also provided financial support for village schools, managed savings clubs, and sponsored mothers' meetings in an effort to improve the lives of those who lived nearby. Through personal contacts with their social inferiors, they engaged in useful work while they helped to preserve the deference upon which their class status depended. There were benefits to be derived from such behavior. As historian Jessica Gerard has pointed out, benevolence was socially approved work that encouraged initiative, allowed women in the landed classes to refine their administrative skills, and provided them with opportunities to enhance their self-esteem as well as with an arena in which they could act independently and impose their wishes on others.[107]

In Alva's experience, members of the American upper classes had never developed the same strong sense of public responsibility. A rich American, she observed, "may or may not be public minded and his wife may or may not be a useful member of the community."[108] So she dismissed American men as potential suitors.[109] In her mind, the only sort of man who could provide Consuelo with a suitable context for living a useful and fulfilled life was an aristocrat with a large estate. Marrying such a man would provide Consuelo an ideal platform from which to perform the sort of public service that Alva had in mind.

Alva was familiar with the international marriage market. Young American women of good breeding from wealthy families had been marrying titled foreigners for years by the time Consuelo was presented to society. As early as the 1820s, Mary Caton, a member of the prominent Carroll family in Maryland, married the Marquis of Wellesley, Viceroy of Ireland.[110] Others followed.[111] In 1874 Jennie Jerome of New York married Lord Randolph Churchill.[112] Alva's friend Minnie Stevens married Sir Arthur Paget in 1878.[113] And in 1888 Sir Michael Herbert wed Belle Wilson.[114] By the end of the century, *Titled Americans: A List of American Ladies Who Have Married Foreigners of Rank* provided biographical information on hundreds of young women who had married men with titles as well as a list of aristocrats searching for marriageable American heiresses.[115] By 1915 there were forty-two American princesses, seventeen American duchesses, thirty-three American viscountesses, and one hundred thirty-six American countesses.[116]

After carefully screening the available candidates, Alva chose Charles Richard John Spencer-Churchill, the ninth Duke of Marlborough, who she believed "could give my daughter that which her equipment invited."[117] She and her London friends Lady Arthur Paget (Minnie Stevens) and the Duchess of Manchester (Consuelo Yznaga, Consuelo's godmother) left no stone unturned to arrange a marriage between the two. Shortly after Consuelo was presented to society in Paris, Alva took her to London where she placed her in the hands of Lady Paget, whose job it was to arrange for Consuelo to meet the eligible young English aristocrat.

All too aware that she was being "critically appraised," Consuelo found her first meeting with Lady Paget extremely humiliating. Apparently unimpressed by Consuelo's appearance and personality, Paget informed Alva that Consuelo's only advantage in the marriage market was that her parents could afford to dress her properly. "It was useless to demur that I was only seventeen," Consuelo explained years later. "Lady Paget was adamant." She insisted that "tulle must give way to satin, the baby *décolletage* to more generous display of neck and arms, naïveté to sophistication." Properly attired to show off her physical attributes as Lady Paget had ordered, Consuelo met the Duke of Marlborough at a dinner party arranged for that purpose.[118] Having set the stage for what she considered to be a brilliant international marriage, Alva, Consuelo said, thereafter belittled anyone other than the duke whose company Consuelo appeared to enjoy.[119]

Alva had reason to be concerned about competing interests. Under her very nose, Consuelo had formed a romantic attachment to Winthrop Rutherford, a young man from a prominent New England family descended from Peter Stuyvesant, the colonial governor of Dutch New York, and John Winthrop, the Puritan governor of the Massachusetts Bay Colony. Physically attractive, well educated, and fifteen years older than Consuelo, he was a man of leisure who enjoyed playing golf and polo.[120] In 1893, Alva had invited Rutherford along with other guests to join her family on her husband's yacht the *Valiant* as it sailed from New York through the Suez Canal to India and Ceylon.[121] Rutherford and Consuelo spent a great deal of time together on that trip, and when it was over they began to court in secret. On her eighteenth birthday, Consuelo agreed to marry him. She did not tell her mother, but in retrospect she realized that Alva was well aware of what was going on. In order to destroy her relationship with Rutherford, Consuelo wrote that her mother "laid her plans with forethought and skill," intercepting the letters she and Rutherford wrote to each other, refusing to admit him to the house, and finally taking her back to London to make sure that the two could not see each other.[122]

During their sojourn in London in 1895, Alva and her friends made sure that Consuelo and the duke met often at the constant round of parties, receptions, and entertainments held during the Season. The duke invited Consuelo and Alva to visit Blenheim Palace, the Marlborough estate in Woodstock near Oxford.[123] What followed had all the drama and pathos of a badly written novel. While they were at Blenheim, Alva offered to reciprocate the duke's hospitality by inviting him to visit them in Newport at the end of the summer. When he accepted her invitation, she and Consuelo returned to the United States to prepare for his arrival. "On reaching Newport my life became that of a prisoner, with my mother and my governess as wardens," Consuelo wrote. Her mother locked her in the house and refused to allow her to see her friends except under closely supervised conditions.

Quite by accident, Consuelo met Rutherford at a party. They had one dance only before Alva whisked her away. When they arrived home, Alva marched her daughter upstairs. There they argued. When Consuelo demanded the right to choose her own husband, Alva unleashed her fury and revealed the lengths that she would go to ensure that she got her way. "I suffered every searing reproach, heard every possible invective hurled at the man I loved," Consuelo remembered. "I was," she wrote, "informed of his [Rutherford's] numerous flirtations, of his well-known love for a married woman, of his desire to marry an heiress. My mother even declared that he would have no children and that there was madness in his family." Despite her mother's vicious verbal attack on Rutherford, Consuelo claimed that for once in her life, she stood her ground, which predictably only infuriated Alva all the more. Their confrontation ended when Alva threatened to shoot Rutherford if Consuelo even considered the possibility of running off with him and then stomped out of the room. Consuelo, left by herself, had no recourse. There was no telephone, her mother had ordered the servants to confiscate her letters, and the porter would not let her out of the house. Hours after their quarrel, Alva sent a houseguest to Consuelo's room to inform her that she had suffered a heart attack because of her daughter's "callous indifference to her feelings" and that she would indeed shoot Rutherford if Consuelo should decide to elope. The pressure was apparently too much for Consuelo. She had never before successfully challenged her mother's authority and considered herself "helpless" under her mother's "domination." "Brought up to obey," she surrendered, broke her engagement, threw herself into the whirl of Newport social life, and prepared to marry a man she did not love.[124]

When the duke arrived, the desire to associate with a British aristocrat overcame any qualms the smart set in Newport had about attending social functions hosted by the just-divorced Mrs. Vanderbilt.[125] It was in the Gothic Room at Marble House that the duke proposed.[126] Consuelo unenthusiastically accepted. Once the duke left, she and her mother left Newport for New York to plan the wedding. Consuelo was a completely passive participant in the process. Alva arranged for the ceremony to be held in St. Thomas's Cathedral in New York City on November 6. She then picked out her daughter's wedding dress, ordered her trousseau, selected her bridesmaids, and, having just divorced Willie K., prohibited Consuelo from receiving wedding gifts from anyone on his side of the family.[127]

The duke left no record of his feelings for Consuelo, but aligning himself with the Vanderbilt family had profound financial implications for him. According to the *Atlanta Constitution,* he was in desperate need of money because his father, the eighth Duke of Marlborough, had mortgaged Blenheim Palace to the hilt and sold many of its precious furnishings at auction.[128] He had to have been aware that in cases where European aristocrats married American heiresses, it was common practice for representatives of both families to negotiate what was called a marriage settlement designed to provide the groom with part of his prospective father-in-law's fortune. Once married, the new husband was expected to use this money, known as a dowry or portion, to support his household and provide for any children that he and his wife might bear.[129]

The duke had every reason to expect Consuelo's father to be very generous. Willie K. settled on the couple an annual income of $100,000 derived from the dividends of 50,000 shares of Beech Creek Railroad Company stock. Despite the fact that the British Married Women's Property Act of 1882 limited a husband's control over his wife's property, he also guaranteed his daughter an additional income of $100,000 a year for her own separate use to ensure her financial independence.[130]

News about the duke, Consuelo, their engagement, and their wedding preparations filled the pages of the nation's newspapers from late September through the first week of November.[131] Again the *New York World* provided the Vanderbilts with free publicity while it used the occasion to engage in social commentary regarding social privilege and class relations. Shortly before the wedding, the *World* ran a human interest story on heiresses titled "How a Millionaire's Daughter Is Prepared for Society" along with an operatic libretto titled "Dedbroke, or the Duke and the Debutante (A Suggestion for a Timely Comic Opera Based upon Current Happenings)." It burlesqued the Duke of Marlborough, identified as "the Duke of Dedbroke (the real thing from England)" and his fiancée Consuelo ("Miss Goldandgilt"). Alva Vanderbilt appeared as "Mrs. Goldandgilt" and two of her friends as "Mrs. Gottmunny" and "Mrs. Rich."[132]

Seemingly oblivious to the negative press that accompanied her daughter's approaching nuptials, Alva could not have been happier about the prospect of becoming the mother of an English duchess. It was obvious even to those who were not invited to attend the affair that she managed the wedding with military precision. "She's a general, every inch of her," declared one bystander on the day of the ceremony.[133] Determined to leave no stone unturned to guarantee that the event would go off without a hitch, Alva even posted a footman outside her daughter's bedroom door on the day of the wedding to prevent Consuelo from escaping and any unauthorized person from entering. As a result, Consuelo spent her last day as an unmarried woman alone and in tears of despair. Just before the ceremony, she remembered feeling "cold and numb as I went down to meet my father and the bridesmaids who were waiting for me." She needed time, she remembered, to wipe away all signs of her distress. As a result, she was late to her own wedding.[134]

While her daughter was trying to compose herself, Alva waited in the cathedral. The guests had been seated and the orchestra and organ had finished playing when it became obvious that the bride and her father were not standing at the back of the church ready to walk down the aisle. As minute after excruciating minute passed, the crowd of three thousand began to murmur, and "the Duke became visibly nervous." A reporter for the *New York Tribune* noted that "his face was almost ashen white. He toyed nervously with his slight mustache, stroked his chin with his left hand and tried to appear unconcerned."[135] Sitting in her pew at the front of the church, Alva's anxiety turned to panic. "My heart grew pale," she confessed later. She could not imagine what had happened and did not know what to do. Much to her relief, the bridal party finally entered the narthex and proceeded down the aisle. The young couple spoke their vows. And the marriage that meant more to the mother than it did to the daughter was consecrated. Alva accepted without question the unlikely story that Consuelo and her father had been delayed because they "had fallen into conversation and forgotten to watch the time" and gave it no further thought.[136]

Headlines featuring the Vanderbilt name and extensive descriptions of the elaborate ceremony appeared on the front pages of newspapers across the country.[137] Not all of the commentary was positive. The *Chicago Daily Tribune,* for example, focused its attention on the cost associated with the affair. Estimating that the Vanderbilts and their guests had spent between $500,000 and $700,000 on the event, it provided its readers with an itemization of some of the expenses that included $6,720 for the bride's wedding attire, $15,000 for the floral arrangements that decorated the church, $450,000 for the purchase of wedding presents, and $100,000 for the guests' wedding clothes.[138] "The matter of taste aside, there is good cause for public condemnation of the lavishness with which money was spent upon the wedding of Miss Vanderbilt to the Duke of Marlborough," its editor argued. It was only because most of the money spent by the Vanderbilts and their friends went to "dressmakers, florists, musicians, caterers, jewelers, and tailors," thus putting food on the table of the working class, that such extravagance could be excused, he wrote.[139]

Having married Consuelo off, Alva turned to her own affairs. Less than a year after her divorce and only a couple of months after her daughter's wedding, she married Oliver Hazard Perry Belmont in a civil ceremony conducted by the mayor of New York. Alva's celebrity guaranteed that even though the ceremony was performed privately, it was national news.[140] A graduate of the St. Paul's School and the U.S. Naval Academy, Alva's new husband was the son of August Belmont, a Jewish banker from Germany who had come to the United States in 1837 to represent the interests of the Rothschild family.[141] Oliver, a man with no need or desire to work for a living, devoted most of his adult life to spending his father's money and enjoying himself. He was essentially a charming but aging playboy who had been a member of the Vanderbilts' social circle for a long time. His Newport mansion, Belcourt, was just down the street from Marble House, and he often accepted invitations to be a guest on the Vanderbilt yacht. In 1887–1888, he accompanied Willie K. and Alva on a cruise around the world, enjoying such amenities as sleeping in one of the ship's seven guest bedrooms, eating meals prepared by one of its three chefs, and playing cards before a fire in the library.[142] When Alva's marriage collapsed during the 1893–1894 cruise, he was on hand to comfort her.[143]

Their marriage was a happy one. "The great power within me to love claimed my whole being," Alva told Sara Bard Field some years after Oliver's death. Being with him, she said, "completed for me a life in its perfection in every sense."[144] The newlyweds bought a house on Fifth Avenue between 54th and 55th Streets and with the help of architect Richard Howland Hunt, the son of Richard Morris Hunt, built a country house called Brookholt on Long Island, which served as their summer residence when they were not living in one of their houses in Newport.[145] While she was married to Belmont, Alva lived in an upper-class cocoon, enjoying a life of self-indulgence and pleasure. "It was an ideal life," she recalled, "full of gaiety and fun."[146] They traveled a great deal. Oliver was fond of gardening, so Alva went to France to study landscape architecture and then planned spectacular gardens for Brookholt.[147]

To prevent the boredom that accompanied associating with the same people all the time, she and her friends arranged elaborate, expensive entertainments when they were in Newport. Typical of such events was an automobile parade and driving contest that she organized along Bellevue Avenue in 1899. On the day of the event, she ordered her florist to attach two enormous floral butterflies to the hood of her electric car in such a way as to make it appear that her chauffeur was driving them in the parade. She modeled the driving contest after a drivers' test used by officials in Paris intended to ensure that taxi drivers were skilled enough to carry passengers safely. While Parisian cabbies had to maneuver their way around lampposts, piles of debris, and cast-iron figures of pedestrians and street peddlers, Alva arranged for "a woman dressed as a nurse" to cross the field with a baby doll "in a perambulator, purposely getting in everybody's way. It was for us to avoid her and cover the course laid out for us across and around the field without driving over the 'baby,'" she told one of her secretaries. "Another obstacle was one of Mr. Belmont's dog carts with a servant in livery seated in it and a wooden horse in the shafts. It had to be an effigy," she explained, "because no real horse at that time would have stood or remained controllable in the midst of all those automobiles."[148] Other memorable events included a barn party held in the coach house at Belcourt where the guests came dressed as "housemaids and dairy maids, valets and grooms," a Chinese ball held to celebrate the construction of the pagoda between Marble House and the sea, and potluck picnics held on Bailey's Beach just down the road and around the corner from Belcourt.[149]

Only the collapse of her daughter's marriage in 1906 marred Alva's contentment. The union between Consuelo and her husband, so carefully orchestrated by her mother, was as unhappy as Alva had expected it to be. Consuelo and the duke were ill-suited for each other. So after the birth of an heir and a spare, they decided to separate.[150]

When it became clear that there was no chance for reconciliation, Alva boarded the steamship *Umbria* and sailed for Liverpool on November 3.[151] Oliver followed her a few weeks later.[152] It took until January 1907 for the two families and their lawyers to reach an agreement on a deed of separation. On January 12, they met at Sunderland House in London to work out the final details of the document.[153] Winston Churchill took the lead in representing the duke's interests. Given the personalities involved, it is not surprising that the negotiations were difficult. According to Churchill's private secretary, Phyllis Moir, Alva was the only person she had ever known who could intimidate her employer. "This formidable female adversary proved too much for him," she wrote in her memoir. She claimed that Churchill was a man who appreciated beauty in a woman but had a rather low opinion of female intellect. According to Moir, Alva subjected him time and again to lashings from her "notoriously sharp tongue." When the negotiations were over, there was no love lost between the two. Thereafter, Churchill could not bear the thought of her, and Alva typically referred to him as "'that dreadful man.'"[154]

In order to preserve the reputations of Consuelo and her husband, the deed of separation made no mention of their dysfunctional relationship and alleged infidelities. It merely provided that the couple would share custody of their children, John Spencer-Churchill, the Marquis of Blanford, and Lord Ivor Spencer-Churchill, and that Consuelo could keep Sunderland House in London. In return, the duke got to keep the $100,000 a year income that Consuelo's father had settled on the couple at the time of their marriage, leaving Consuelo to live off her separate estate.[155]

Alva may have regretted that her daughter's marriage was a failure, but she died believing that her efforts on Consuelo's behalf were well intentioned and that, in the end, her strategy for ensuring her daughter's happiness had ultimately succeeded. She maintained that by providing her daughter with the skills to successfully engage in public service, she had guaranteed that Consuelo would find fulfillment outside marriage and that Consuelo's willingness to use those skills had saved her from the temptation to indulge in "selfish grief and introspective melancholy" when it became apparent that her marriage was doomed.[156]

The plan seems to have worked. Having conscientiously fulfilled her philanthropic responsibilities as a duchess to those who lived on the Marlborough estates, Consuelo broadened the focus of her service to others after her separation. She immersed herself in social welfare campaigns designed to improve the lives of women and children in London. Not only did she open a home for prisoners' wives, a lodging house for working women, and a recreation facility for working girls, but she also served on a national commission to investigate the declining birth rate in Britain. She ran for a seat on the London County Council, founded the Women's Municipal Party, and joined the English woman suffrage movement. In the process, she created her own circle of friends. Through Sidney and Beatrice Webb, she met H. G. Wells and George Bernard Shaw as well as other Fabian socialists. And she invited scholars, writers, and social activists to grace her drawing room, drink her wine, and eat at her dining table.[157]

Once they had helped to settle Consuelo's affairs, the Belmonts returned to the United States. Unfortunately, they had very little time to enjoy each other's company. Oliver died in June 1908 from an infection resulting from appendicitis surgery.[158] Predictably, the distraught

Alva was once more subjected to the scrutiny of the press. Both the *Times* and the *World* issued daily bulletins updating their readers concerning the state of Oliver's health. They then reported his death and covered his funeral.[159] True to form, the *World* accompanied its obituary with the sensational revelation that a woman in Galveston, Texas, claiming to be Oliver's only living child, intended to make a claim against his estate.[160]

Horrified and grief stricken, Alva fled to Newport shortly after the funeral. "She arrived at Belcourt at 9:30 AM and Marble House at 11:30 AM," wrote her superintendent William Gilmour in his diary. "She looked very badly indeed," he noted. She stayed for almost a week and then left for Europe with her son William, his wife, and a professionally trained nurse, leaving her lawyers to deal with the scandal and settle Oliver's estate.[161]

In March 1909 she returned to Newport. Arriving in a driving rainstorm, she met with Gilmour to check on her property but seemed distracted and not very interested in what he had to say. She stayed for only four hours.[162]

In the months that followed, however, she began to emerge from her insulated life as a society matron. Desperate for something to do and armed with the settlement from her divorce as well as an inheritance of over a million dollars, she slowly began exploiting her celebrity and her financial resources to promote the political, economic, and social interests of women.[163]

FACING TOP. The Mobile, Alabama, house where Alva was born in 1853. *Courtesy of the Historic Mobile Preservation Society*

FACING BOTTOM. William Kissam Vanderbilt, grandson of Commodore Vanderbilt and Alva's first husband. *Courtesy of the Preservation Society of Newport County*

ABOVE. Alva's mansion on Fifth Avenue in New York City. *Courtesy of the New York Historical Society*

Alva as hostess of the Vanderbilt Costume Ball in 1883.
*Courtesy of the New York Historical Society*

Alva's architectural triumph, Marble House in Newport, Rhode Island. *Courtesy of the Preservation Society of Newport County*

Portrait of Alva as a young matron. *Courtesy of the Preservation Society of Newport County*

Alva with Consuelo and Harold in Paris. *Courtesy of the Preservation Society of Newport County*

Alva's daughter, Consuelo, as a young bride in 1895.
*Courtesy of the Preservation Society of Newport County*

Alva's oldest son, William Kissam Vanderbilt Jr., a noted sportsman. *Courtesy of the Library of Congress*

ABOVE. Harold Stirling Vanderbilt, Alva's younger son, a renowned yachtsman and master bridge player. *Courtesy of Vanderbilt University*

LEFT. Alva's second husband, Oliver Hazard Perry Belmont. *Courtesy of the Library of Congress*

Inez Milholland and Alva on their way to England in 1910.
*Courtesy of the Sewall-Belmont House and Museum*

“Farmerettes” working at Alva’s Brookholt School of Agriculture during the summer of 1911. *Courtesy of the Library of Congress*

ABOVE. Alva's friends rehearse "Melinda and Her Sisters," a suffrage operetta performed in 1916. *Courtesy of the Library of Congress*

RIGHT. Alva's private secretary during the summer of 1917, Sara Bard Field. *Courtesy of the Library of Congress*

Alva as a wealthy New York socialite. *Courtesy of the Sewall-Belmont House and Museum*

Alice Paul, leader of the National Woman's Party. *Courtesy of the Sewall-Belmont House and Museum*

Doris Stevens, suffragist and equal rights advocate. *Courtesy of the Schlesinger Library, Radcliffe Institute, Harvard University*

ABOVE. Alva Vanderbilt Belmont, president of the National Woman's Party. *Courtesy of the Sewell-Belmont House and Museum*

FACING. Alice Paul greets Alva on the steps of the National Woman's Party headquarters. *Courtesy of the Schlesinger Library, Radcliffe Institute, Harvard University*

# 3 A Sex Battle

DURING HER DAYS AS A VANDERBILT, Alva engaged in the conventional sorts of philanthropy: founding a home for ill and convalescent children and supervising the building of an Episcopalian church near her home on Long Island. But she never expressed any interest in social reform or political activism.[1] When she returned from Europe in 1909 after the death of her husband, however, she found her circumstances much altered. Besides the fact that two of her sisters had died, her divorce, widowhood, and self-imposed exile to Europe left her estranged from many of her old associates.[2] She had long nurtured a deep resentment of male power and privilege. She possessed an intellect open to new ideas, an enormous amount of energy, considerable administrative ability, and a great deal of money. And not only had her daughter, Consuelo, taken up the cause of woman's rights in England but one of her best friends, Kitty (Katherine) Duer Mackay, the wife of Clarence Mackay, the founder of International Telephone and Telegraph, had also become a suffragist.[3]

In 1908, Mackay organized the Equal Franchise League, hosted suffrage meetings in her home, and arranged a series of public lectures on the subject of woman's rights in one of New York's theaters.[4] In late March of that year, Kitty invited Alva to attend a suffrage meeting at the exclusive Colony Club in New York City. There Alva met Carrie Chapman Catt; Harriot Stanton Blatch, the daughter of woman's rights advocate Elizabeth Cady Stanton; Fanny Villard, the daughter of abolitionist William Lloyd Garrison; Ida Tarbell, the muckraker;

and Ida Husted Harper. All were prominent members of the National American Woman Suffrage Association (NAWSA).[5] Alva had little time to get involved, however. She left for Europe shortly after her husband's death in June.

At loose ends when she returned from Europe in 1909, Alva accepted an invitation from Mackay to attend a lecture series featuring Harper, who had been a close friend of Susan B. Anthony. Afterwards Harper, who was always interested in recruiting new members, took Alva to NAWSA meetings held at the Martha Washington Hotel in New York. What struck Alva about those meetings was that while those in attendance talked about woman's rights, they seemed incapable of taking any action likely to change women's position in American society. "The audience, always approximately the same audience, seemed to consist only of old and convinced suffragists," she lamented. They appeared to have no idea how to promote the cause.[6]

The atmosphere at those meetings reflected the general condition of the suffrage movement at the time. Efforts to win the vote for women had started in upstate New York in 1846 when six farm women petitioned the state constitutional convention in Albany to grant women suffrage.[7] Two years later, those who attended the Seneca Falls Woman's Rights Convention made the same demand.[8] An argument over the issue of black suffrage after the Civil War split woman's suffrage advocates into two groups—the National Woman Suffrage Association and the American Woman Suffrage Association—which did not unite until 1890. After that, the leaders of the newly created NAWSA initiated a strategy for winning the vote that focused on convincing state legislators to add a woman suffrage amendment to their state constitutions. By the time Alva became interested in the issue, only Wyoming, Idaho, Utah, and Colorado had granted women the right to vote. NAWSA, whose headquarters was located in the small town of Warren, Ohio, was isolated from the seats of political power. And its campaign to win suffrage in state-by-state campaigns had stalled.[9] What the movement needed was new blood, an infusion of cash, and a willingness to implement new strategies.

A woman who had devoted her energy and intellect to fighting her way to the pinnacle of New York society, a woman who had helped design and supervise the building of a series of spectacular mansions, a woman who had managed to marry her daughter off to the most eligible bachelor in Europe, Alva needed something to occupy her time, stimulate her intellect, and give meaning to her life. In short, she needed a new project. So in March 1909 she invited NAWSA's president, Anna Howard Shaw, to dine. Shaw reported to her board a few days after the event: "We staid [*sic*] and talked suffrage until nearly one o'clock. . . . We talked so late that I missed my train and had to stay over at the hotel another night, but I got her for a life member of the National Association before leaving. . . . I think she will help us financially by and by."[10]

In an effort to involve Alva in the affairs of NAWSA, Shaw invited her to attend the International Suffrage Alliance convention to be held in London at the end of April. Alva accepted her invitation, went to London, and attended the conference. She said later that while she found most of the international delegates "very serious, very respectable, [and] very placid," they appeared to be very much like their American counterparts. She despaired of their ever accomplishing anything.[11] The English militants, however, were another matter.

By the time Alva arrived in England in 1909, the English suffrage movement had split into two competing factions. The larger group was the National Union of Women's Suffrage Societies (NU) led by the imminently respectable and dignified Millicent Garrett Fawcett.[12] The Women's Social and Political Union (WSPU), founded in 1903 by Manchester labor activists Emmeline Pankhurst and her daughters Christabel and Sylvia, endorsed a militant approach to the issue of woman suffrage. Their strategy was to create a mass movement whose supporters were willing to engage in behavior considered shocking and therefore newsworthy. The idea was to provoke discussion of the issue. In order to accomplish their goal, WSPU members not only attended political rallies and heckled public officials about their position on the issue of suffrage but also organized large public demonstrations designed to attract the attention of the press.[13]

By 1909, the Pankhursts had moved the headquarters of the WSPU from Manchester to London where they and their supporters marched on Parliament, "paid unwelcome calls" on the prime minister at Number 10 Downing Street, and regularly interrupted speeches by members of Parliament and cabinet ministers. During a march on Parliament led by Emmeline Pankhurst on June 29, 1909, thirteen suffragists systematically broke windows at the offices of the Privy

Council, Treasury, and Home Office. Arrested and imprisoned for their efforts, they protested by going on a hunger strike.[14]

When she was in London, Alva was completely riveted by what she considered to be the WSPU's "lively and picturesque" militancy. She purchased a box for a suffrage rally held in Albert Hall in order to witness the English suffragists' efforts to create a political spectacle designed to promote their cause. She found the experience exhilarating. She was equally impressed with English suffrage parades where woman's rights supporters, carrying "inspiring banners" and "flaming torches," marched through the streets of London. These sights, she dramatically recalled, "moved me not only to quiet tears, but to a determined resolve that American women must not lag behind this stupendous march of women toward the glory of liberty."[15]

Alva claimed that she identified with the English suffragettes, as the militants were called, because she was "a born rebel" who had since childhood harbored a deep resentment about the "degrading position of women."[16] That may have been true, but there were other factors that may have influenced her. The WSPU eagerly recruited well-connected women of the English upper class whose male relatives were noted for their political and social influence. The support of Lady Constance Lytton, sister of the Earl of Lytton; Charlotte Despard, sister of General Sir John French; Anne Cobden Sanderson, daughter of Liberal reformer Richard Cobden; and Margaret Haig (later Lady Rhondda), daughter of the wealthy Liberal member of parliament D. A. Thomas, all gave militant suffrage activity social cachet and blessed it with a measure of respectability.[17]

By 1909, the WSPU was a well-organized propaganda machine with a staff of seventy-five and a budget of over £21,000. It was as much a commercial enterprise as it was a political one. Its entrepreneurial supporters ran shops that sold suffrage merchandise such as jewelry, china, soap, and Christmas cards. And its leaders were able to convince fashionable West End milliners such as Debenham and Freebody, Marshall and Snellgrove, and Burberrys to advertise in their newspaper, *Votes for Women.* Indeed, high-end shopkeepers went out of their way to exploit the appeal of the suffrage movement. One milliner advertised a coat designed specifically for suffragettes made of green and purple fabric, the colors of the WSPU. Another shopkeeper sold purple, white, and green underwear. A fountain pen manufacturer advertised writing instruments inscribed with "Votes for Women."[18] In short, supporting the WSPU was considered both fashionable and good business in some London circles. And Alva, if nothing else, considered herself fashionable.

Having planned many spectacles of her own and having developed some expertise in attracting the attention of the press, Alva appreciated the publicity value of parades, demonstrations, and consumer goods. The strategies utilized by the English suffragettes were certainly more dramatic and newsworthy than those of either the NAWSA or the more conservative English suffragists. She was also drawn to the charismatic Emmeline Pankhurst, whom she described as "a flaming torch in the night which lighted my way."[19] And as a woman who had created a public persona but had not yet found a public voice, she was impressed by the bold rhetoric of militant suffrage speakers.

Inspired by what she had seen and heard in London, she declared herself ready to engage in what she called "a sex battle."[20] In her mind, her willingness to sacrifice herself to improve the condition of women had begun with her divorce suit in 1895. Because of the treatment she had received after her divorce, she could not help but sympathize with female suffrage advocates who "men, press and 'society' abused."[21] But more importantly, she saw that "English women were commanding the attention of the world."[22] Becoming a militant suffragist could provide her the opportunity to expand the celebrity she had so carefully nurtured and at the same time exploit her access to the press to promote a cause that would benefit all American women.

She returned from the London convention energized by her experience and completely politicized. With missionary zeal, she set about to reinvigorate the American suffrage movement by rallying support from those not yet converted to the idea that women should have the right to vote. Her goal, as she put it, was to "go out and convert the multitude."[23] At the same time, however, she was politically astute enough to understand that public spectacles had limited utility in the sense that they accomplished "nothing" in a "practical" sense. She knew that winning the vote could only be achieved by implementing a "definite program."[24]

She attended a suffrage meeting in a rented hotel room in New York City to find only fifteen women seated in the audience, which only confirmed that there was a great deal of work to be done. Disheartened but not deterred, she concluded that the problem was that the public knew little or nothing about woman suffrage and that the strategies employed up to that point to publicize the movement had been totally inadequate. Armed with energy, enthusiasm, enormous resources, and a sense of urgency that demanded that "something . . . be done at once," she began her career as a suffrage publicist.[25]

It being summer, she began her efforts to promote the idea of woman's rights in Newport, Rhode Island, a place she considered to be the "summer-publicity center of the nation." She invited Julia Ward Howe, author of the "Battle Hymn of the Republic," and Anna Howard Shaw, president of NAWSA, to come to Marble House to give suffrage lectures on August 24, 1909, and scheduled a third lecture to be held four days later. In order to encourage attendance and raise money for suffrage at the same time, she arranged for the sale of tickets that allowed the holder to both attend the lecture and tour the first floor of her Newport mansion. The inducement appears to have worked. People, many of them architects and artists from Maine to Michigan, wrote for tickets. Newspapers estimated that over 1100 people attended the two events. Publicity for the cause was what she wanted, and she was happy with the publicity she got. "The event was heralded from coast to coast and across the continent," she remembered. "Articles, cartoons, not always approving, photographs, editorial comment—mostly abuse—followed in the wake of it."[26]

Once the lectures were over, she left Newport for New York determined to continue her public relations efforts on behalf of woman's rights. A flurry of activity followed. She told reporters that she had ordered her architect to build a large room in her new residence at 477 Madison Avenue to serve as a lecture hall for suffragists.[27] And having convinced the NAWSA and the New York State Woman Suffrage Association to move their headquarters to New York City, she rented the seventeenth floor of a Fifth Avenue office building in order to provide them and her own newly minted Political Equality Association (PEA) with office space. Such close proximity, she believed, would increase opportunities for suffragists to share resources and collaborate on strategy. Experience had taught her that image management was an important component in campaigns designed to harness the power of the press. So in order to more systematically exploit her access to reporters, she hired Ida Husted Harper and a staff of assistants to direct a newly created suffrage press bureau.[28] To whet the appetite of the fourth estate, she notified the *New York Times* that she intended to energize the suffrage movement and publicize its activities by borrowing tactics used by the English suffragettes. "I have studied the question of suffrage in England thoroughly," she told reporters, "and I am convinced that more militant methods must be adopted in this country if we hope to succeed."[29] A few days later she told another reporter, "I don't believe in knocking down policemen and forcing yourself into offices where you're not wanted, and getting arrested, and all that sort of thing, but more street meetings, more enthusiasm wouldn't do the cause any harm."[30]

Continually frustrated by genteel suffragists who seemed to prefer "preachment and propaganda" to militant action, she began pressing local politicians to support votes for women. As the November elections approached, she sent suffrage field-workers to Buffalo, Albany, Syracuse, Rochester, and Troy to engage politicians running for the state legislature in discussions regarding their willingness to support woman suffrage. And she sent a series of questions regarding woman suffrage to one of the candidates running for mayor of New York demanding that he respond publicly or face the prospect of being heckled.[31]

Such strategies were both innovative and newsworthy. The newspapers could not get enough of her. They had made her a celebrity. She was their creature, and they were not about to let her go. Typical of the news coverage of her activities was an interview conducted by *New York World* columnist Kate Carew at Belmont's PEA office in December. Carew claimed to have arrived at the suffrage headquarters expecting to talk with a somewhat intimidating "large and aggressive" woman of the world. Much to her surprise, she found Belmont to be slender and small. And it soon became obvious that Alva was also "a serious, practical, masterful woman with an uncommon amount of brain and a great fund of energy and ambition." In order to illustrate her point, Carew asked Alva whether she considered the baby or the ballot more important to women. Belmont, she wrote, responded thoughtfully: "They are interwoven in a curious way which shows that woman's right to political equality with man is part and parcel of her rights and longings as a mother." It is with great sadness, Belmont continued, that having established an intimate relationship with her son during his childhood, a mother must watch both the intimacy and the respect that is due from him diminish when he gets old enough to understand that she plays no role in his political education and that her position vis-à-vis men is one of inferiority.[32] The interview was a journalistic coup for Carew. The editors placed her story on the first page of the editorial section of the paper and accompanied it with pen-and-ink drawings of Belmont and a cartoon illustrating her point.

The sort of name recognition that resulted from such stories provided Alva with the opportunity to place articles supporting suffrage in public affairs magazines. She argued that women needed the vote because while some women were well represented by their male relatives, others were not. "Overworked, underpaid women, the mother toiling for hungry children, the drunkard's wife, the woman of the scarlet letter, the wife replaced by one younger and fairer" had to rely on their own resources and the vote would help them do so, she pointed out to the readers of the *North American Review* in November.[33]

Having thrust herself so unexpectedly into the political life of the nation, she took pleasure in the attention she received. She was gratified when the press began to accuse her of "being 'too active.'" It meant that because of her efforts the issue of woman suffrage was getting the attention it deserved.[34]

The actions of New York City's female shirtwaist workers provided yet another opportunity for her to publicize the cause of women's rights. In November 1909, as many as 18,000 young garment workers marched out of their factories to picket their employers as a way of protesting their low wages and deplorable working conditions.[35]

Alva was already sensitive to the plight of working women. Why this was true is unclear. Her interest in wages and working conditions may have been a product of her association with the Pankhursts, who had begun their public careers as labor organizers. Whatever the reason for her concern, it predated the strike. In September 1909, she had published an article in the *New York American* arguing that political freedom and economic independence were essential for women. Women had entered the workforce for good, she told her readers. "The duty now facing us is to improve the conditions under which women work and to help them obtain an adequate price for their labor." The best way to do that, she asserted, was to provide them with the right to vote. Convinced that labor could play an important role in the suffrage campaign, she conferred with United Mine Workers' leader John Mitchell at the NAWSA's New York headquarters shortly before the strike in order to solicit from him an endorsement of woman suffrage.[36]

The self-sacrificing militancy of the shirtwaist workers—their willingness to forgo their wages for a principle they believed in, to picket in front of their factories in inclement weather, to face verbal harassment, physical abuse, and the humiliation of arrest and imprisonment—appealed to Alva, convincing her that recruiting working women might be just the thing suffragists needed to help energize their movement. In support of the strikers, she helped organize a protester's march through the Bowery and Lower East Side and rented the 6000-seat Hippodrome in midtown Manhattan for a pro-strike rally. When it became clear that the shirtwaist workers needed from $1.50 to $3.00 a week in benefits to support themselves, she solicited strike-fund money from her dinner guests to the tune of $1425. Together with Anne Morgan, daughter of banking tycoon J. P. Morgan, she sponsored a benefit at the exclusive Colony Club which raised another $1300 for the strikers. She loaned her car to the Women's Trade Union League (WTUL) to be used in a parade publicizing the cause of women strikers. Accompanied by her lawyer, she even visited the night court in Greenwich Village, where shirtwaist workers were being arraigned. As the strike dragged on, she helped to arrange another mass meeting in Carnegie Hall, and when the strike finally ended in February, she gave a party for strike leaders at Delmonico's restaurant.[37] What Alva Belmont did was news, so all of her efforts were duly reported in the city's major newspapers.

Reaction to her efforts was mixed. While shirtwaist workers may have been grateful for her help, many members of the NAWSA were ambivalent about promoting an alliance with working women. And some labor leaders, many of whom were socialists, as well as members of the WTUL were suspicious of her motives, saying that she was merely exploiting working women in order to expand the base for suffrage. William Randolph Hearst's *New York Journal* supported Alva's efforts, but conservative periodicals like *Century* magazine found the whole situation alarming.[38] The important point was that she got a reaction and in the process promoted the cause of both suffrage and labor.

Alva's work with the strikers reinforced her desire to build a broad base of support for the movement. Toward that end, she met with Irene Moorman, president of the Negro Women's Business League, and Mrs. S. J. S. Garnet, representing the Colored Woman's Equal Suffrage League of Brooklyn, at her PEA office in mid-January 1910 in order to explore ways in which they could work together to promote woman's rights to vote.[39] On February 6, 1910, she, Ella Hawley Crosset, president of the New York State Woman Suffrage Association, and civil rights advocate Fanny Garrison Villard attended a meeting at the Mount Olive Baptist Church on West 53rd Street. Speaking before a crowd of two hundred, she endorsed the idea of racial equality and the expansion of suffrage to all American citizens at what the *New York Times* identified as "the first colored meeting in the cause of woman suffrage to be held in the city."[40]

At the same time, she began to realize that she could not help build a mass movement from headquarters hidden on the seventeenth floor of a Manhattan office building. So in an effort to make suffrage more visible, she initiated plans to open street-front suffrage settlement clubs in and around the city to serve as satellite branches of her PEA. Her first was a suffrage settlement in Harlem at 84 E. 111 Street, which opened in early February 1910.[41]

By the time she was done, she had established eleven suffrage clubs located in Manhattan, the Bronx, Brooklyn, and Long Island designed to attract a diverse group of people ranging from nurses, artists, physicians, and musicians to ordinary wage earners. In these clubs she organized suffrage meetings, public speaking classes, music programs, and reading rooms. She also opened a lunchroom run by suffrage supporters where working-class women could purchase a nutritious meal for as little as five cents. Wealthy enough to hire a staff to run her organization and its satellites, she insisted on personally supervising their activities.[42]

Such efforts were, of course, time-consuming and very expensive, and Alva insisted on getting credit for her leadership and generosity. In a press release to the newspapers, she claimed that between August 1909 and March 1910, she had spent over $40,000 to support the suffrage movement, including over $8,000 in rent for the office suite that served as PEA, NAWSA, and New York state suffrage association headquarters, another $8,000 for partitioning the space and furnishing it, $12,000 for maintaining the NAWSA press bureau, and $2,400 for paying the salaries of suffrage organizers.[43] At a June meeting of the PEA, she claimed to have reached over 18,000 people by holding suffrage meetings. She said that she and her co-workers had distributed over 22,000 pamphlets, 95,000 buttons, and 60,000 postcards, and that her staff had sent out thousands of letters. She was particularly pleased to report that PEA activities had been mentioned over 17,000 times in the nation's newspapers.[44] Given the fact that the PEA had been in existence for less than a year, her claims were no doubt exaggerated. Nevertheless, it is clear that she knew how to grab the headlines.

Leaving her suffrage storefront settlements in charge of staff, Alva, accompanied by fellow suffragist Inez Milholland, traveled to England during the summer of 1910.[45] By that time, the English suffragists had prevailed upon the House of Commons to consider a suffrage bill, known as the Conciliation Bill. In order to solicit support for its passage, over 10,000 of its supporters marched through London on June 18. On July 11 and 12, Alva sat in the gallery of the House of Commons to watch the bill pass its second reading. Alva then agreed to be interviewed by a reporter from the *New York Times*. She not only expressed her continuing support for the militant tactics of the English suffragettes but also demanded that the rights of American women be expanded. Women in the United States needed the right to vote, she insisted, but their married women's property rights also needed to be ensured and they deserved to have custody rights over their children.[46]

Since three readings were required for passage on the Conciliation Bill, the WSPU held a large rally in Hyde Park on July 23 to demonstrate public support for the legislation. They erected forty platforms intended to accommodate the 150 speakers who were scheduled to address suffrage supporters and onlookers.[47]

Alva returned to the United States in September with a heightened appreciation of the sort of personal sacrifice that leading the suffrage movement might demand. She insisted that American suffragists needed to "give themselves and their life to the public." She wrote in retrospect that she "did not think anyone who stood for or led in this great reform had a right to consider merely her personal preferences." When a woman joined the suffrage movement, she needed to accept the fact that "she had become a public person" and that she would have to deal with "public disapproval."[48]

Alva's continuing concern for working women manifested itself during the winter of 1910–1911, when she began making plans to establish a farm school for women on about 200 acres of her Long Island estate. She sought applications, hired an instructor, and admitted her first class of twenty "farmerettes," who arrived to begin their agricultural education in March.[49] She intended the Brookholt School of Agriculture to provide women employed in factories, offices, and shops a healthy alternative to working in the city. Establishing such a school had public relations value. It stood as an embodiment of her philanthropy and commitment to the welfare of women.[50] Unfortunately, the experiment was a complete failure. By the spring of 1912, the women were gone, and the stock that had been placed in their care had been sold.[51]

Convinced that she had overextended herself by trying to run so many suffrage settlements and that they had served their "purpose as advertising and propaganda centers," she began closing them down in the fall of 1911. As a way of centralizing her efforts, she purchased two buildings on East 41st Street just off 5th Avenue and furnished them to serve as PEA headquarters at a combined estimated cost of $320,000. She not only set up another cafeteria in one of the buildings but also created a Department of Hygiene, or what the press called her "beauty shop."[52] If she had learned anything at all from her years as a leader of society, she had learned the importance of appearances. Knowing that it was common for the press to depict woman's rights advocates as unattractive, she admitted that she "wanted women representing themselves to the world as suffrage advocates to look their best."[53] It was her intention that suffragists be as well groomed as they were well informed. In her beauty shop, prospective woman's rights supporters could listen to lectures on health and personal hygiene delivered by physicians and purchase such items as toothpaste, soap, and corn removers.[54]

A journalist working for William Randolph Hearst credited Alva for almost single-handedly changing the way the New York suffragists presented themselves. She claimed that originally "the clothes that suffragists wore when they went about petitioning were grim as shrouds." Clearly, presenting a logical critique of an unjust political system in "unbecoming clothes . . . hadn't worked in sixty years," she pointed out. It was under Alva's leadership, she said, that women not only began to dress fashionably but "the smartest drawing rooms in the country echoed with the applause of jeweled hands as one inconsistency after another in the judicial system was brought forward and ridiculed."[55]

Such strategies perpetuated Alva's celebrity. She understood that accessibility facilitated publicity and made sure that journalists were on the spot to report that she was intent on supervising every aspect of her new enterprise. They described her as arriving for work at ten each morning with a flourish: Her carriage arrived. Her footman jumped down from his seat, opened her door, and stood at attention until she disappeared into the building. Reporters found the whole scene captivating. They described how she haughtily swept into her office and then turned to her work. "Mrs. Belmont is everywhere," noted one reporter. "One moment she is giving a word of instruction to the peach-faced girl who sells liquid shampoo . . . the next she is watching Chloe of the kitchen range steaming rice."[56]

When she was not tending to business at PEA headquarters, she engaged in other suffrage activities. In April 1912, she began publishing a weekly column in the society section of the *Chicago Sunday Tribune*, using it as a platform for articulating her feminist philosophy and as a way to try to influence the outcome of the November elections.[57] Her approach to women's participation in public affairs combined anti-capitalist rhetoric with maternalism. She claimed that because women had special responsibilities as mothers, they had an important role to play in reforming society. She relentlessly attacked those who opposed suffrage, expressed contempt for politicians who claimed to represent the interest of the people, and identified the benefits to be derived from giving all women access to the ballot. She focused her wrath on the titans of industry, the political bosses who carried out their orders, and the male civil servants who failed to ensure that homes in their cities were clean and well ventilated; that sidewalks, streets, and backyards were free of filth and debris; that the food supply was wholesome; that the public bath system was accessible and sanitary; and that public schools were good.[58] She criticized religious leaders who, instead of preaching God's word and concerning themselves with the poor, allowed their churches to become what she dubbed "Seventh Day Houses" that provided social entertainment for the wealthy men who served on their vestries.[59] And she expressed contempt for the "feeblemindedness of the male electorate," whose impotence allowed such arrangements to continue.[60]

She began her series by pointing out that the world was arranged for the comfort and pleasure of men. Women and children were the victims of that arrangement, she declared. She noted, for example, that "predatory" men felt free to engage in extramarital sex and then infect their wives with venereal disease while employers forced female wage earners to work in unhealthful conditions, thus making it impossible for women to fulfill their maternal responsibilities to bear and rear healthy children.[61] She repeated a point she had made seven months earlier in the *World To-Day* that while men had willingly given women responsibility for preserving the sanctity of the home and rearing children, they had neglected to give them the means to do so.[62] Only through the vote, she argued, could women protect their families from such threats.[63]

An even more serious problem for women, in her opinion, was the alliance of industrialists and political bosses who turned a blind eye to the needs of the average citizen. "The money interests in collusion with the politicians form a plutocracy," she wrote. The result, she suggested, was that in the United States there was no such thing as a free market economy. Trusts run by the titans of industry controlled wages, the supply of consumer products, prices, and government policies regarding such matters as tariffs—a situation which resulted in raising the cost of living for everyone. Given those circumstances, she argued, it was virtually impossible for ordinary people to adequately house, feed, and clothe their children.[64] "Today," she wrote, "the corporation employer virtually holds in bond the toiler everywhere—in mine, factory, railroad and shop—and is now stretching out and enslaving the small merchant and dealer." She insisted that all workers had a vested interest in changing this situation but that the six million women who engaged in wage labor had no way to do so without being able to vote.[65]

Alva was particularly critical of upper-class women who failed to assume a leadership position in efforts to expand woman's rights. She claimed that opposition to woman suffrage was "most bitter" and "aggressive" in their households. She described them as "silly," clinging women who rarely voiced their own opinions and vapidly spent their days doing nothing but amusing themselves. It was a waste, she declared, that their only accomplishments were in bearing sons for their husbands and enhancing their husbands' "consequence by winning social victories." Such women, she charged, whether "for the sake either of the luxury or wealth she may thus obtain, or for fear of facing life alone" were nothing more than "paid legitimate prostitute[s]." And it was a disgrace, she opined, that they "heartily echo[ed] their masterful lords" in their opposition to woman suffrage.[66] She called upon society matrons to re-educate themselves, to assert their individualism, to become self-supporting and self-reliant, to find outlets for their ambition, and to train themselves to fulfill the demands of citizenship if for no other reason than they should be concerned about the way their tax money was spent.[67]

Alva was convinced that women would eventually gain the right to vote. But in the process, she warned, woman's rights advocates had to be "vigilant and active" in their effort to promote the idea of suffrage by asking candidates for public office about their position on the issue. They should understand, she told them, that assurances and promises would not be enough. Politicians, she pointed out, "are not inconvenienced with retentive memories."[68] But since promises were all suffrage supporters had at the moment, she advised her readers that the Progressive Party under the leadership of Theodore Roosevelt was more likely to give women the vote than either the Democrats or Republicans.[69] She may have been right. But Woodrow Wilson, a Democrat, won the election, and he was no supporter of woman suffrage.

While she was acting the part of journalist on behalf of suffrage, she also joined over 10,000 suffrage supporters who marched the fifty or so city blocks from Washington Square to Carnegie Hall for a rally on the evening of May 4, 1912. Dressed in white, Alva waited on the sidewalk to lead a group of shop girls who did not get off work until six. Once they all took their places in the parade, she marched alone at the head of their column. "She had the appearance of a brave soldier facing fire, looking straight ahead," said a *New York Times* reporter.[70] A brave soldier she was. Inexplicably for a woman who had spent her adult life courting the attention of the press, she found marching in the suffrage parade an excruciatingly painful experience. "To a woman brought up as I was, it was a terrible ordeal," she told her daughter,

Consuelo.[71] However uncomfortable she may have found that venue, at least one columnist, Beatrice Fairfax, credited her appearance with forcing politicians to take suffrage seriously. "The greatest shove ever given to the suffrage movement will always be that lady's appearance at the head of a suffrage parade in New York City," the journalist wrote in her memoir years afterward.[72]

Shortly after the parade, Alva left New York to open Marble House for the season and set up a suffrage headquarters in Newport in order to raise money and recruit support for the cause among the city's summer residents.[73] When she returned to New York City in the fall she again took up the cause of working women. In January 1913, she attended a rally at the Hippodrome held to offer support to striking garment workers. And when the newspapers charged that wage-earning ticket holders had caused a riot in the lobby, she challenged their version of what had happened. From where she had been sitting, she saw no riot, she said. The gathering, she reported, had been "as orderly as a church meeting." Indeed, she claimed to have seen "rowdier behavior at fashionable weddings."[74]

In February, she testified before a New York State legislature committee investigating the police, working women, and prostitution in New York City. Warning the committee that trafficking in girls for immoral purposes was increasing, Alva recommended that the legislature authorize the city to hire policewomen to help patrol its vice districts. Under her plan, policewomen could compel reluctant policemen to arrest the men who accosted women in the street and the testimony of policewomen would carry the same weight as policemen. "Without in any way depreciating the value of the policeman," she told the state's legislators, "it seems to me . . . [that] he is not qualified to deal with delinquent girls without the help of a woman."[75] In April, she wrote to the secretary of the Committee on Criminal Courts in New York suggesting that rather than solicit the state government for funds to deal with young prostitutes, they should ask the state legislature to pass a law authorizing the "arrest [of] every man, rich or poor, young or old, who traffics in human bodies." Fining each "heavily according to his means" would provide the revenue necessary to build a refuge for his "victims," she argued.[76]

Shortly thereafter, she returned to England to monitor the activities of the English suffragettes, visit her daughter, and attend the

International Congress of the Woman Suffrage Alliance to be held in Budapest.[77] Militancy was then at its height in London. Eighteen months before, Parliament had dissolved before the suffrage bill had a chance to pass its third reading.[78] The Pankhursts and members of the WSPU responded by initiating a policy of vandalism, assault, bombing, arson, and sabotage which included breaking windows and attacking the Royal Mail Service by pouring acid, ink, and tar into mailboxes in London and other cities.[79] By 1913, engaging in illegal activities had escalated. Members of the WSPU claimed responsibility for burning suffrage slogans on the putting greens of private golf clubs, smashing a case holding the crown jewels in the Tower of London, cutting telephone and telegraph lines between London and Glasgow, burning the orchid house at Kew Gardens, smashing the windows of exclusive London clubs, and burning down the refreshment stand in Regents Park.[80] The intent was to make such a nuisance of themselves that the government would acquiesce to their demands just to be rid of them. The government's response was to arrest and imprison the perpetrators they could identify and find.

Before Alva arrived in England, Emmeline Pankhurst had been arrested, convicted, and sentenced to three years' imprisonment for having firebombed the house of Lloyd George, a prominent member of Parliament. Her response was to go on a hunger strike. The government responded by passing what was called the Cat and Mouse Act, a law providing that prisoners whose health was damaged by hunger striking be released to recuperate and then rearrested.[81]

Alva supported the WSPU's defiance of the law and the destruction of property that accompanied their militant campaign. In hindsight, she declared it hypocritical for people, who were preparing to engage in a "great world conflagration," to declare "force," when used by "female furies" as "ethically bad." "How men so deprecate 'force' when used by women," she said. "Used by them for their own liberties it becomes a sacred thing and glorious in their eyes." She saw a gendered difference between men's war for democracy and women's war for civil rights. As she pointed out, when men go to war, they intend to kill their opponents while women only intend to kill "the IDEA held by their opponents."[82]

It is also clear that she was furious about the government's force-feeding policy. When the subject came up during an interview with a reporter, she lost her temper: "Look at the shameful torture of forcible feeding that goes on in your prisons! You have maimed several women already. . . . The whole world is ashamed of you." After what women had been forced to put up with from a "tyrannical" and "hypocritical" government, she continued, the destruction of property by fire and bombs was more than justified. She declared herself unwilling to pass judgment on the hunger strikers. They had to accept responsibility for their own actions. But she insisted that force feeding must end.[83]

Alva left London, attended the Budapest Conference in the middle of June, and then retired to a villa outside Deauville on the English Channel in Normandy. There she entertained Christabel Pankhurst, who had fled to Paris in March 1912 to escape arrest and confinement.[84] Intent on doing all she could to promote the cause of women at home and abroad, Alva generously provided Pankhurst with a quiet, luxurious retreat where she could write suffrage propaganda and direct the affairs of the WSPU from afar without fear of government harassment.

Alva was completely captivated by her guest, a woman she regarded as powerful, charming, perceptive, and brilliant. She fondly remembered their conversations, their "moonlit walks in the garden overlooking the sea," and their rides together through the countryside.[85] Since her entry into suffrage work, Alva had made it a point to seek out the company of talented, attractive young women. Christabel, like Inez Milholland before her, was all that and more. Petite and slender with brown hair and deep blue eyes, Christabel was passionate about the cause of suffrage and willing to suffer the consequences of being the brains behind the reign of terror that the suffragettes were imposing on the British government for refusing to give women the vote.[86] She was a woman after Alva's own heart. Alva never forgot their summer together. Indulging in a propensity to romanticize this heroine of the English suffrage movement, she vividly remembered "this slip of a girl" with moonlight falling on her "brave, heroic young face" discussing "with vivid imagination and penetrating wisdom the great tragedy of womankind."[87]

That summer, Alva's chateau was, as she put it, a "mecca" for distinguished guests whom she invited to meet and talk with Pankhurst about suffrage and the international tensions that would eventually erupt in war.[88] The *New York Times* even reported that Alva tried to broker a truce between the suffragettes and the British government by arranging at dinner party at the Ritz in Paris so that Christabel and selected members of Parliament could devise "some graceful way of allowing the English Government to back out of its present disagreeable predicament with the militant suffragettes." Her effort failed; Christabel was apparently unwilling to negotiate.[89]

Immersing herself in affairs related to suffrage for most of the summer abroad only made Alva more exasperated with what she considered to be the timidity and ineffectiveness of NAWSA leaders at home. She was increasingly "tired of having to pull along with me a heavy mass of suffrage conservatism."[90]

But it was not just suffrage that she was concerned about. No doubt inspired by Christabel, she announced in September that she intended to continue her campaign against prostitution.[91] Later that month she agreed to help sponsor the performance of a play titled *The Guilty Man* which advocated making all children legitimate at birth and legalizing birth control, including abortion.[92] And in December she wrote a letter, which was published in the *New York Times*, supporting the screening of *The Inside of the White Slave Traffic*, a film on prostitution. "The existence and rapidly increasing enormity of the white slave traffic in every section of the world will not be ignored with impunity, and, in my judgment, no more effective way has yet been devised to arouse the public to its responsibility toward the abolition of this terrible evil than the film referred to," she declared.[93]

Meanwhile in October, she used her connections to resolve the issue of whether Christabel's mother, Emmeline Pankhurst, should be admitted to the United States for a fund-raising tour. When she heard that Emmeline had been detained at Ellis Island, she sent her lawyer, Herbert Reeves, to investigate and then to petition for a writ of habeas corpus from the commissioner of immigration. She also offered to post a bond to ensure Pankhurst's good behavior.[94] When government authorities were finally convinced that Pankhurst was not among those who qualified as "dynamiters, arsonists, seditionists, silly fulminators, nihilistic flouters and mannish Amazons," she was released and allowed to go about her business.[95]

It was in December 1913, at a NAWSA convention in Washington, D.C., that Alva met Alice Paul.[96] Paul was the epitome of the "new woman." She was young, middle class, college educated, and like many of her contemporaries, less interested in marriage than she was in public service.[97] The daughter of a banker, Paul was a graduate of Swarthmore and had done graduate work at both the University of Pennsylvania and the London School of Economics. While she was in England, she joined the WSPU. In 1909, she was arrested and imprisoned for her suffrage activities and participated along with other jailed suffragists in a series of hunger strikes. Returning to the United States in 1910 to recuperate, she finished her PhD and joined the NAWSA. With NAWSA president Carrie Chapman Catt's blessing, Paul and her friend Lucy Burns went to Washington in 1913 to lobby Congress as the head of an arm of the suffrage organization called the Congressional Committee (CC).[98] Paul had unimpeachable reform credentials and a history of militancy. She was also a compelling speaker with what appeared to Alva to be a clear understanding of the political and financial problems facing the suffrage movement.[99]

Described by her co-workers as "slender and frail-looking," self-sacrificing, indomitable, and occasionally ruthless, she was a charismatic figure.[100] "She is the most extraordinary woman," said Mabel Vernon, who had gone to Swarthmore with Paul. "She's no bigger than a wisp of hay, but she has the most deep and beautiful violet-blue eyes, and when they look at you and ask you to do something," it was impossible to refuse.[101] Sara Bard Field, who worked with Paul, agreed completely. "If Miss Paul had been a general in the army she would have known exactly what her troops would do and have them do it without any flinching whatsoever," she said. "I don't mean that she was dictatorial either. She had a way of just assuming this was what you wanted to do because it was good for the party."[102] It was not through affection that she influenced people, said Doris Stevens, another of Paul's recruits. It was through "a vital force which is indefinable but of which one simply cannot be unaware. Aiming primarily at the intellect of an audience or an individual, she almost never fails to win an emotional allegiance." Paul was such a successful but "silent adversary" that some of her associates called her "the Silent Bullet." When she asked someone to perform a task that they were unlikely to want to perform, she merely sat back and listened quietly to their objections. When they finished, she repeated her request, and they inevitably agreed to do as they were told.[103]

Paul eschewed the democratic model of governance adopted by the NAWSA for that of a highly structured hierarchy. She chaired the CC; Lucy Burns served as vice chairman; and Mary Beard, Crystal Eastman Benedict, and Dora Lewis acted as their advisors.[104] Although Paul sought the opinions of her associates and depended on staff members, including field-workers, to do much of the organization's work, everyone knew who was in charge. Under her management, power was centralized and lines of authority were clear. Because of these factors, those outside her inner circle had only limited opportunities to wield power.

Before Alva left for Europe to attend the Budapest Conference in the spring of 1913, Paul and Burns had already begun implementing the sort of attention-getting strategies inspired by those of the WSPU. In January of that year, they began organizing a suffrage parade to be held in Washington on March 3, the day before Woodrow Wilson was to be inaugurated president of the United States. Modeled on the public demonstrations sponsored by the English suffragettes, it was to be a spectacular event during which an estimated eight thousand woman suffrage supporters, accompanied by twenty-six floats, ten bands, six mounted heralds, six mounted brigades, and six chariots marched down Pennsylvania Avenue from the Capitol, past the Treasury and the White House, demanding that women be given the right to vote.[105]

This was just the sort of activity that might ordinarily have appealed to Alva. So Caroline I. Reilly, a New York suffragist, offered to broker an effort to recruit her and thereby exploit her celebrity status and her money. She wrote to Burns assuring her that Alva was interested in their activities and that she might be persuaded to participate in the suffrage events they were planning in Washington if they could provide an appropriate venue for her.[106] Alva had suggested to Reilly that she might come to Washington for the pre-inaugural suffrage festivities, but she was unwilling to be treated as a mere bystander. At the same time, however, she made it clear that she thought it "silly to ride in a chariot, a float or sit on a throne." The challenge, then, was to tailor an invitation that would accommodate Alva's sense of entitlement. Hoping to lure the rich socialite to Washington, Reilly asked if Alva could sit with other dignitaries on the reviewing stand so that she could see the parade as something more than an ordinary spectator.[107] The underlying message in Reilly's request made it plain that it would be a good idea to give Alva special treatment. No one, Reilly suggested, could reasonably expect a woman of Alva's age and social status to come all the way to Washington to stand on a street corner to watch the parade.

Burns was aware of the financial benefits to be derived from involving Alva in the parade and pageant, so she passed Reilly's letter on to Glenna Smith Tinnen, the woman in charge of parade arrangements, attaching the following note: "Apparently Mrs. Belmont doesn't . . . want to walk. Could she be used as a figure in the pageant? Have you ever seen her, & do you think she could be made to do? She is a newspaper item. And once here [she] would probably contribute." She then signed the note, "Greedily, L. Burns."[108] Perhaps because she was extraordinarily busy or perhaps because she did not appreciate what might be gained from including the rich society woman in their plans, Tinnen did not send Alva one of the elegant engraved invitations that served as the ticket to sit on the reviewing stand.[109] Instead, she invited her to sit on a float, an honor that Alva courteously declined.[110] As inauguration day approached, Alva made no plans to travel to Washington. Months passed before another opportunity arose to attract her attention and solicit her support.

It was clear that Paul and Burns understood the advantages to be derived from soliciting Alva's support. Suffrage activists were typically women of modest means who found it necessary to support their activism by earning money.[111] There were exceptions, of course. Rich women such as Olivia Sage, Mary Elizabeth Garrett, and Harriot Stanton Blatch could be counted on to provide the movement with both financial support and social cachet.[112] Like them, Alva was an immensely wealthy and deeply committed feminist, but she also had political connections that Paul's organization could access only through someone like her. Alva's second husband had served a term in Congress, and she was socially connected to some of the most important politicians and bureaucrats in Washington.[113] As her efforts to liberate Emmeline Pankhurst from her imprisonment on Ellis Island had proved, her money and political connections could be used to benefit the suffrage movement. Like other socialites, Alva also had experience planning banquets, balls, and conferences, and better yet, had the means to both sponsor and pay for events that could involve hundreds of people who might not under normal circumstances take an interest in suffrage.

The prospect of associating with someone of Alva's social status could be counted on to help attract the interest and financial support of those with social aspirations as well as those who provided services to the wealthy. Indeed, Mary Beard assured Paul that "every swell" in Washington would fall all over themselves to attend any event that Alva decided to sponsor. "Our committee can't reach that element as she can and we need its money and support," she pointed out. All they needed to do, she suggested, was let Alva sponsor a meeting, arrange for whatever speakers she wanted, invite her rich friends and acquaintances, and take up a collection for the organization's benefit.[114]

By the time Alva returned from Europe in the fall of 1913, she was tired of the constant petty bickering that plagued the leadership of the NAWSA and was fed up with its conservatism.[115] It was becoming increasingly clear that there was no place in the NAWSA for her to exert any real influence over policy or strategy.[116] The final straw came in December at the NAWSA convention when she tried to persuade the organization's leaders that they should move their headquarters from New York to Washington so that they would be able to lobby Congress more effectively. She found it particularly galling when they tabled her resolution.[117] Convinced that she did not have the influence that her financial contributions should have given her, Alva was ready to find some other avenue to promote the cause of suffrage.

Paul and her associates began courting Alva shortly thereafter. By that time, they too had split with the NAWSA. The media attention that the CC parade received prompted the Senate Suffrage Committee to pass a resolution calling for a vote on the suffrage amendment, the first time it had seriously been considered since its introduction in 1878. Paul and her associates considered this a great victory. But NAWSA leaders, aware that passage was unlikely, considered such a vote premature and worried that a negative vote would do nothing to advance their cause.[118] Moreover, on the last day of their convention in December 1913, Paul had given a report on her lobbying activities as chair of the CC and an accounting of her expenditures. During that report, it became apparent to NAWSA leaders that Paul had failed to deposit money raised on behalf of the CC in the NASWA's account. They also suspected that she was in the process of setting up an affiliate organization, one that would not have to rely on or answer to NAWSA's leadership. Paul wanted the Congressional Union for Woman Suffrage (CU), as her new association was to be called, to engage in a more partisan, militant strategy than had been the case with the NAWSA. All efforts on the part of NAWSA leaders to keep Paul, Burns, and their supporters in the fold failed.[119] So Paul and her associates declared their independence.[120]

Timing was important. The CU had a small loyal base but very little money. After noting that Alva could "give a lot," Mary Beard encouraged Burns to come to New York, meet Alva, and "arrange matters in a friendly way but with a clear understanding of her position."[121] At the same time, Crystal Eastman Benedict put pressure on Paul to pay Alva a visit, extending her an invitation from Belmont to spend the night with her. "She's [referring to Alva] crazy about the CU," Benedict wrote. "I think she's *all right* and means to give the work a big gift."[122] Later that month, it was Paul who accepted a dinner invitation from Alva. After their meal, they stayed up until two in the morning discussing the suffrage campaign. Paul remembered their conversation as interminable but considered her time well spent.[123]

Despite Alva's access to the press and the potential her wealth had for providing the sort of financial support that the militants needed, not all of Paul's associates were enthusiastic about recruiting her. A public figure with tremendous energy and strong opinions, she had grown used to demanding and receiving her fair share of attention, being in control, giving orders, and having them obeyed. By 1914 she had been involved in the woman's rights movement long enough to feel that she understood the challenges that suffragists faced and to have devised strategies that she believed would help win the vote. She was determined that in return for her financial support she be given a position on the CU advisory board and assurance that her opinions would count for something. "Mrs. B. is quite keen about the CU," Benedict wrote in a letter to Burns on January 9, 1914, but "says quite frankly that she won't give money unless she has some representation on it[s board]. . . . I don't think Mrs. B would want to interfere or dictate. She just doesn't like to be made a baby of—to be used just for money and not for work or advice."[124] Fellow suffragist Mary Beard made the same observation: "Mrs. Belmont is justified in not wanting to be considered merely a money bag," she wrote to Burns; "she wants to be asked for her opinion now and then just to be a human being."[125] A few days later she reiterated her point when she again wrote to Burns, "If we treat her as a being capable of thought she will be a valuable ally, without interfering unduly too."[126]

Women of means commonly demanded the kind of influence and authority that Alva made a condition of her support. Take Nettie McCormick, the widow of Cyrus McCormick, inventor and developer of the McCormick reaper and the man to whom Alva's father sold their house in New York in 1866. Between 1887 and 1915, she gave money for building construction to Tusculum College in Greenville, Tennessee, a school that trained Presbyterian ministers. But she reserved the right to dictate the amount to be spent on the buildings, to decide which architect was to design them, to appoint her lawyer to monitor the solicitation of construction bids, and to choose the furnishings. Moreover, she did not feel it an imposition to demand that the college president visit the construction site every day "to assure that she was paying for the very best materials and workmanship."[127]

Margaret Dreier Robins of Chicago exerted similar power as president and chief benefactor of the National Women's Trade Union League (NWTUL), an organization founded in 1903 to help wage-earning women form unions and lobby for protective legislation. Funding NWTUL activities depended almost entirely upon the generosity of rich philanthropists. So Robins dipped into her personal resources and solicited donations from her friends.[128] Because of her money, her social contacts, and her fund-raising skills, Robins had accumulated unprecedented power within the organization by 1911. As NWTUL member Pauline Newman put it in a letter to Rose Schneiderman, "Mrs. Knefler [president of the St. Louis league] is perfectly right when she says the League is owned and controlled by one person. . . . I find that Mrs. Robins pays everybody's salary, all other necessary expenses, and as a consequence she has no opposition in the entire organization."[129]

Mary Elizabeth Garrett of Baltimore provides a third example of what historian Kathleen Waters Sander has characterized as "coercive philanthropy." A dedicated suffragist and heiress to a railroad fortune, Garrett directed her considerable resources toward providing women with educational opportunities. By raising money to support the establishment of a medical school at Johns Hopkins and offering to donate over $300,000 to its endowment, she held the trustees of the university hostage to her demand that women be allowed to study medicine on the same basis as men. When the medical school opened in 1893, three women had been admitted to the nation's first graduate school of medicine.[130]

Dealing with donors who wanted to run things was an occupational hazard for leaders of institutions and reform organizations dependent upon the generosity of the very rich to support their programs. So while Benedict and Beard thought that giving Alva the leadership position she wanted was only fair, others felt justifiably concerned about how the reallocation of power within their organization might diminish their ability to accomplish their goals. It was for that reason that Katharine Houghton Hepburn opposed efforts to solicit Alva's support. Belmont, she pointed out, was "in the habit of running things absolutely" and would surely try to control the policy of the organization.[131]

Alva's impact on the power structure of the organization, however, was not the only concern of CU insiders. Used to doing things her own way and to receiving a good deal of attention and deference from those who associated with her and sought her support, Alva was also hard to deal with on a personal level. For this reason Hepburn warned that the CU should beware of welcoming Alva. "She really enjoys eternally fussing about details, and would use up all your energy and then would not be satisfied," she wrote.[132]

The inner circle of CU supporters also worried that rich women had reputations for enthusiastically taking up a cause only to drop their support when they got bored with it. Conventional wisdom had it that the enthusiasm and generosity of the upper class was not something you could count on over the long haul, particularly when it came to social reform. Hepburn, for one, was skeptical about the level of Alva's commitment. She feared that Alva had "none of the idealism that would make her give in large amounts either in money or personal devotion."[133] Even Beard, who supported the idea of recruiting Alva, later admitted that her "'progressive' passion" might soon "blow over."[134]

Alva sensed their skepticism. She was savvy enough to realize that reinventing oneself was not easy. And she understood that people often had little or no confidence in the sincerity of wealthy society matrons who expressed interest in matters relating to progressive social and political reform. After all, rich women benefited from the social and economic inequities that characterized life in the early twentieth century, and their privileged positions typically kept them insulated against the need to acknowledge those inequities. "The vulgar idea is that the society woman has no heart, no soul, no idealism," Alva said. She knew that this preconceived notion would produce some doubt about her motives and the level of her commitment.[135] When she joined the suffrage movement in 1909, she had felt it necessary to assure the public that her support of suffrage was not a "fad." "I sometimes regret that I have money, for many persons think that to give money to a cause ends all interest of the donor in the cause," she told a group of reporters. "They think it is like throwing a bone to a strange dog. One cares nothing for the bone and perhaps less for the dog. Not so with me in this cause." She went on to say that she not only had money to spend on promoting the idea that women should have the right to vote but would also invest her time and energy in the suffrage movement because she felt that "only to spend money in such a cause is unworthy of it." The movement needed workers as well as money, and she intended to provide the leadership necessary to convince her friends and acquaintances to support suffrage.[136]

CU leaders were also concerned that if it became known that a woman such as Belmont gave them particularly generous donations, it might discourage the bulk of CU supporters from continuing to contribute. From the beginning, the suffragists depended upon a large number of small donations to finance their campaign. Most of these donations fell in the $1–$10 range.[137] Their supporters typically did not work for wages, had little ready cash, and, although they had charge accounts and paid the bills, their husbands usually signed the checks.[138]

Sensitive to the effort that many women had to exert in order to financially support suffrage, Harriet Taylor Upton, a former NAWSA treasurer, had warned that when ordinary supporters heard that someone with as much money as Alva had sent the organization thousands of dollars, they might stop giving: "Women who used to give a dollar [may think] its [*sic*] not worth the while to send such a drib. So our apparent prosperity [may well be] our undoing."[139] Upton understood that small contributions to the CU served suffrage in a variety of ways. First, suffragists were in the process of creating what they hoped would be a mass movement, and those contributions served as confirmation of their success in appealing to a wide range of supporters. Second, since small donors often had to make personal sacrifices to send them money, their donations stood as testimony to their commitment to suffrage. Finally, while checks of one or two thousand dollars helped in times of financial crisis or in support of special projects, it was the steady stream of small donations that allowed the CU staff to establish a dependable cash flow and carry out their work on a day-to-day basis. So from Upton's point of view, suffrage leaders needed to take care not to alienate their supporters by making their sacrifice seem unnecessary.

In the end, those who understood that one "could not accept a heavy contributor without giving her a great deal of power" won the day.[140] It was important to the CU to exploit both Alva's name and money. Alice Paul wrote to Mary Beard on January 9, 1914, "Can you persuade Mrs. B. to make a pledge before Sunday so we can announce it at Mrs. Kent's meeting?"[141] Her request was premature. But once Alva was assured that she would have a place on the CU's Executive Committee, she withdrew her support from the NAWSA and, at the end of the month, sent a note to Paul pledging her support for CU activities along with a check for $5000 to help pay for them.[142] In February, she became a member of the Executive Committee.[143] She told the press that she believed that Washington should be the focus of the suffrage campaign and that "inasmuch as the National Association did not see fit to agree with me, I decided to swing my influence where I thought it would prove more effective."[144]

Almost immediately she began to solicit money from her friends for the benefit of the CU and to think about ways to promote the CU in the press.[145] By the end of 1914, she had donated $12,600 to the organization, which comprised about half of all the money raised that year.[146] She also had begun looking for a building in Washington to house the CU's lobbying operation. The *Washington Post* welcomed her with open arms, noting that she was "a most estimable woman whose wonderful ability as a leader and capacity for successful achievement in charitable and educational work has been universally recognized."[147]

It is unclear how upset the leaders of the NAWSA were about her defection. From 1908 until women got the vote in 1920, Katharine Dexter McCormick, Cyrus and Nettie McCormick's daughter-in-law, provided funds for that organization's activities. And when Mrs. Frank Leslie (Miriam Florence Leslie) died in 1914, she bequeathed Carrie Chapman Catt almost a million dollars to be used at her discretion to support activities that would lead to the enfranchisement of women.[148]

It was to Paul's advantage to exploit Alva's money, her fund-raising expertise, her administrative skills, and her seemingly unending supply of ideas about how to promote the cause of suffrage. Confident that Alva had the experience, connections, resources, and personal staff to carry out her ideas without tapping into the assets of the CU, Paul turned her largest donor into what today would be called a special projects manager. When Alva came up with a scheme intended to raise money and publicize the suffrage campaign, Paul simply stepped aside and let her make whatever arrangements were necessary to carry it out. By keeping her busy, Paul adopted a creative but passive strategy to ensure that Alva did not interfere unduly with the management of the CU.

Money and initiative were not the only benefits to be derived from Alva's association with the CU (soon to become the National Woman's Party). A scrapbook compiled by members of Alva's staff contained almost 300 pages of articles from a wide range of newspapers such as the *Milwaukee Sentinel* and the *Dallas Morning News* chronicling her role in the suffrage movement from June to December 1909.[149] In 1910, Ida Husted Harper, head of the NAWSA Press Bureau, credited the impressive increase in press coverage of suffrage activities to Alva's association with the movement.[150]

But managing Alva's dealings with the press could be a problem for other suffrage leaders. Alva had a vile temper, and when it was directed at reporters, she was likely to throw them out of her office.[151] And she resisted even well-intentioned attempts to collaborate on composing press releases, as Caroline Reilly discovered shortly after Alva joined the CU. On January 31, 1914, Reilly wrote to Burns saying that Belmont was anxious to submit a pro-suffrage article to the Hearst papers describing the CU and its program. Reilly understood the importance of Alva's connection with the Hearsts and suggested that Burns write the article. She would edit it, she said, and then give it to Alva who would submit it.[152] When the article was finished, Reilly delivered it to Alva who began composing an introduction to the piece that was particularly critical of the Progressives. CU leaders were determined not to do or say anything that might alienate the only political party who had come out in support of woman suffrage. But when Reilly suggested that Alva rework the offending passages, Alva "flew into a rage"—saying "that if she had to be dictated to she would do nothing; that when she was requested to take any action, no matter what the nature of it might be, she must be left to decide just how it shall be done. She knew what was required, better than anyone else, and her method must be pursued or none at all."[153] In this case, it turned out to be none at all.

The most immediate issues facing Alva and the CU in 1914 were political and financial. By the time Alva took her place on the CU board, Paul and her associates were in the process of developing a strategy for dealing with what became known as the Shafroth-Palmer amendment. This proposal, sponsored by the NAWSA, Democratic Senator John Franklin Shafroth of Colorado, and Democratic Representative Alexander Mitchell Palmer of Pennsylvania, was a state initiative effort that required states to hold referenda on woman suffrage when 8 percent of those who had voted in the last state election signed a petition calling for it.[154] The alternative proposal, popularly known as the Susan B. Anthony amendment, sponsored by Republican Senator Joseph Little Bristow of Kansas and Republican Representative Frank Wheeler Mondell of Wyoming, provided for a federal constitutional amendment providing that no one be denied the vote on the state or federal level because of their sex. This proposal had been languishing for almost twenty-seven years.

Arguments in favor of the Shafroth-Palmer approach included the belief that the South—dedicated to the theory of states' rights, determined to control the vote within its borders, and distrustful of federal authority—might be more sympathetic to the idea of woman's suffrage if provisions for it were initiated by the states. Supporters also pointed out that it was being proposed by two Democrats at a time when the Democrats controlled Congress, which meant that, in theory at least, it would be easier to pass than a Republican-sponsored measure. The third argument in its favor was that if, under its provisions, enough states passed referenda providing women the right to vote, it would make it easier to pass a federal amendment.

Both Alva and the other members of the CU supported the Susan B. Anthony amendment which would have provided federal protection for woman suffrage. But it was clear to them that they needed the time to garner more support for it. Their strategy was to postpone the vote on the Bristow-Mondell bill until they could be sure that it would pass.

NAWSA strategists wanted an immediate vote on the Bristow-Mondell proposal. Like CU leaders, they expected it to be defeated. In that event, they intended to keep the issue of woman's suffrage alive by having the alternative Shafroth-Palmer introduced.[155]

Taking advantage of her first opportunity to exert some political influence on behalf of the CU board, Alva sent a threatening telegram on March 6 to Arizona Senator Henry F. Ashurst, a Democrat and suffrage supporter. It read in part: "If you allow suffrage amendment to go to vote now I shall consider you absolutely false to our interests and shall not hesitate to make that fact known in important places. Those who have asked you to push the amendment to vote now are not genuinely interested in its immediate success. They are Progressives and are using you."

Alva's way of trying to influence the situation was certainly in character. She was an opinionated bully. But it was also both politically naïve and a strategic miscalculation. Ashurst responded both by reading the telegram aloud on the floor of the Senate and writing Alva that there was nothing he could do about scheduling a vote. All an embarrassed Alva could do was write back that she had only written to warn him because she had come to believe that the Progressives wanted the credit for having supported the suffrage amendment and were, therefore, determined that his effort, which would benefit the Democrats, should fail.[156]

Despite the CU's desire to postpone the issue, the Senate voted on the Bristow-Mondell version of the Anthony amendment on March 19. It failed to pass by eleven votes. A House committee subsequently voted it out without recommending it, which ensured that it would not pass there either.[157]

Meanwhile, other matters needed attention. While there was support for suffrage in the Northeast and the West, southern women were slow to take up the cause. Alva was convinced that success for the movement depended upon its having national appeal. So after southern suffragists organized the Southern States Woman Suffrage Association (SSWS) Conference in November 1913, Alva began corresponding with its president, Kate Gordon, in order to solicit her support for the

Susan B. Anthony amendment. Even though as a southerner she was unenthusiastic about federal amendments in general, Gordon needed money to run her organization. So she responded positively to Alva's overtures, acknowledging that NAWSA's Shafroth-Palmer amendment was an unfortunate effort that only diminished the possibility that the Anthony amendment might pass. Reassured that the group would not work against the CU's program, Alva sent Gordon $11,000 in two installments, asking her to keep the name of the donor secret. A woman with southern roots, Alva also assured Gordon that she was sensitive to how the issues of race and states' rights might influence the southern suffrage movement.[158] "I plead guilty to so strong a desire for the political emancipation of women that I am not at all particular as to how it shall be granted," she is alleged to have said later.[159]

At the same time, the CU was planning a fund-raising ball to be held at the Willard Hotel in Washington, D.C., on April 21, a suffrage rally to be held near Grant's Tomb in Manhattan on May 2, and a parade and rally to be held in Washington's Belasco Theater on May 9. Alva served on the ball planning committee. Her prestige guaranteed that those with social aspirations in the Washington area were pathetically eager to participate in the event. Within days of her arrival she had managed to recruit the wives of prominent politicians from both parties to serve as patronesses of the fund-raiser and to ensure the goodwill of local philanthropic organizations by negotiating a date for the event that would not interfere with their fund-raising efforts.[160]

In May, Alva left New York for Newport where she intended to spend the summer.[161] Once she arrived, she notified CU leaders that she wanted to establish yet another suffrage headquarters in the summer resort. Then, anticipating the arrival of her daughter, the Duchess of Marlborough, she began to plan a conference to be held in July which was designed to bring together social reform leaders from all over the country. That convention of notable women was to be followed by a CU conference to be held in August. In early July, Paul sent field-worker Doris Stevens to open the headquarters, raise money to furnish and support it, convince the residents of Newport to open their drawing rooms for suffrage meetings, help Alva with the conferences, and serve as her secretary and companion.[162]

The July convention resembled that which Alva had organized in 1909. Only this time the draw was her duchess of a daughter and the exquisite new Chinese tea house that she had just built on the lawn of Marble House. She sold tickets for two dollars for entry and an additional three dollars for a tour of Marble House and its grounds. Guests were greeted by tables full of suffrage literature as well as displays of suffrage pencils and fans. On the grounds, society leaders such as Mamie Fish, Tessie Oelrichs, and Gloria Vanderbilt mingled with reformers such as Julia Lathrop, head of the U.S. Children's Bureau; Chicago superintendent of schools Ella Flagg Young; the leader of the National Consumers' League, Florence Kelley; and Rose Schneiderman of the National Women's Trade Union League.[163]

Some of the participants were more comfortable than others in the setting that Alva provided for the conference. Schneiderman, who worked as a labor organizer, later claimed to have left the conference after having spent only one night sleeping in the Oelrichs' mansion. A Jewish immigrant of Polish origin, she found the whole event not only "high-faluting" but unlikely to accomplish anything. "I was furious at myself for going," she wrote in her memoir, "and furious with Mrs. Belmont for spending money on the pavilion and for charging sight seers five dollars to see the inside of her house (even though she spent it for the cause)."[164]

Others with similar distaste for associating with the rich declined Alva's invitation to attend. "I can't do the Newport stunt," Mary Beard told Alice Paul in a letter. "I shall probably be the only one who, for labor attachments, feels that participation in the Newport plans is inadvisable."[165] A week later she added that while she understood that the conference would result in a great deal of publicity for the cause, she remained "a pure coward" and had definitely decided that she would not attend.[166]

The August CU conference drew as much newspaper coverage as Beard had predicted. Alva managed to entice over 150 suffrage supporters to Newport. During the first business meeting, held at Marble House, those present passed a resolution denouncing the Shafroth-Palmer amendment.[167] At a subsequent meeting, Paul, with Alva's encouragement, outlined the CU's strategy for the upcoming election. It provided that if Congress did not pass the Susan B. Anthony amendment before the November election, the CU intended to organize campaigns in those western states where women already had the right to vote to defeat Democrats running for the House of

Representatives. This was in essence a program patterned after that being followed by the English suffragists, who held the majority party in Parliament responsible for the government's failure to give women the vote. CU members were enthusiastic enough about the proposed program to pledge $10,000 to support it. Alva provided half of that amount.[168]

The impact of their anti-Democratic campaign was mixed. Only twenty of the forty-three Democratic congressmen running in states where the CU was active won their seats. On a national level, Republicans gained more seats than the Democrats, but the Democrats retained enough seats to control the House.[169]

The outbreak of World War I in August 1914 had little immediate impact on the activities of the CU. But it prompted Alva once more to make an effort to tend to the needs of working women. In January 1915, she turned her PEA headquarters lunchroom into a soup kitchen that served meals to indigent working women who had lost their jobs when the declining demand for American exports closed shops and factories in New York City.[170] By the end of the month, she and her friends were providing as many as ninety women a day with food, wool stockings, underwear, and shoes. By the first week in February, the number of women benefiting from Alva's benevolence was estimated to be over 2000.[171]

By this time, eleven states, all of them west of the Mississippi, had granted women the right to vote.[172] While New York suffragists were engaged in the last stages of what turned out to be an unsuccessful referendum campaign, suffragists associated with the CU began their efforts to pressure Woodrow Wilson into declaring his support for their cause. On May 17, 1915, Alva's secretary, Florence Harmon, representing the PEA, and Mabel Schofield, an English suffragette representing the CU, attempted to deliver a letter to the president while he was attending a banquet on the nineteenth floor of the Biltmore Hotel in New York City. The missive asked politely that he meet with a delegation of suffrage supporters before he left the city. The two women evaded the secret service but could not get close enough to Wilson to deliver their note. Not to be deterred, they followed him in a taxi when he left the hotel and ended up delivering the letter to his stenographer.[173] The incident infuriated the leaders of the NAWSA, who, condemning the tactics of the two women as "undignified and preposterous," believed it would hinder their efforts to organize support for woman suffrage in New York state.[174]

Undiscouraged, the militants devised another plan to get his attention. After holding a suffrage convention at the San Francisco Panama-Pacific Exposition in September 1915, the CU sent Sara Bard Field and Frances Joliffe by car from California to Washington, D.C., with a suffrage petition over 18,000 feet long containing more than 500,000 signatures. Their arrival was timed to coincide with the CU national convention to be held in early December.[175] In anticipation of the petition's arrival, CU staff members began organizing a well-publicized suffrage parade complete with demonstrators dressed in flowing robes of suffrage colors—purple, gold, and white—and a women's liberty bell mounted on a truck. On December 6, as a raw winter wind whipped down Pennsylvania Avenue, Alva and other suffragists arrived at the steps of the Capitol to present the monster petition to their staunch supporter Congressman Mondell, who in turn introduced a version of the Susan B. Anthony amendment to the House of Representatives. Meanwhile, three hundred suffragists met with President Wilson in the East Room of the White House to ask for his support.[176] The next day, delegates representing both suffrage supporters and their opponents testified before the Democratic National Committee at the Willard Hotel.[177] That evening, Alva entertained suffragists, socialites, and politicians at a reception at Cameron House, a building located just off Lafayette Park near the White House that she had rented to serve as the CU's Washington headquarters.[178] From there the CU would launch its final campaign to ensure the passage of a suffrage amendment.

The following year, 1916, proved to be a time of growth for the CU. The sort of attention that their activities and Alva's celebrity brought to the group guaranteed that their fund-raising and recruiting efforts would be successful. Louisine Havemeyer, Elizabeth Seldon Rogers, and Eunice Dana Brannan, all wealthy socialites, followed Alva's lead and joined the organization.[179] In February, Alva collaborated with composer Elsa Maxwell to present a suffrage operetta in two acts called *Melinda and Her Sisters,* followed by a midnight supper in honor of the governor's wife in the grand ballroom of the Waldorf-Astoria in New York City. The satire featured both professional actors and debutantes with bit parts. The sale of boxes, tickets, programs, the libretto, and sheet music netted over $8000 and three days of newspaper headlines for the CU. Various and sundry Vanderbilts, Belmonts, DuPonts, Goulds, and Havemeyers attended the performance.[180]

Alva had worked hard to support suffrage and wanted to take some time off. So she invited four friends to accompany her on a month's cruise on the *Seminole.* The yacht left Long Island on the first of July and sailed the Atlantic coast, putting in at various ports including Sag Harbor and Newport, R.I.[181] While she continued to raise money for the cause, her summer vacation marked the beginning of her withdrawal from militant suffrage activism.

With membership roles increasing and money filling their coffers, Paul and her staff began plans to initiate a nonviolent picketing campaign in front of the White House beginning in 1917 to protest Wilson's refusal to use his influence to promote woman suffrage.[182] Beginning at 10 AM on a dreary January 10, the CU's "silent sentinels" marched from their headquarters to take up their position on either side of the two main gates of the president's residence. Ignoring the damp, raw weather, they stood wearing gold, purple, and white ribbons over their coats and holding banners asking, "Mr. President, what will you do for woman suffrage?" Much to their dismay, they got no immediate response from those in the White House.[183]

Suffrage picketing was controversial. Not surprisingly, Carrie Chapman Catt, president of the NAWSA, opposed the strategy, issuing a statement saying that the CU was making an "error in picketing the White House."[184] But Harriot Stanton Blatch, daughter of Elizabeth Cady Stanton, thought picketing an excellent idea and held an "indignation meeting" to raise money to cover the costs of the demonstrations.[185] Alva did not object to the picketing, but she was over sixty years old and was not prepared to protest Wilson's lack of enthusiasm for woman's rights by standing in the freezing cold of the D.C. winter holding a banner. Instead, she remained in Florida and sent Paul a check for $5000 to help pay for whatever expenses the picketing campaign might incur.[186] A reporter for the *New York World* editorialized with the headline, "Mrs. Belmont Gives $5000 to 'Attack' the White House."[187]

Not surprisingly, the picketing campaign caught the attention of the media. It also attracted bystanders who could not resist the temptation to harass the picketers as they peacefully marched back and forth carrying their suffrage banners. The police arrested the picketers, who were convicted of trespass and obstructing traffic. They refused to pay their fines, so the judge ordered them to be incarcerated in the Occoquan workhouse in Virginia. Among them were Florence Bayard Hilles of Wilmington, Delaware, whose father had been secretary of state and ambassador to Great Britain under President Grover Cleveland; Eunice Dana Brannan, whose father, Charles Dana, was publisher of the *New York Sun;* and Dora Lewis of Philadelphia, who had served on Alice Paul's Executive Committee since 1913.[188]

When the prisoners arrived at the workhouse, the matrons ordered them to surrender their personal belongings, including their wedding rings, money, glasses, and toiletries. The demonstrators then sat down at tables in a large dining hall where under a rule of silence they ate what Doris Stevens described as "dirty sour soup." Their next stop was the dormitory where the matrons forced them to undress and stand naked. Once they had showered, a prison uniform consisting of underwear of unbleached muslin, shapeless Mother Hubbard dresses, thick cotton stockings, and heavy, utilitarian shoes replaced the fashionable clothes they had been wearing when they were arrested. They slept on cots alongside prostitutes.[189]

Alva continued to support the efforts of the militants from afar. In the midst of opening her Newport home for the summer, she spoke out in favor of what they were doing in a letter to the editors of the New York press. "Picketing is just an advance form of demonstration which the women are forced to make in order to call to the attention of a resisting Government and an indifferent mass of people the claim of women . . . to participate in the Government on equal terms with men," she declared.[190] By publishing her letter, the press assured Alva that her invisibility did not mean she had been forgotten. Her reputation as a militant feminist and staunch supporter of women's political activism was still intact, and her carefully orchestrated public image was preserved.

# 4 Immortalizing the Lady in Affecting Prose

WHILE ALICE PAUL and her militant compatriots were picketing the White House, going to jail, and refusing to eat during the summer of 1917, Alva could be found sitting within earshot of the Atlantic Ocean, drinking lemonade in her Chinese pagoda in the sweltering heat of the Newport summer, and dictating her memoir to a young, socialist, anti-war activist named Sara Bard Field. They spent almost two months together producing a manuscript chronicling Alva's life and accomplishments. Day after day, Alva talked, and Field took notes. Then, while Alva entertained guests, Field spent her evenings trying to make sense of what she had written.

Since Alva left no papers, we can only speculate about why she decided to engage in this private exercise in self-discovery and public disclosure. In some ways, it is predictable that she should think it worth her time to write a memoir. Alva was not by nature introspective, but she had always craved the attention of others. And her ability to attract that attention encouraged her to develop an exaggerated sense of her own importance. So writing a memoir was in some ways just another manifestation of her self-absorption. As literary critic Paul John Eakin has put it, she was, like many autobiographers, an "opportunist with an itch for notoriety."[1]

Her celebrity status and the newspaper headlines that accompanied it had demonstrated that the public had an insatiable interest both in the way she lived and in her opinions on a wide range of public policy issues, including labor reform, prostitution, child-rearing, and the Monroe Doctrine.[2] The problem was that while newspapers provided her with name recognition, they controlled the way her story was told. Publishing a memoir would provide her the opportunity to frame her own story.

Moreover, while she had worked actively in the campaign to improve the condition of women in the United States since 1909, she appears to have been somewhat insecure about her status within the women's movement. She knew from personal experience that while it was common for women of wealth to engage in philanthropy, it was unusual for them to support causes whose purpose was to challenge the distribution of social and political power. Because of this reality, she seems to have been afraid that people might not take her contributions of time and money seriously. And she was determined to get credit for what she considered to be the personal and financial sacrifices that accompanied her feminist activism. Writing and publishing her memoir offered the opportunity not only to claim a prominent place for herself in the annals of suffrage history alongside woman's rights advocates such as Elizabeth Cady Stanton, Susan B. Anthony, Carrie Chapman Catt, and Alice Paul but also to shape the collective memory of the suffrage movement itself.

She also appears to have felt that a chronicle of her life might be a useful way to explain to her family, her friends, her suffrage colleagues, and the general public how and why her transformation from being an apolitical society diva to a militant feminist took place.[3] This required her to identify the characteristics and experiences that might explain not only her outrage at women's subordinate status but also why she chose to take the actions she did to remedy that situation. So sometime in 1915 at the age of sixty-two, she decided it was time to sort out her memories and arrange them in some sort of coherent order. It was time to make sense of her life.

Alva was many things, but she was no writer. So she searched for someone to help her with the memoir project. She was quite clear about the sort of person she wanted to hire. She wanted a secretary and companion "with writing ability and pleasing presence" who would "look after her affairs, write her speeches, care for her books, represent her when she cannot be present at affairs . . . and generally be brains for her."[4] Since there was no employment or placement service to whom she might turn, she consulted Doris Stevens, a CU fieldworker whom she had recently met at the Panama-Pacific Exposition.[5]

More than willing to act as facilitator, Stevens contacted Field, a friend, fellow suffragist, and aspiring poet, to tell her about the possibility of working for Belmont. Stevens assured Field that it was common for Belmont to hire young suffrage sympathizers to work for her and that at one time or another both Ida Husted Harper and Inez Milholland had been employed by the rich society matron. At the same time, however, she warned Field that the work would be "exacting" and that "the old lady" was extraordinarily demanding. But she also pointed out that taking the job might provide Field with access to people with money and influence and through them other employment or publishing opportunities. After all, she noted, Belmont was "human" and once she grew "fond of a person" she did whatever she could to promote their interests.[6]

Almost thirty years Alva's junior, Field was born in Cincinnati, Ohio, in 1882. She spent most of her childhood in Detroit where her father worked as a purchasing agent in the wholesale food business. After graduating from high school in 1900, she married Albert Ehrgott, a Baptist minister who took her to Rangoon, Burma, where he served as a missionary. There she bore a son, Albert. After the family returned to the United States, they settled first in Connecticut and then in Cleveland where she gave birth to a daughter and involved herself in progressive social reform work.

In 1910, the family moved to Portland, Oregon. There she worked as a paid organizer for the suffrage movement. It was while they were in Portland that one of her acquaintances, Clarence Darrow, introduced her to Charles Erskine Scott Wood, a maritime lawyer. A gifted artist and writer, he was a man known for his liberal views and political anarchism. She found him fascinating. The fact that he was thirty years her senior and a married man did not deter her from falling madly in love with him.

As she grew more and more attached to Wood, she grew increasingly estranged from her husband. So in 1913, she took her daughter to Nevada to file for divorce and continue her suffrage work. When her divorce was granted, she worked out a joint custody arrangement with her former husband that provided her the time and space to pursue her own interests. He cared for the children during the week at his home in Berkeley. She was responsible for them on weekends and during vacations. Unfortunately, marriage to Wood was not possible. His wife, a Catholic, refused to give him a divorce.[7]

A writer without a reliable source of income, Field wanted to be financially independent and very much resented her economic dependence on her lover.[8] She needed money but had a few qualms about working for Belmont. As she pointed out to Wood, she knew virtually nothing about the state of the suffrage campaign in the East, did not have much experience being a secretary, and did not believe that she was "temperamentally" suited to being a servant.[9] As a socialist and self-avowed intellectual, she was also hostile to the upper class, regarding them, as she said in a letter to Wood, as "smug robbers" and "mindless creatures of inherited wealth" who produced nothing, thought only of themselves, and lived lives of "self-indulgence and unvirtuous sloth."[10]

Before she spent the summer in Newport, Field had no difficulty believing that Belmont had "the usual lack of brains and culture of rich people who have depended on their looks and their money to win them place and applause." And she accepted without question Stevens's observation that Belmont's "psychology is quite that of the plutocratic class."[11] She was also slightly put off by what she perceived to be a strange possessiveness on Belmont's part. It appeared to her that she was somehow being expropriated. Mrs. Belmont "has fastened onto me with a strange desire," she wrote to Wood. "The old lady was actually affectionate the Sunday we both spoke together. She seems gluttonous to get at my spirit and to have it hers just as she buys gowns and jewels."

However much Field may have been flattered by Belmont's attention, her reservations about working for her remained. "On the whole," Field told Wood, "she is *hard*-flinty, brutal to her 'inferiors' and I shall find it hard to deal with such material either in discourse or in literary interpretation." Those issues, she feared, might unduly influence the way she wrote Belmont's reminiscences and make it difficult for her to produce a manuscript that would meet both Belmont's expectations and her own literary standards. If she could make ends meet, she would not take the job, she confessed. But she was well aware that she could not afford to "tell Belmont's money to go to hell!"[12] So she began negotiating the terms of her employment in August. Those negotiations continued into the New Year.

Field was flattered by Alva's attention but wrote to Wood, "she is a queer, smart, calculating old lady and too sharp to let anyone she thinks valuable slip thro [*sic*] her fingers. I am, if I will, to return to her in the spring, go to Newport and there immortalize the lady in affecting prose."[13] Field understood from Stevens that Belmont was prepared to offer her $1000 a month and provide her housing so she would have few expenses. Field found those terms acceptable, but expressed the fear that working for Belmont might require her to sell her soul. "I expect to pay in spiritual coin for every dollar I get from her," she told Wood. "She is a terror and I cringe at the thought of her buying me."[14]

Alva was clearly in no hurry to begin the project, so it was not until mid-June 1917, nearly two years after Stevens had recommended Field to Belmont, that the two finally reached an agreement. Alva wrote to Field that she expected her to arrive in Newport in the middle of July, would arrange a room for her near Marble House, and hoped she would stay until the first week in September and then plan to resume work that winter, if necessary, in order to complete the manuscript.[15] In early July Alva sent Field a check to cover her traveling expenses.[16] Looking forward to earning some money and gaining entrée into eastern literary circles, Field dutifully arrived at Marble House to begin her work.

It is unlikely that Alva had ever spent much time with anyone quite like Field. Alva's social circle had always been small. During her childhood, her parents carefully chose her friends.[17] After she married, she had little opportunity to establish close relationships with anyone outside the Vanderbilt-Belmont social circle. Only after she became a widow, joined the suffrage movement, and began to take an interest in the welfare of working women did she begin to socialize with people outside her own class. By that time, she had grown bored with her society friends, whom she contemptuously described to Field as "undereducated, parasitic, frivolous, self-centered lapdogs of wealth," women with "sawdust brains" and "wax faces" whose sole purpose in life was to marry a rich man and then keep him.[18]

By hiring Field to serve as her secretary and companion, Alva quite consciously decided to spend her summer revealing the most intimate details of her life to a woman deeply committed to woman's rights but one who was also known to consort with such anti-war socialist intellectuals as Max Eastman, the editor of *The Masses,* the journalist John Reed, and the historian Charles Beard.[19] Like Paul, Field was a perfect example of the "new woman" who had come of age at the turn of the century and was part of a generation of self-supporting, independent-minded women who often rejected conventional domesticity in order to dedicate their lives to expanding educational, vocational, and public service opportunities for themselves and other women.[20]

It is equally unlikely that Alva gave much thought to how Field's outlook on life might influence the manuscript she was expected to produce. Like Alva, Field brought her own agenda to the memoir project. Field thought of herself as a serious writer. For her, writing was both a "profession" and "an art."[21] Transcription of her notes and the production of a compelling, readable narrative from them was an intensely creative process for her. Like other aspiring writers, she wanted to publish what she wrote. Selling the memoir manuscript to a reputable editor would serve as confirmation of her literary talents, and royalties from the book would help her support herself and her children. Moreover, she had taken seriously Stevens's point about how working for Belmont might provide her entrée into the eastern publishing establishment and was determined to use the contacts she made by working as Belmont's secretary to help advance her career.[22]

In addition, Field approached the writing project with a clearly articulated sense of mission common to many reformers who believed in the inevitability of social change. She convinced herself that she could single-handedly convince Belmont to embrace an expansive form of social justice that went well beyond the rather narrow goal of providing American women with the right to vote. "I have sworn to the gods," she told Wood, "to try to help this dominant, fearless old Lady see the light—more light than she now sees." Field was convinced that Alva could be a valuable ally to those with socialist sympathies not only because she had money but also because, as she told Wood, when she adopted a cause as her own "not God nor the devil can frighten her off."[23]

While Alva may have been open to discussing Field's advanced ideas, her experience working with the disadvantaged had convinced her that there were limits to what could be done to level society. Not surprisingly, she tended to see life from the narrowness of her own experience. She had done her best, she told Field, to get women out of the city and onto the land, but the experiment had failed miserably. Try as she might, Field found it impossible to convince Alva that "the evils which centuries had been making" could not be so easily resolved "or the fact that man's desire itself had been stunted with poverty and misery."[24]

The memoir project also provided Field with an opportunity to engage in social commentary as well as practice her craft as a creative writer. She was sensitive to the power of language and the difficulties inherent in using it to try to capture lived experience in such a way as to allow her readers to experience Alva's life vicariously. She hoped that the narrative that she produced could be more than just an engaging chronicle of a rich woman's life. And she wanted to use her skills as a writer to give Alva's experiences enough substance and meaning so that she could use them to speak to a wide variety of audiences about the state of American society in general and the condition of American women in particular.

She did not find Alva particularly helpful in the pursuit of that lofty goal. It was not that she found the story of Alva's life uninteresting. Indeed, she found much of what Alva told her fascinating. "Her early childhood in its slave-owning environment, her move to New York, her father's sadness in being torn between his non-secession persuasion and his Southern love and sympathies—these and much, much more, I noted with keen interest," Field told Wood.[25] She found Alva's description of her participation in the 1909–1910 shirtwaist workers' strike even more riveting. The way Alva told the story, Field said, "would have done credit to Aeneas himself or Odysus [*sic*]."[26]

It appeared to her, however, that Alva was either too distracted by minutiae of life or too lacking in intellectual sophistication to see and understand the broader social implications of what she was saying. In a letter to her lover, Field wrote, "I think you will be interested in what she has fearlessly said in her divorce chapter. Of course there is not the developed philosophy you and I might make as foundation for a discussion of divorce but I cannot put that in. It would not be her. . . . She herself little knows the import of much she is uttering. In that respect she is like the Oracle at Delphi—a priestess on a tripod saying that of which she has little actual knowledge."[27] And in another letter she complained, "She is often so vague that I have to define all her ideas myself and I hope to god she will stand for some of the things I have interpolated. Of course after all this is *her* life not mine and I have no right to put my views into her mouth unless she subscribes to them and thus makes them her own."[28]

At the same time, however, Field was perfectly willing to shape the emerging narrative by interrupting their conversations "with a hundred questions." And if Alva did not elaborate on a topic that she found interesting, she prodded her employer "by suggestion and interrogation." Moreover, she confessed to Wood that as she transcribed her notes in the evening, she spent time "filling them in," elaborating on Belmont's "thoughts in accord with her expressed ideas" and then adding notes and comments of her own.[29]

The process of producing a memoir manuscript was also heavily influenced by the tensions inherent in the fact that Field found herself in an unfamiliar social milieu. She found living in Newport and associating with some of the wealthiest people in the world, people she was predisposed to despise, unnerving. Alva's attitude toward and treatment of those who provided her services determined the quality of their lives, the duties they performed, and their personal and professional relationship with her. Both Field and her employer were well aware of that fact. Having developed a wide variety of bullying strategies at a very young age, Alva generally got what she wanted when she wanted it. That reality governed the way Alva related to the women she employed.

By accepting a position as Belmont's private secretary and companion, Field became a domestic servant whose position within the household was ambiguous, a situation she found awkward and uncomfortable. Like governesses, private secretaries were not ordinary servants.[30] Besides knowing how to frame an invitation or letter of regret, write a thank-you note, balance a checkbook, and keep a calendar as well as execute plans for extravagant dinner parties, receptions, and balls, ideal private secretaries needed to be well bred, well mannered, well spoken, well dressed, and discreet. And like private secretaries in the corporate world, personal attractiveness combined with a pleasant personality, a sense of responsibility, trustworthiness, honesty, and loyalty were of considerable value. It was also helpful if a private secretary had no life of her own and was willing to be at her employer's beck and call at any time of the day or night.[31]

Unlike most domestic servants, private secretaries had a public role to play. They had to be able to relate to a wide variety of rich, well-born, socially and/or politically prominent individuals and conduct themselves appropriately at everything from business meetings and garden parties to the opera. Like the administrative assistants of corporate executives, they were often called upon to serve as their employers' alter ego, represent their interests, and protect them from unwanted distractions or solicitations.

Because of the intimacy of their relationship with their employer, private secretaries were compelled to live the fiction that they belonged in the world of the rich and powerful despite the fact that employers such as Belmont used a wide variety of strategies—including gestures of generosity, demands for deference and gratitude, emotional bullying, disrespect for their personal privacy, and reminders of their economic dependence—to expose that fiction and disabuse them of any exaggerated notions they might harbor about their social position.[32] No matter how well educated and genteel, no matter how personalized and intimate their relationship with her, no matter how much maternal concern she bestowed on them, no matter how many times she treated them as one of her family, Alva was not willing to allow her secretaries to forget that they were, in the end, merely employees.[33]

By the time she employed Field, Alva was used to handling personal servants. But for Field, being a servant was a new experience. There was nothing in her previous life that could have prepared her for it. So it is not surprising that the summer the two women spent together in Rhode Island was fraught with considerable tension and some conflict.

Field found the process of being incorporated into the world of the fabulously wealthy as disorienting as it was seductive. Initially, she appears to have been bewildered by what she was experiencing. She arrived in Newport prepared to settle into a cottage or apartment of her own only to find herself ensconced in an entire suite of rooms at Marble House. The Belmont mansion was a house in which the routines, smells, and sounds of daily living were muted. Beds were made, clothes laid out, fires lit, furniture dusted, and floors swept by invisible hands in her absence. It was an environment in which needs were anticipated, negating the need for communication. Served meals in the dining room, she was unaware of their preparation downstairs in the kitchen. Unobtrusive servants filled her wine glass without being asked to do so. Even more disconcerting, the ladies' maid who had been assigned to her insisted on not just running her bathwater but bathing her as well. If that were not bad enough, Field felt that when Alva introduced her to her friends and associates, she did so in a way that made Field feel as if she were some exotic creature on exhibition.[34]

As an avowed socialist suspicious of those with wealth and power, Field found it necessary to adjust to a lifestyle for which she had nothing but contempt. Uncomfortable living at Marble House, embarrassed by the fact that her maid expected to do many of the "menial tasks" that she was quite used to performing for herself, and bored with the social events that Alva insisted that she attend, Field began the summer expressing hostility, incredulity, and distaste for the life she found herself living.[35] Writing to Wood, she said, "I was never so surrounded by luxury and never so unhappily (in one way) as I now am." She had the use of one of Alva's cars and was "waited upon by footmen, butler, maids, and chauffeurs," she told him. She had the sense that as long as it did not inconvenience her employer, she would continue to be "treated with a sort of sumptuous consideration, fed delicacies by the soft moving servants, given delicious drinks when suffering from heat and generally coddled and made soft." Incorporated into the household but not really belonging to it, she felt like a "little sister of the rich," she confessed.[36]

That she found the materialism inherent in her new lifestyle addictive was even more disturbing. The longer she lived in the privileged environment of Marble House, the boundaries between the luxuries that she enjoyed and those that she wished to receive expanded. In the process, she began to understand that while she was being well paid, there were limits to Alva's generosity. "She takes me to little shops here where she buys for her already over-laden wardrobe exquisite cob-webly garments for outside and underwear. But never once has she offered to buy me a thread," she complained. "I think she believes my constant presence in Marble House with its luxuries at my disposal are all the extras—and more than all that a 'poor friend' ought to expect."[37]

The disparity between the lives of the very rich whom she met in Newport and those of ordinary people continued to bother Field.

After only a few weeks, she wrote to Wood in complete frustration, "Save the world from the rule of these creatures. Their spirits have been castrated. They produce nothing. They don't even have spiritual intercourse one with another. They babble and simper and murmur and look sweet and never commune. They think only of themselves. They are lost in their own darkness."[38] Despite the fact that she was being well treated, she told Wood that she "would be ashamed to be happy here." Her socialist sensibilities led her to conclude that she was "so identified with the race that I can never enjoy this excessive and unpardonable over-abundance while the world starves both materially and spiritually. This place of wealth, of palaces and idleness, of luxurious inanity and extravagant worthlessness instead of feeding me with beauty only reminds me the more of the terrible suffering in hot cities and war-weary Europe. . . . So much power in the hands of such colossal Ignorance! So much bounty in the hands of Selfishness incarnate."[39]

Dealing with Field must have posed some problems for Alva as well. She seems to have sensed Field's discomfort and to have understood the need to establish a bond of trust and empathy with her new secretary. Tyrannizing over Field, as she apparently did over other servants, simply would not do. Instead, her strategy seems to have been to ensure Field's comfort and establish a modicum of personal intimacy with her. She made it clear that she enjoyed Field's company, took her shopping, and sent for her personal physician when Field was not feeling well.[40] She even took an interest in Field's personal circumstances and shared the most intimate details of her own love life with her new private secretary.[41]

The strategy seems to have worked. At first alienated by her employer's social position, wealth, and lifestyle, Field's attitude toward Alva began to soften as she spent more time with her. However much contempt she had for Alva's friends, she came to see Belmont as strong and resolute. "She is a character," Field wrote to Wood. "What she lacks in gentleness, she makes up in justice; what she fails to grasp through subtle intellectual power, she often grasps through a fierce maternal passion."[42]

As the summer progressed, Field came to appreciate how bored Alva was and how desperate she was for love. "Poor lonely soul," Field wrote to Wood, "for she is poor in many ways and in every way lonely.

My heart aches for her—selfish to the core and weighted down from babyhood with the heaviness of too much possession."[43] A few days later, she wrote, "The old lady is softening so much as our contacts multiply. She is not the same arrogant person I first knew. No one can be who has shown her heart to another."[44] Indeed, Alva indicated in a variety of ways that she had become attached to Field. When Field left Newport for a few days to visit family in Waterbury, Connecticut, for example, Alva kissed her good-bye and, as Field put it, "in her grim Lady Macbeth way said, 'I'll miss you.'" Apparently taken aback at such an unexpected gesture, Field concluded that "Mrs. B really hated to have me go these few days."[45]

Field was also touched by what she learned about the reality of Alva's life. Indeed, she admitted that Alva's description of the circumstances under which she married William Kissam Vanderbilt brought tears to her eyes. Alva framed the circumstances of the marriage as an act of self-sacrifice. And Field accepted it as such, telling Wood that her employer had as much as sold herself to Vanderbilt out of a "truly noble desire to save her Father who was slowing dying of worry and anxiety over his failing business." For Field, Alva's sexual innocence only made the circumstances of her marriage all the more disgraceful, "sordid," and sad. But she also thought that Alva's willingness to share the intimate details of her marriage revealed an "inner heart" that, as she put it, "could have been loved into beauty" but sadly had "been steeled against its own finer and softer emotions."[46]

However much she came to sympathize with Alva's circumstances and to enjoy her company, Field was determined to preserve her own independence in terms of space and time. She convinced her employer that she needed to rent rooms in town rather than continue to live in the mansion by disingenuously arguing that she would be able to get more work done that way.[47] She demanded Sundays off, so she could spend her time as she wished. And she reserved the right to refuse dinner invitations from Alva.[48]

Dinner invitations were a problem for Field. As Alva's companion, she was expected to attend social functions to which she would not under normal circumstances have been invited. Despite her disdain for many of those who lived in the mansions on Bellevue Avenue, Alva had an active social life which involved giving and attending dinner parties. On more than one occasion, she insisted that Field attend.

Field was ambivalent about this part of her job. She remembered having been flattered that Alva wanted to include her, noting that at the time she "was young and not unattractive." But she found that she had little or nothing in common with most of Alva's guests and found their company boring and their conversation inane.[49] So occasionally eating with them was an extremely unpleasant experience. One evening, after working all day, she had returned to her boarding house too tired either to work or to take a walk, when Alva called and invited her to dine. In need of a diversion, Field agreed to return to Marble House. The evening was a dismal failure from her point of view and only confirmed her low opinion of Belmont's so-called friends. The men, she reported, all drank too much wine, one made a pass at her, and when she spurned his advances apparently told his friends that she was a "virago."[50]

So she refused to return to Marble House for dinner when she thought she could get away with it. Doing so clearly served as confirmation that despite the fact that Alva was paying for her time, her writing expertise, and her company, she still had some control over her life. One day, for example, Field was drinking iced tea on the porch late in the afternoon when Alva's youngest son, Harold, unexpectedly arrived. She was surprised to find the young man "a rather serious, thoughtful boy, a bit prideful but not at all bumptious and without hauteur." She was soon engaged in a discussion with him about the advisability of America's entry into World War I. Field, a pacifist, could not contain her surprise that Harold agreed with her that for the United States to declare war on Germany would be a mistake. "That did not sound like the plutocratic defense of Organized murder that I had expected," she told Wood later. She and Harold chatted amiably, afternoon turned into evening, and she rose to bid him good-bye. But when she did so, he begged her to stay. She politely expressed her regret and returned to her boarding house. It was clear to her that Belmont was pleased that she and Harold had "struck it off well," but she was not prepared for what happened next.

About an hour before dinner was to be served at Marble House, the phone rang. It was Mrs. B, as Field called her employer. "She was quite excited," Field reported to Wood. "'Can't you get dressed quickly and come over for dinner?'" she asked. It seems that Harold was insistent that she join them and would not accept no for an answer. Field, however, was tired from the heat and note-taking and determined to stay her ground. The thought of dressing in her evening clothes, traipsing back to the Belmont mansion, and being agreeable all evening did not appeal to her in the least. "I think my positive refusal was as much of a surprise as her son's interest in having me return," she told Wood. In fact, she was a little surprised herself at her declaration of independence. "What! I refuse the invitation of a Vanderbilt—sought as the most desirable eligible in all the land," she wrote. "What if it was merely a dinner invitation—he is a Vanderbilt, the heir to untold millions. Everyone does as he asks. That was all implied in their displeased replies to my refusal." She claimed that she had not refused simply "for effect." She was "honestly tired," she said. In retrospect, Field was convinced that her refusal had caused her to "have gone up a peg in" Alva's estimation.[51]

As the summer progressed, Field was continually surprised by Alva's lack of affection for her Newport society friends, people she had known and associated with for years. Puzzled by the hypocrisy inherent in Alva's contempt, Field asked her one day why she continued to socialize with so many people she considered superficial and ignorant. "I'm getting out of it [society] all as fast as I can," Alva responded. At the same time, however, she was well aware that those in her social circle had worked out an unspoken agreement of philanthropic reciprocity that required them to give donations to each other's favorite charities whether they sympathized with the purpose of that charity or not. Doing so had the practical effect of providing a more or less secure and continuing source of income for the worthy causes sponsored by members of the social elite. Alice Paul's organization, now known as the National Woman's Party, needed all the financial support it could muster. So for Alva, simply dropping out of society was not really an option. "I only identify myself with this set enough to have some influence with them and get money for causes out of them," she told Field. What she could do, however, was to limit her social activity, a change in her behavior that apparently caused some talk in Newport.[52]

Despite all of her efforts to convert them to the cause of suffrage, few of Alva's Newport society friends had any sympathy for woman's rights. Preserving their social status and enjoying life was their most pressing concern. Alva found that reality frustrating. One day, Field was working in the library at Marble House, when Alva returned from playing bridge. She swept into the room in a huff and throwing her gloves down on the table exclaimed, "I *loathe* these people! . . . They care for nothing but money." Taken aback, Field pointed out that it was strange that she felt that way since she had a great deal of money. Predictably, Alva got testy and responded, "Surely I have. Money is power."[53]

That said it all. Alva was, of course, as obsessed with money as the rest of her crowd. She had enjoyed the possession of it long enough to appreciate that it provided the ultimate protection and security from most of the vagaries of life. Money allowed her to do anything she wanted. It gave her prerogatives and influence that she would not otherwise have had. The difference between her and her rich friends, as she saw it, was that while she cared deeply about having money, she also cared deeply about woman's rights. Her feeling of superiority came from the belief that she was doing something with her money that went beyond ensuring her personal comfort and that of her children. She was using it as a tool to produce fundamental changes in gender relationships and to provide women with unprecedented political influence.

As Field and Alva spent more and more time together, the business that they conducted was increasingly interspersed with personal conversations about matters relating to their private lives. Only a few weeks after she arrived, for example, Alva asked Field about her children and marital status. "Yesterday in the Gothic Room of Marble House I talked of you to Mrs. Belmont," Field wrote to Wood. The conversation, she said, went something like this.

"'Are you in love—Doris gave me to understand you are?'

And I said simply 'Yes, I love someone.'

She softened perceptibly at this.

'He is not young though,' she said.

'No.'

'And he is married?'

'Yes.'

'And he cannot get free to marry you?'

'No.'

'And he is not rich?'

'No.'

'Then what in heaven's name will you get out of it?' She asked and she was angry. She thinks women are fools for weakness."

Alva's best advice was for Field to marry again if only for her children's sakes. It was money that gave children the advantages they needed to succeed in life, she told her secretary. And she again pointed out that it was "money which alone has power." There was nothing to be gained by basing a marriage on "sentimental romance," she said. That being the case, she offered to find Field a rich husband, an offer that Field politely refused.[54]

Field was appalled by the suggestion that she marry for money. Marriage as a contractual arrangement designed to promote the material and social advantage of a man, a woman, and their children could not have been less appealing to her. Such a suggestion only reinforced her dim view of the upper class where marriage was nothing more than a business transaction and marrying for money was a fact of life.

Alva attempted to further cement their friendship by sharing her feelings for a young man named Ralph Bloomer, a bachelor in his thirties who may have helped her negotiate the sale of one or more of her homes.[55] "She talks to me freely of him, searches the whole world for contemporary women who have married much younger men," Field reported.[56]

Bloomer eventually arrived at Marble House for a visit. Field was more impressed with him than she had expected to be. He turned out to be a "clean looking, clean living chap, neither drinks nor smokes (athletic influence while at Harvard) and with a wholesome love of out-door life and sports and especially flowers." What made him even more appealing to Field was that "he is sick of insipid society women."[57] It was apparent to Field that whatever hopes Alva might have had for her relationship with Bloomer, it could never be anything more than platonic.

Experience taught Field that her employer was capable of expressing interest in the personal lives of those who lived and worked in her household and affection for those who served her. But in the end, she concluded that Alva's expressions of interest and concern were merely a way to dominate them: "When it came to any personal relationship with the women who served her there was no sense of right then; there was just determination to have power over them, which money had and which allowed her to be dictatorial and even at times cruel."[58] Field saw a real discrepancy between Alva's attitude toward the working class in the abstract and working-class individuals in particular. She was impressed by Alva's willingness to support working-class causes such as the shirtwaist strike of 1909–1910. But she was appalled by Alva's treatment of her servants. "Her treatment of her women servants was so abominable they all hated her," she remembered. But Alva paid good wages and they needed the money.[59] In return for their paycheck, however, they had to put up with her temper tantrums. One night when Field was still living in Marble House, Alva's ladies' maid knocked on her door and burst into the room crying. Apparently Alva had hit her with a hairbrush because she was not quick enough in putting up Alva's hair.[60]

As Belmont and Field got to know each other and began negotiating a mutually satisfactory working relationship, they proceeded with the memoir project. Field's day typically started when a chauffeur drove up to her boarding house in a "smart but hot limousine." In the morning she and Alva ran errands or did some shopping. In the afternoon after lunch they worked on the memoir manuscript.[61] Field believed that Alva enjoyed the hours they spent together.[62] And despite her misgivings she had originally had about working for Alva, she admitted that time did not drag during the afternoons the two of them spent time together. "She wears well," she told Wood.[63]

Their conversations may have been engaging, but Field found transcribing her notes, organizing the raw material that Alva provided, and writing a coherent first draft of the memoir an extremely tedious exercise. "The work drags a little," she wrote Wood. She felt as if she were writing catalog copy, she complained. Her only comfort was the thought that she could fill in the "dramatic interest and pathos" that would be needed to make the manuscript readable in subsequent drafts.[64]

Field faced an enormous challenge as a writer. The dynamics of Alva's narrative—her facial expressions, the tone of her voice, and her body language—got filtered out in the process of note-taking.[65] It was Field's job to edit and organize what she heard. She had to work with a verbal narrative presented spontaneously and therefore lacking in nuance. She had to establish literary standards high enough to satisfy both her own sense of professionalism and those of a reputable publisher. And she had to use her own judgment to identify her potential audience and anticipate what content would be most appealing to them. At the same time, however, she was constrained by her employer's desire to control her own story. Publication without Belmont's approval was not possible.

By the end of the summer, the two women had produced a ninety-one-page manuscript that began with descriptions of Alva's pedigree and childhood. By focusing on Alva's youthful resentment of male privilege, her thwarted ambition, and her obsessive desire for personal independence, Field established the groundwork for explaining the eventual appeal that feminism had for Alva and the source of her insight into women's subordination. She used subsequent discussions of Alva's building projects; her attitudes toward marriage, divorce, and motherhood; and her trips abroad to illustrate how Alva came to understand the world in feminist terms.

As Field transcribed her notes and began writing her first draft of the manuscript, she played an active role in shaping Alva's story. She followed her notes closely, quoting from them often.[66] But by highlighting issues that provided information that she thought might be significant for their dramatic effect, market potential, or explanatory usefulness as well as those that were important to her personally, Field appropriated what she heard to manipulate the narrative. She told a good story—but it was as much her story as it was Alva's. So once again, Alva lost the power to make herself for public consumption.

The life narrative that emerged is grounded in the feminist sympathies of both women, an ideology that gave their lives coherence and meaning. Take the issue of divorce, for example. It was a matter that interested Field and about which she had strong feelings. So it is not surprising that she filtered the story of Alva's failed first marriage and her divorce through her own experience, her sensitivity to women's subordination, and her socialist sensibilities.[67]

Alva was very candid about the reasons for her divorce and the conduct of the divorce proceedings. Particularly vivid were her memories of her lawyer's attempts to discourage her from filing suit. She told Field that he kept warning her that it would be a mistake to initiate divorce proceedings. Wealthy men controlled both society and the courts, he pointed out, and would do everything they could to make her life miserable if she divorced her husband.[68] It is clear from Field's notes that Alva interpreted her lawyer's warnings as a sincere effort to protect her from the social consequences of her proposed action. Field's socialist sensibilities led her to be less generous in her interpretation of his advice. She maintained that it was not Alva he wanted to protect but the interests of her class. "She [Alva] gives much brave information on the way [Joseph] Choate, her lawyer, wanted her to protect Wealth from any assault by the public," Field wrote to Wood. "She sees that as a corporation lawyer it was his business to come to the defense of both Organized Wealth or individual rich men. And she says so."[69]

For Alva, getting a divorce was not just a personal victory over attempts on the part of men like her husband and their lawyers to preserve male privileges and exploit, intimidate, and control women for their own benefit but also an opportunity to give other women in her circumstances the backbone they seemed to need to rid themselves of their own philandering husbands. She told Field that when she decided to petition the State of New York for a divorce, she did so, in part, as a way to give "many women courage to step away from their bondage."[70] According to Field, Alva envisioned herself as "a sort of female knight" who was intent on rescuing other women by providing them with an example that a woman could prevail over whatever overwhelming forces were placed in her way.[71] Speaking for Alva in the manuscript, Field wrote, "When they saw I had overcome massed opposition, and combated powerful enemies and enmities, they, too, stepped out from their unlovely position."[72] Alva was not the first New York socialite to divorce her husband, but she viewed herself as a "pioneer" who made divorce socially acceptable.[73]

For Field, however, the whole story of Alva's divorce was not so much a tale of individual triumph or a step toward gender equality as it was a commentary on the social and economic inequities that accompanied the development of capitalism. Field wrote in the manuscript (though not in her notes) that Choate "argued from the standpoint of a true representative of Organized Wealth." He feared that social unrest would inevitably result from concentrating immense fortunes in the hands of a privileged few. It was his belief, she argued, that "if the people saw that those handling immense fortunes were profligate in their living . . . the outcry against Wealth would increase" and the people "would demand that these uncrowned kings be dethroned." Thus, in her view, it was not surprising that Choate urged Alva to place class interests over her own. It was predictable that he would do everything he could to preserve the power of those who employed him, including encouraging those who threatened to expose the hypocrisy of the upper class to be "silent where its sins were concerned."[74]

Field's feminism also provided the framework for describing other aspects of Alva's life. Belmont's travels were extensive, but Field did not think the topic very interesting except to the degree that it provided the context for understanding Alva's eventual work in the woman's rights movement.[75] "I am writing of her travels—but only such phases of them as had any particular urge toward her ultimate life work and faith," Field wrote to Wood.[76] With Alva's prompting, Field portrayed travel as having provided her employer with a general education and insight into women's social and economic positions in different cultures. Alva learned about the world, Field wrote, through experience, observation, and personal interaction with people whom she met and in the process absorbed lessons in comparative religion, the history of Western culture, and art appreciation.[77]

Travel also apparently stimulated Alva's latent feminist sensibilities. Alva visited many important historic and cultural sites during her married life. But the ones that impressed her the most, according to Field, were "those things which were in some way connected with women." Her visit to the Taj Mahal in Agra served as a perfect example. Alva remembered being impressed by the realization that, as she put it to Field, "one man had appreciated the sweetness, beauty and ability of a woman" enough to build a monument to her. It was a testimony to the potential of woman's leadership, she said.[78]

In the manuscript, Field elaborated on this theme. Alva thought of the Taj as more than a stunningly beautiful mausoleum, Field wrote. Because it was built at "a time when woman was still given so little actual consideration in momentous affairs and in a country where the sacred cow was of more importance than woman's soul," she considered it a sacred feminist shrine. For Alva, "the delicate minarets" were indeed aesthetically pleasing architectural decorations. But, according to Field, as Alva reflected on their significance and meaning, she began to see that they "pointed to a living hope of what all women might become to the world and of how the world might someday cherish them, not as weak creatures needing protection but as comrades with men protecting the world."[79]

Field treated discussion of other aspects of Alva's life in a similar fashion. She pictured Alva's architectural achievements as an expression of her response to the social convention that prevented her from becoming an engineer or an architect.[80] Alva considered designing and decorating Marble House and its Chinese tea house to be one of her greatest accomplishments. Field claimed that the art in the Gothic Room in Marble House featuring Luca Della Robbia's "Virgin and Child" was particularly meaningful to Alva. Alva told Field, as she sat taking notes, that the "masterpiece of the collection" displayed in the Gothic Room was Della Robbia's.[81] Field elaborated on that comment, writing that not only had Alva quite self-consciously placed it in the same position of importance as "given in a cathedral to the altar," but that she also believed that its figure of the mother of Christ helped inspire and promote her feminist activism. "The childish innocence of the Madonna combined with mature sorrow which is the outgrowth of maternal love, represent all that is best in Woman's soul," Field wrote. And to emphasize the point, she added, "Sometimes in the heat and fret of battle for woman's emancipation when the goal was hidden by the din of combat, I have turned to this Virgin mother's face for inspiration."[82]

In the process of incorporating Alva's views on gender discrimination, marriage, and motherhood in the text, Field elaborated on her notes to produce a commentary on and analysis of the status of women in the United States. She turned a random remark about playing with boys into a ten-page discussion about how social convention limited girls' activities and thwarted their aspirations.[83] Similarly, she turned three pages of cryptic notes on Consuelo's wedding to the Duke of Marlborough into a rambling, fourteen-page, feminist critique of marriage in general and a commentary on the marriage of American heiresses to European aristocrats in particular.[84] "If some god should visit this earth and order all homes to uncover at the same time the heart's secrets concerning marriage," Field wrote, "such a stench would go up as would overpower us all. The marriage institution is protected from utter disintegration to-day by the meek long suffering of women who feel it is their religious duty to endure the sorrows from marriage rather than to annul it."[85]

Both Belmont and Field had divorced their husbands, and Field was in love with a man whose Catholic wife refused to free him from his marriage vows. There is every reason to believe that she and Belmont were in complete agreement about the advisability of easing the restrictions on divorce when, as Field put it in the typescript, "the element of spontaneous desire to perpetuate the mating has gone."[86]

Indeed, in Field's papers there appears a short essay written in Alva's hand critiquing the ease with which people were allowed to marry and the difficulty they had getting a divorce when the marriage proved to be a mistake. "It has always seemed to me that had I the power to frame laws governing the granting of licenses to those desiring to marry, I would construct a board of trustees who alone were entitled to issue such permits," Alva wrote. Composed of mature men and women, "it would have it in its power to refuse the license if in its judgment—evil not good would come of the aspired union." It was her hope, she said, that the inability to get a license would postpone the "thoughtless, hasty" unions of "frivolous, flighty" individuals.[87]

Alva was equally critical of divorce law. "Divorce laws should be made easier," she told Field.[88] "We seem content to divest ourselves of all responsibilities by making as stringent and binding as possible all law to help unbind those who through either youth, impulse, or of impaired judgment—have fettered themselves with a yoke the carrying of which is unbearable," she wrote in her essay.[89]

Given the fact that Field actually wrote the memoir manuscript, it is sometimes difficult to determine where what Alva believed and said ends and where Field's literary license begins. Take, for example, the topic of arranged marriages between American heiresses and European aristocrats. Alva apparently told Field that she was "perfectly aware of the [negative] feeling that exists in certain classes of America about alliances of rich American girls with foreign nobility." Many such marriages failed, she is alleged to have said, so there was valid basis for criticism. But she insisted that arranged international marriages were no more subject to failure than any other. "The reason the world believes all marriages between rich American girls and the foreign nobility are doomed to failure is because whenever such a failure occurs, the whole world knows about it," Field wrote in the memoir. "Gilded sin is so much more interesting that ragged sin. Scandle [*sic*] dressed in ermine and purple is much more salacious than scandle in overalls or a kitchen apron. The wickedness enacted in a palace has a fascination that no village can possibly lend. . . . Therefore, while a hundred thousand marriages between Susan Smiths and John Browns come to a tragic end and no one but an insignificant circle know anything about it, the few marriages of the titled nobility with rich American girls which have likewise proved disastrous are known all over the earth."[90] Discussion of this matter does not appear in Field's notes. And it is unlikely that Alva would have articulated her comments on the matter in terms of "gilded sin" or would have referred to the salaciousness of scandal as dressed in "ermine and purple." In this case, it appears that Field put her own words into Alva's mouth. In doing so, she claimed for herself the role of artist, creating evocative images that were likely to be more memorable and to convey more clearly the message she intended than had she used straightforward prose.

It is equally difficult to assess the degree to which Field's attitude toward motherhood influenced the approach she took to Alva's comments on the subject. Field had two children but did not engage in mothering full time. A woman of varied interests and professional ambitions, she made an attempt to separate her life as a writer from her life as a mother when she arranged to share custody of her children with her ex-husband. That, combined with the fact that she did not accept Belmont's offer to pay to have her children with her during the summer they spent together, suggests some ambivalence on Field's part about the demands that motherhood made on a woman's life.[91]

Whatever Field's attitude toward motherhood, she portrayed Alva as a loving and attentive parent, but one who, in retrospect, regretted the devotion she showered on her children.[92] As we have seen, Alva took great pride in the time and effort she devoted to their development. "I gave them an exclusive devotion. I considered their welfare before all else. I lived in their lives and cultivated no other life apart from them for myself," Field wrote in the memoir.[93] By 1917 Alva's children were grown, and she had begun to have some reservations about the sacrifices she had made. "I dedicated the best years of my life to rearing, influencing, and developing those three beings," she told Field. "Often later on in thinking of how much greater and wiser I individually could have been if I had thought more of my own development, I have almost regretted the exclusiveness of my devotion." This issue clearly resonated with Field. She wrote in her notes, "elaborate on this."[94]

And elaborate she did. Field began her nine-page critique of motherhood with a quote from Bertrand Russell noting that "all women are not necessarily maternal." Despite the fact that "there is every degree of maternal desire," she wrote, few women willingly acknowledged the ambivalence they feel about fulfilling a mother's responsibilities. The reality was, she said, that most women were not instinctively maternal. They simply married and had children in order to support themselves. So like "any other employee [who] seeks the approval of his employer," she continued, they tend to tell their husbands what they know will please them and in order to earn their keep, they do what is expected of them.[95] In such cases, mothering had little to do with women's inborn love of children and everything to do with economic survival. If marriage was merely "legalized prostitution," as Alva contemptuously suggested, some mothers were nothing more than well-paid nannies.[96]

Speaking for Alva, Field went on to say that for a mother to devote herself exclusively to her children and to consider their welfare above her own was at the very least unwarranted and at the very worst a "crime." "I deplore the eternal sacrifice of women for another or others," she wrote. There should be no inherent conflict between motherhood and individualism, she continued. Instead of focusing all of their energy on rearing children, women needed to balance their lives between duty to themselves and duty to their family, she argued. Women are misguided if they think that children needed coddling, constant attention, and exhausting care, she declared. What children really needed was a mother who could provide them with "wise direction and loving guidance."[97] So, she concluded, a woman's children would benefit if she spent some of her time developing her own personality and intellect. Having expanded her perspective on life and prepared herself to be of benefit to society after her children were grown, she would save herself from "a living extinction" when no one any longer needed her undivided attention.[98] A woman who failed to establish some balance in her life, was, as Field put it with considerable literary flourish, like "a diamond already cut and ready to sparkle as she can find light" but one whose gem-like "lustre" was likely to be "lost for the sake of children who may be only imitations."[99]

Again it is hard to tell where what Alva actually said ends and what Field wanted to say begins. This problem in no way diminishes the significance of what Field wrote. Field may have been contemptuous of Alva's intellect, but her notes show that Alva, like other feminists such as Charlotte Perkins Gilman and Harriot Stanton Blatch, understood the principles at stake and the limited choices for personal development available to those whose primary responsibility was to care for young children.[100] So by interpolating what Alva said about gender discrimination, marriage, divorce, and child-rearing, Field's text became something more than just a memoir. It articulated the general thrust of intergenerational and cross-class feminist thought in the early twentieth century.

Field's own feminist instincts combined with her knowledge that Alva would have final approval over the manuscript that she was producing could not help but frame the way that she used the material that Alva gave her. While Field may have been willing to rant in her private letters about the self-absorption and sense of privilege she saw among Newport's rich, it would have been impolitic to do so in her manuscript. So Field followed Alva's lead by making connections between childhood experiences and adult political activism. A description of Alva's physical attack on a boy who dared to "giggle and snicker" at her clothes in Sunday School, which was intended to teach the young man "not to make fun of girls," for example, served as the foundation for teaching grown men in government to take women and their demands for equal rights seriously.[101]

However conflicted her personal feelings about her employer, Field never forgot that, in the end, their relationship was a contractual one and that she had accepted the position as Belmont's secretary and companion for professional and financial reasons. Apparently by the end of July, however, Alva began to have second thoughts about publishing her memoir, and her interest in the project was waning. She never explained why. But Field speculated that a number of factors may have had an influence on her declining enthusiasm for the project. It was possible, she said, that despite the fact that she would never have put anything in the manuscript that her employer did not want there, Alva may have regretted being so candid about her private affairs. It was clear to Field that Alva had not anticipated how complicated and time-consuming writing a publishable memoir could be. Moreover, Alva was "capricious" and inclined to change her mind, Field observed, so it was also possible that having spent what she considered to be enough time on the project, she simply turned her attention to what she considered to be more important matters.[102]

Whatever the case, in a letter to Wood, Field wrote, "Mrs. B. told me she is not going to publish this book now—probably not have it done till after her death. This means that while I get the immediate little cash there is in it, there will be no publisher's door open to me through it. As you know, this was a substantial part of my hope. You can understand my disappointment."[103]

As if to add insult to injury, Alva also told Field that she was having her lawyer draw up papers that would protect her rights and those of her heirs to the manuscript. Field responded by insisting that her right and that of her children to a percentage of the profit when the manuscript was published be guaranteed.[104]

The frustrated Field was beginning to feel exploited. She was proud of her ability to write good prose, defensive about how much creative energy it took to translate her cryptic notes into an engaging narrative, and resentful of the feeling that Alva did not really appreciate what she was paying for. "I am very sorry I did not charge her more money for the work," she wrote to Wood. "I work practically all day and it is creative brain labor on which there is no price. She knows she is getting me dirt cheap and in her secret, selfish heart she rejoices at the bargain."[105]

But it was not just the money or control over the manuscript that bothered Field. She needed Alva to approve of her work for both personal and professional reasons. So as she finished rough drafts of the first chapters, she read them to her employer. In a letter to Wood, she attributed Alva's lack of enthusiasm for her early efforts not to their lack of literary merit but rather to a desire on Alva's part to make sure that she would not have to pay for more than she had originally bargained for. She did eventually get the praise that she was looking for, however. "Yesterday when I had finished reading her the chapter on her child life in Newport, she could not restrain her pleasure," she wrote. "So I know, indeed, I felt it before, that she likes what I am doing." Such praise was even more significant since Field admitted to Wood that what she had written was "rough," a draft representing "the merest skeleton" of what she eventually hoped to produce.[106]

Thus encouraged, Field continued her work on the manuscript and by mid-August claimed to have completed drafts of nine chapters which chronicled Alva's life up until her entrance into the suffrage movement. She and Alva agreed that the rest of the memoir would be based on her notes and the newspaper clippings that Alva had collected over the years. The *Atlantic Monthly* had expressed interest in seeing the manuscript, she told Wood. She hoped that she could complete the book by spring and then somehow convince Alva to publish it.[107]

By the end of the summer, Field had worked out an editing procedure with Belmont. Alva told her to revise the chapters she had already written, make a copy, and then send the manuscript to her so that she could add her own revisions. Field was not sure how much time Alva was willing to devote to the manuscript once she received her copy since her attentiveness to the project had to be sandwiched between her fall sojourn on Long Island and the pre-Christmas "social whirl" in New York City. But Field told Wood that she was "curious in the extreme to see what she [Alva] will make of it."

Field was justifiably sensitive to Alva's comments and criticisms, which focused on both content and style. Alva had already made it clear that she did not find the text very "interesting." Predictably, she felt that Field "was inclined to slight the things the world is interested in for those that the few intellectuals care about." Field was resigned to Alva's desire to edit what she had written but contemptuous of the choices she was likely to make, acknowledging that Alva's sense of what was important was likely to stand in stark contrast to her own. "You will find that what she considers the world is interested in are the number of bridesmaids at Consuelo's wedding, the descriptions of their clothes etc. etc.," she wrote to Wood. On more significant issues such as "her own moral adventures (or immoral ones)," Field lamented, "she has nothing to say." Yet Field was convinced that the potential value of the book lay not in Alva's actions or experiences but rather in what it had to say about Alva's ideas, which Field admitted were—with some padding, expanding, and enlarging on her part—"interesting and worth recording at some length."

Field and Alva clearly had very different ways of expressing themselves. "I think she is stung with the fact that the style is too fluent and too spiritualized to be her and that, of course, is a grave fault of my work," she wrote to Wood in a rare moment of self-criticism. "I ought to have made it *her* in style as well as in content if possible. My only excuse is that her life is, after all, very meager, 'thin stuff' . . . and I had to pad and expand and enlarge so much that it became too much for me."[108]

In November, Alva wrote to Field that she had read the manuscript. "So far I agree with you that it is somewhat pedantic and all of the humor and light and shadows of existence seem to have been left out." But she was convinced that Field's literary sensitivity and writing skills would enable her to turn it into "something which most people will find of interest to read."[109]

In the end, Field believed that the book she was writing would have historical and literary significance, but not necessarily the sort that Alva anticipated. As we have seen, Field's experience working with Alva and living in Newport had provided her entrée into a world completely alien from any she had ever experienced. That being the case, she began to see ways in which the material that Alva was providing could be used to appeal to an even wider audience than either she or her employer had planned. She found Alva's life story fascinating. "I am studying her for my own interest quite apart from her autobiography," Field told Wood. She had begun toying with the idea of writing a romantic novel using a Belmont figure as its tragic heroine. Doing so, she pointed out, would allow her to control the plot and put in material that Alva was hesitant to include in her memoir. "There are phases vivid and I believe universal in their significance but because such phases come from the depths one wishes to keep hidden, they will not come out in her autobiography but the world ought to profit by them in some other form," she wrote to Wood. A fictionalized version of Alva's life would give her the license to include such sensitive material.

She was particularly struck by the literary opportunities inherent in building her story around Belmont's claim that she married in order to save her family from penury. Doing so would allow her to address the problem of what happened when circumstance and social convention denied women of talent and ambition the opportunity to follow their dreams. Her heroine, she said, would be destined "never to know wings and the upper air. It is Aspiration wrapped about with heavy chains of gold and anchored to the earth with self."[110] She believed that the potential market for such a tale was enormous and that she could combine the telling of a good story with an underlying feminist message.

In the end, however, the relationship between the two women foundered on quarrels about money. While Field was at Newport, they quarreled over travel money, causing Field to call Alva "stingy" and express a wish that she was "through with this job."[111] After the summer was over, they quarreled over the terms of their agreement when Alva refused to pay Field for continuing to work on the manuscript.[112] Unwilling to press the matter, Field angrily let it drop. Belmont, she wrote, "ought to be ashamed of herself." She could clearly afford to pay her for the time she spent revising the manuscript and adding the material on Belmont's suffrage work. But Field was unwilling to argue over money. She told Wood that writing was not something she could pin a price on and announced it time for her to turn her attention to creating something of real literary substance. She was through with "this Belmont stuff." And she was through with Belmont as well. Their mutual friend, Doris Stevens, apparently wrote to say that Alva was considering the possibility of hiring Field as her "permanent literary secretary at five hundred [dollars] a month." Field told Wood that if Belmont broached the subject with her, she would refuse, saying: "I would not work for her for five thousand a month."[113]

Field's sojourn in Newport during the summer of 1917 only confirmed her contempt for the rich. After she left, she told Wood that she hoped that what she had written would serve "as an indictment of a monstrosity—for that is what this over-rich element are." She hated them, "their ideas, their psychology," she continued. And although they were the products of "a bad system and an evil environment," she found them "loathsome."[114]

Field and Belmont never resumed their collaboration. In February 1918, Alva wrote to Field that she should not begin work on the rest of the book until they could discuss it in person. She had been busy, she explained, and had not had time to revise the draft that Field had written. There was no hurry, she assured Field, since she had no immediate plans to publish.[115] She wrote to Field again in early October 1918 to say that there was no need for her to come East any time soon since she still had not worked on the manuscript.[116] A few weeks later, Field's son, Albert, died in an automobile accident.[117] Field was emotionally devastated by her son's death and in no position to continue the writing and editing that needed to be done.

When Alva finally heard about Albert's death in early January 1919, she wrote a condolence letter. "Dear friend," it began, "I don't know what to say to you. For a long while I have thought of you, I have known of your mental and physical pain and with my heart over flowing with knowledge of it all, still I have not known what to write." Having expressed her sympathy, however, she assured Field that in the end the death of her son was all for the best since it left her free to pursue the work for which God had intended her. "All great human personal love," Alva wrote, stood in the way of work intended to advance the cause of "all mankind." Apparently forgetting that Field had a daughter, Alva compared Field to Christ, who was destined to "stand alone, stripped, cold, almost homeless" without husband or child. "You," she wrote, "who gave always so much, whose very pulse beat only for others, whose heart and mind blossomed with great human sympathy, must know, that to have been called upon to meet this last supreme sacrifice, is because you are one of the choosen [*sic*] ones." It was all right for Field to grieve and weep, she wrote, but she should eventually "cast off the yoke of sorrow" and "rise from those tears, the new woman."[118] One can only gasp at Alva's insensitivity. Field could not have taken much comfort in her words.

The two women never met again, and the manuscript remained unfinished.[119] Interest in it did continue, however. In 1925, Brenda Ueland, a staff writer for the magazine *Liberty* published in New York, wrote to Field on behalf of its editor asking about the Belmont memoir. Was the manuscript complete? she asked. And did Field think that Belmont would be interested in selling it? She assured Field that the magazine had a large circulation and suggested that publishing the memoir first in the *Liberty* would help to create a market for single copies. Field would benefit from such exposure, she wrote. "Surely you could make some money and some journalistic reputation out of it too," she suggested.[120] It is unclear whether or not Field responded to her inquiry.

After Alva's death in 1933, another editor approached Field about publishing the manuscript. It was clear to her by that time, however, that Alva's ex-husband did not want his former wife's memoir to be published and was willing to use his influence to make sure that the manuscript was not circulated. Under such circumstances, Field was unwilling to pursue the matter. She knew that the memoir needed a great deal of work to make it publishable, and she had begun to have reservations, as she put it, about making "money out of something" that was supposed to have been written by Belmont and would have been published under Belmont's name.[121]

When Field left Newport, she returned to the West Coast. Wood finally gave up his law practice, left his wife, and began cohabiting with her in San Francisco. The two of them bought a home together. Called "The Cats," it sat perched on a hill near Santa Cruz, California. There they wrote poetry and entertained friends interested in literature and radical politics.[122] Field remained an ardent suffrage advocate throughout the 1910s. But once the vote was won, she turned her attention to the campaign to promote world peace and birth control.[123] She published her first collection of poetry, *The Pale Woman,* in 1927.[124] Five years later, Wood's wife died. Field and Wood finally married in 1938.[125] After Wood died in 1944, Field moved to Berkeley to be near her daughter. She died in 1974.[126]

If the newspapers, with Alva's encouragement, "made" her into a social celebrity known for her social and political activism, so did Field make Alva Belmont into a woman of ideas, a woman quite capable of critiquing the status of women in American society, impatient with anyone or anything that impeded the advance of feminist reform, and determined to do her part to bring about social change.

While Alva did tell Field that she thought the text that she had written had emphasized issues that would have appeal to only a small number of intellectuals, there is no evidence that she objected to the way Field portrayed her—a feminist heroine whose personality and life experiences compelled her to challenge the power of men, question the subordination of women, and demand that women grasp opportunities for economic independence and self-ownership so that they could stand on their own.

# 5 Belmont's Orphan Child

AFTER HER SUMMER with Field was over, Alva returned to New York. From there she continued to offer the CU, now known as the National Woman's Party (NWP), both money and moral support.[1] Paul credited Alva for the name change. Mrs. Belmont preferred it, she said, and since she was providing them with operating funds and no one objected, it was an easy way to keep her happy and involved. The effort paid off. "Belmont was so pleased . . . and so full of interest that she . . . pledged . . . [a] tremendous sum of money" to the new organization, Paul remembered.[2]

Alva did not participate in suffrage activities that fall. Her invisibility meant that when the State of New York granted women suffrage in early November 1917, her name was nowhere to be seen in the press coverage.[3] It was Anna Howard Shaw and Carrie Chapman Catt of the NAWSA who got all of the attention. Infuriated, Alva called reporters to a press conference at the headquarters of the PEA. "I have received letters and telegrams from all over the country . . . asking why, in the recording of the New York State victory, the name of the woman responsible for it—my own—was never mentioned by a person or a paper," she indignantly told them. Maybe Shaw and Catt had "forgotten who is responsible for this victory," she continued. "But I don't care. I shall go down in history."

The *New York World*'s coverage of her statement was absolutely gleeful. "Mrs. O. H. P. Belmont is miffed," it said. "She feels that Hamlet has been left out of the cast; then in the magnificent drama of the

Suffrage victory in this State the woman who should have played a stellar role has been forgotten." Unconvinced that she deserved credit for the enfranchisement of women in New York, it noted that while she may have brought the NAWSA to New York City and donated money to pay for its headquarters in 1914, she had since allied herself with the NWP and had made it known that she considered state campaigns a "needless waste of money and energy."[4]

On the heels of the New York victory, the U.S. House of Representatives finally passed the Susan B. Anthony amendment.[5] At the time, Alva was in Florida enjoying the warm weather and raising money for the NWP in Miami, Ft. Myers, and Palm Beach.[6] When Paul proposed putting more pressure on Wilson by burning his speeches in the urns that dotted Lafayette Park across from the White House, Alva reluctantly supported the effort. She was concerned that the strategy might backfire on the NWP and make it even more difficult to raise money to support the suffrage campaign.[7]

Alva remained out of sight (and out of mind) until December 1918, when she gave her PEA headquarters in New York City to the Salvation Army. "Mrs. O. H. P. Belmont's suffrage shop . . . famous for the votes-for-women cold creams and lip salves, which did so much to make woman suffrage and beauty synonymous in New York City, and for the votes-for-women beef stew and apple pie, which made many a convert to the cause before suffrage orators got in a word, passed into history yesterday," said the *New York Tribune.* Henceforth, it would serve as sleeping quarters for 160 veterans and a snack bar where ex-soldiers could get donuts and coffee for free.[8]

By the time Congress began its session in May 1919, Wilson had publicly come out in support of a suffrage amendment. On May 21, the House of Representatives again passed the suffrage amendment by a vote of 304–89. The Senate followed suit on June 4.[9]

It is unclear what role the NWP's militant tactics played in the amendment's passage. The *New York Times* credited the pressure that the NWP activists placed on members of Congress through the use of an elaborate card-index system containing information on each of them combined with the masterful coordination of state and national campaigns as key factors in guaranteeing the success of their campaign.[10] Thomas Marshall, Wilson's vice president, had a different perspective. Women got the vote, he said, because the militants wore down Congress's resistance. Congressmen simply got tired of hearing "the everlasting clatter of the militant suffragists." Passing the suffrage amendment along to the states was merely an act of self-defense, he continued. Once Congress had dispensed with it, they could proceed to consider matters of more importance to the nation.[11] What worked with Alva's mother appears to have also worked with Washington's politicians. Wearing down the opposition got the suffragists what they wanted.

Alva took no part in the campaign to organize state support for the amendment's ratification. When on August 18, 1920, the Tennessee legislature approved its passage, the amendment became part of the U.S. Constitution, but Alva was nowhere to be seen.

Again, private matters proved distracting. Separated from her husband for fourteen years, Consuelo wanted to remarry and, thus, needed a divorce. The duke was more than willing to cooperate. He wanted to marry Gladys Deacon, his mistress. However, when Consuelo consulted her lawyer, he explained that not only must she prove that her husband had committed adultery, but she must also show that he would not consider resuming his role as her husband. The second condition proved troublesome since it required that the duke and duchess again cohabit, if only temporarily. So in March, the couple, accompanied by the duke's sister, agreed to live together for a few days at Consuelo's residence at Crowhurst. When the duke left, he sent her a letter saying in essence that he was deserting her. Consuelo responded as she was forced by law to do. She sued him for what was called "restitution of conjugal rights." When the duke refused to comply with the injunction, she was free to file for a divorce.[12] The court entered the decree of divorce in November. Meanwhile, Alva was trying to put her affairs in order so that she could leave the United States to spend the winter with her daughter.[13]

Despite her lack of participation in the last phase of the suffrage campaign, Alva's contributions of time and money were critical to its success. It could be argued, however, that her celebrity status was her greatest gift to the woman's rights movement. Given the amount of publicity devoted to Alva and her suffrage activities, it is clear that both moderate suffragists in the NAWSA and the more militant activists in the NWP benefited from her ability to harness the power of the press. With social and financial capital to spend, she could solicit interest in woman's rights from journalists, the established members of society, and those who identified with them. When Alva joined the CU in 1914, her reputation preceded her. As Mary Beard pointed out to Paul, "She [Alva] is always a good press story up and down the land." Beard was convinced that the CU could get "fine press notices" in the South and West, if they could convince Alva to campaign in those areas.[14]

But the movement also needed the support of ordinary Americans. And in order to solicit that support, suffrage leaders exploited the general public's fascination with the lives of public figures such as Belmont and in the process created for themselves a public space where discussion of suffrage could became an ordinary topic of conversation. Suffrage organizations could not do this on their own. Subscribers to NAWSA's *Woman's Journal* and the NWP's *The Suffragist* did not represent a large percentage of the American population and did not need to be convinced that woman's suffrage was a goal worth fighting for. Only the popular press could generate the kind of interest that was essential for the success of the woman's suffrage movement. It was the cult of personality that Alva successfully cultivated that provided suffrage activists with the sort of press coverage that gave them entrée to the private spaces inhabited by average Americans whose support was crucial to the passage and ratification of the Nineteenth Amendment.

The wide variety of stories about Alva that appeared in papers such as the *Times* and the *World* helped to personalize the public's understanding of what it meant to be rich and a woman. Vicarious involvement in her life allowed ordinary people to appreciate the aesthetic value of the stately mansions that she built, to sense the humiliation that she suffered at the hands of her philandering husband, to enjoy the celebration of her daughter's marriage, and to share her grief when her second husband unexpectedly died. Journalistically produced visions of Alva Vanderbilt and then Alva Belmont as homemaker, wife, mother, and widow provided the reading public with comforting and familiar images suggesting similarities of life circumstance that had the potential for bridging the economic and social gaps that separated the very rich from those of more modest means. Her carefully crafted public image—lady bountiful who was willing to devote herself and her fortune to promote equal rights for women less fortunate than herself—combined ideas about noblesse oblige and the changing role of women in American society. Militancy, however disconcerting in a woman, could be seen as somewhat less distressful when it was exhibited by someone who clearly had a vested interest in the preservation of the social and economic status quo. Because her celebrity gave her social authority, she was able to give not only respectability but a certain degree of cachet to the idea that women in the highest circles of society could be and were legitimate agents of political and social change.

Once their goal had been accomplished, suffrage activists had to decide whether to continue their struggle for woman's rights or turn to other matters. Some, like Lucy Burns, retired from political activism.[15] Others continued their work in social and political reform. The members of the NAWSA voted to disband and form the League of Women Voters in order to educate women so that they could competently carry out their responsibilities as full-fledged citizens. Feminists interested in social welfare legislation formed the Women's Joint Congressional Committee in November 1920.[16]

Winning the vote did not diminish Alva's interest in woman's rights. She had no wish to see the NWP disband. After all, the leadership position she enjoyed through her affiliation with that organization provided her with a legitimate platform from which to carry on her public life. So she was determined to spearhead an effort to expand its work.[17] At the NWP Executive Committee meeting in July 1920, shortly before ratification, she suggested that in the post-suffrage era the organization dedicate itself to a campaign designed to bring about the abolition of gender discrimination both at home and abroad.[18] Subsequently at the September NWP conference held at her mansion on Long Island, Beacon Towers, she made it clear that she expected the NWP to expand its efforts to promote female equality.[19]

Having laid the groundwork for an equal rights campaign, she left for England in November 1920.[20] In her absence, those who remained in the NWP began the process of redefining their purpose and planning their new campaign.[21] It took them two years. At their national conference in November 1922, they adopted a "Declaration of Principles." In content this statement was essentially the same as the Declaration of Sentiments adopted by the Seneca Falls convention in 1848. The NWP, like early woman's rights advocates, committed itself to demanding equal access to education, employment, civil service jobs, and the ministry for women. It demanded equal pay for equal work and equality before the law. And it declared that a woman had a right to her own body, a right to control her own property, a right to divorce, and a right to custody of her children. "Women shall no longer be in any form of subjection to man in law or in custom, but shall in every way be on an equal plane in rights, as she has always been and will continue to be, in responsibilities and obligations," it said.[22]

The equal rights campaign envisioned in that statement was national in scope. Alva, however, was determined that there be an international component to the crusade as well. Because she had lived in France and was well traveled, her perspective on woman's rights was not nation-bound. Indeed, her ambition was to improve the condition of women around the world. She also had a personal interest in the matter. When Consuelo married the Duke of Marlborough, her claim to American citizenship became ambiguous.

In the early nineteenth century, common law, which held that marriage had no effect on the nationality of either husbands or wives, applied in the United States. Following the example of both the British and French, Congress passed a naturalization act in 1855 that conferred automatic citizenship on alien free white women who married American men. Unfortunately, the position of American women who married aliens remained unresolved. On a practical level, disagreement among politicians, the courts, and executive agencies such as the Department of State and the Department of Justice regarding the status of women who married foreigners led to the implementation of four separate policies regarding them. Sometimes they were denied their American citizenship, sometimes they were denied it only if they moved abroad, sometimes their citizenship was merely suspended, and sometimes their citizenship was preserved. To clear up and simplify such matters, Congress passed an expatriation act in 1907 declaring that any woman who married a foreign national automatically lost her American citizenship. The retroactivity of this law and its application to women such as the Duchess of Marlborough, who married in 1895, remained unclear.[23]

Despite the fact that Consuelo had no trouble entering the United States when she came home to visit, uncertainty about her daughter's claim to American citizenship bothered Alva.[24] She found the fact that Consuelo, a native-born American, had become "a foreign subject" through marriage galling and was willing to put her considerable financial resources behind a campaign intended to remedy Consuelo's unfortunate situation. "If [Consuelo] won't refrain from losing her nationality we have to fix up the whole world law so this cannot happen to women," she told Doris Stevens.[25] From Alva's point of view, the sort of gender discrimination that preserved a man's citizenship rights and took away those of a woman was intolerable.

None of the NWP stalwarts, upon whose shoulders would lay the responsibility for actually carrying out a new crusade, were enthusiastic about starting an international equal rights initiative. Paul was exhausted, felt responsible for paying off the debt of over $10,000 accumulated by the NWP during the suffrage campaign, and wanted to take some time off to study law, an effort intended in part to provide her the expertise to argue effectively for the passage of an equal rights amendment to the U.S. Constitution.[26] Ambivalent about Alva's new pet project, she believed that the passage of such an amendment would guarantee women equal treatment before the law, thus making a separate campaign for equal nationality rights redundant.[27]

Stevens was equally unenthusiastic. About to make a new life for herself by marrying Dudley Field Malone, she believed that only a few legal experts really understood the intricacies of international law regarding citizenship, and she doubted that ordinary woman's rights supporters would take any interest in the issue. She appreciated the fact that Alva had a personal stake in the matter, but it appeared to her to be a class issue that affected the small number of rich heiresses who were marrying European aristocrats.[28]

NWP leaders had other concerns as well. There was virtually no money in their bank account. Their membership had declined. They had almost no staff.[29] It was not clear how much time Belmont was willing to spend in the United States to help conduct the campaign. And they were not sure that dividing their efforts and resources between soliciting support for an equal rights amendment and at the same time financing an international crusade calling for the formulation and passage of an equal rights treaty and an equal nationality treaty was a good idea. Congress had already begun to discuss the possibility of passing legislation designed to address the problem of citizenship as it affected American women.[30] So it was possible that the problem of protecting U.S. women's citizenship rights might slowly but surely be resolved without any special effort on their part. Moreover, campaigning for equal rights put them on a collision course with many of their former suffragist allies as well as some international feminists, who believed that women needed to be protected rather than guaranteed equality with men.[31]

Despite their misgivings, however, Paul convinced the delegates at the NWP convention held in February 1921 to approve Alva's plan to engage in both national and international work.[32] Assuming that the NWP's financial well-being and an equal rights campaign's success would be dependent in part upon Alva's generosity, Paul, who had resigned as head of the NWP in February, arranged for her to be elected president of the organization in October 1921.[33]

Thus encouraged, Alva proceeded with a plan to provide the NWP with visibility as well as a material symbol of substance, permanence, and legitimacy by negotiating the purchase of a new headquarters in Washington, D.C., across the street from the Capitol at 21–25 First Street NE. It was a building of historical significance. President Monroe had been inaugurated there and Congress had used it as their meeting place from 1815 to 1819. By the time she paid the taxes and insurance and supervised the renovation and furnishing of what had been known as "the Old Capitol," she had spent over $156,000.[34] She intended the new NWP headquarters to provide NWP members with easy access to Congress. But she was also determined that the building and the party who owned it serve the interests of women exclusively. So in order to ensure that men would never have any influence in the organization, she stipulated in the deed of gift that bestowed the building on the NWP that it would revert to her estate if the leaders of the association ever employed a man or made him an officer in the organization.[35]

For Paul and the board to have given over the leadership of the NWP to Alva was not as much of an abdication of power as it would seem. By that time it was clear that their principal benefactress, who was in her late sixties, intended to spend most of her time in France where she had just bought a chateau.[36] Thus, her newly acquired position within the NWP was for all practical purposes likely to be an honorary one. That being the case, it was clear that someone else would actually run the organization. The chair of the National Committee ultimately assumed that responsibility.[37]

Alva was honored by the NWP's gesture of support and appreciation. But she realized that if she was going to be an effective leader, she was going to have to find someone whom she could depend on to help her. Paul was the obvious choice. So beginning on October 15, 1921, she began paying Paul's salary and expenses.[38] She also needed someone to organize an international campaign and to represent her interests when she was unable to do so. The person who seemed to be the most likely candidate for the job of lieutenant was NWP fieldworker Doris Stevens.

Younger than Belmont by almost forty years, Stevens was born in Omaha, Nebraska.[39] While she was attending Oberlin College, she became involved in the suffrage movement. She taught after graduation and then began associating with left-wing political activists in Greenwich Village and Croton-on-Hudson, New York.[40] In 1913 she met Alva at a NAWSA convention in Washington, D.C.[41] The next year, just as Alva was switching her allegiance away from the NAWSA, Stevens accepted a job working for Paul and the CU.[42] Once Alva joined the militants, Paul assigned Stevens to work with Belmont as a liaison. Stevens helped Alva organize a National Votes for Women Ball at the Willard Hotel in early 1914 and then joined her in Newport that summer to set up a suffrage headquarters and help plan a suffrage convention at Marble House. In 1915 at Alva's request, Stevens set up a CU headquarters in New York City and then went to San Francisco to organize the woman's suffrage convention to be held during the Panama-Pacific Exposition.[43] Until the ratification of the suffrage amendment in 1920, Stevens remained on the CU/NWP payroll but spent a good deal of her time coordinating Alva's suffrage work with that of the CU/NWP.[44]

Stevens and Alva worked well together. Stevens's feminist credentials were impressive. She was efficient, hardworking, and resourceful. And it helped that she did not mind taking orders. Moreover, she appears to have been willing to accept Alva's assumption that part of her job was to act as both secretary and companion. Typically, when Stevens was with Alva, she worked out of a hotel room, a rooming house, or one of Alva's mansions. That meant that when their official work was done, they found themselves together with time on their hands. It was common for Alva to ask Stevens to read to her, play cards with her, go shopping with her, spend the night with her, accompany her to dinner parties and the theater, help her entertain guests, and listen sympathetically to her personal problems.[45] It was quite a bargain for Belmont. Stevens's salary at the time was only $100 a month.[46]

In return for such services, Belmont adopted the same kind of maternal interest in Stevens's well-being that she had shown for Field. During their 1918 trip to Florida to campaign for woman suffrage, Belmont decided that it was her obligation to find Stevens a rich husband. The man she selected was, as Stevens put it, "a very rich but commonplace widower" whom Stevens had met once in Belmont's home in New York. Belmont, Stevens wrote, "very carefully explained to me how much he had, secured an invitation from him for me to be his house guest with her in Florida, which I declined, and explained that a marriage to him would help relieve her of the burden of having to carry on which she considered to be a heavy financial load." Not willing to let it go at that, Belmont demanded that Stevens's prospective suitor drive his car all night from Palm Beach across the state and through "a jungle" to the place where Stevens was "getting up meetings and raising money, peremptorily demanding that I come at once" to join her as his house guest. Stevens refused to cooperate. Belmont was so exasperated and angry that she reneged on her agreement to pay Stevens's railroad fare home.[47]

Perhaps one of the reasons that Stevens proved to be so effective in her work with Alva was that she managed to figure out how to finance it with such finesse. Associating with Alva was an expensive enterprise. The society matron stayed in only the best hotels, asked Stevens to accompany her to fancy dinner parties, and frequented exclusive resorts. Stevens was a woman with limited personal resources, and her salary from the NWP and the occasional check she received from Alva did not begin to cover some of the expenses she incurred as she helped conduct NWP business. In 1918, for example, she was in Florida and found it necessary "to live at a very expensive hotel in Palm Beach, which was ridiculously beyond my capacity to pay, and yet I had to pay it."[48] In order to avoid embarrassment and make as few financial demands on the NWP as possible, she habitually spent her own money.[49]

Buying the proper clothes necessary to appear in public with Belmont, give speeches, or solicit donations from potential patrons was also a serious drain on her resources. It almost immediately became clear that if she was going to appear with Alva or on her behalf, she was going to need a much larger and more expensive wardrobe than otherwise might have been the case.[50] From time to time Alva offered her some of her cast-off clothing. The garments were both stylish and beautifully made but were more appropriate for an aging society matron than a young professional woman. Stevens investigated the possibility of having them remade but found that the tailoring charges cost more than buying new clothes.[51] So she purchased what clothes she needed on credit. She recalled that it took her "months to pay the bills I contracted for just simple, ordinary clothes to make myself presentable at Palm Beach and other places, and the same was true of Newport. I had to buy things in Washington and pay $5 a month for a long time." Alva, as might have been expected, remained oblivious to the seriousness of the problem.[52] But that, of course, was what made Stevens such a desirable associate. She never complained or discussed the problem, thus sparing Alva the need to concern herself with such matters.

Stevens continued to act as a part-time but wage-earning suffrage field-worker and part-time but unpaid private secretary and companion until just before the suffrage amendment was ratified. At that point, Belmont decided to go to Europe. She had worked with Stevens for almost seven years, had great respect for her work, and enjoyed her company, so she offered to pay all of Stevens's expenses if she would agree to accompany her. Stevens had never been abroad, so she welcomed the opportunity to take advantage of a free trip.[53]

In anticipation of their departure, Stevens gave up her job with the NWP.[54] But then Alva postponed the trip. Unemployed, Stevens's only option was to depend upon Belmont's largesse. Doing so, of course, made her particularly vulnerable to Belmont's propensity to try to control the lives of those with whom she associated. "The last half of 1919 and throughout 1920 she pretty well told me when to come and when to go and where to be," Stevens remembered. "She was appropriating more and more of my time, dictating to me the kind of clothes I should wear. If she didn't like a hat she told me not to wear it again." Belmont even demanded that an unwilling Stevens get her hair bobbed and threatened to cut it off herself if Stevens failed to comply.[55]

As a dependent, Stevens continued to do as Alva asked. That included writing the first of what Alva hoped would be a series of articles outlining her early suffrage activities.[56] While Sara Bard Field's portrait of Belmont, written two years before, represented an attempt to explore and explain the development of Belmont's feminist ideology, Stevens's twenty-five-page typescript focused on how Belmont expressed that ideology on a practical level in her work as a suffragist. Beginning with her 1909 trip to London to attend a meeting of the International Woman Suffrage Alliance, it explained Alva's interest in woman's rights issues, chronicled the increasing appeal that militancy as a suffrage tactic had for her, and described her efforts to make a place for herself as a suffrage leader by using both her celebrity to initiate a public relations campaign on behalf of the movement and her money to support suffrage activities. Intended to celebrate her importance to the suffrage campaign, the article ended with her explanation of why she switched her allegiance to the NWP.[57]

Stevens appears to have filtered the story dictated by Belmont through her own values and experience in much the same way as Field had done. The difference is that Stevens was not an intellectual like Field. She was a field-worker who raised money and organized support for the cause. So it was not feminist ideology that was important in this version of Alva's life as a suffragist; it was what she did with those ideas. The Belmont who emerged from the pages of that manuscript was a practical strategist, a woman of action.

It was apparently Alva's intent that the article be published. It was not, perhaps because it was never sent out for consideration or perhaps because those interested in publishing information about the woman suffrage movement were more interested in current events than they were in suffrage history. Whatever the case, Stevens filed the typescript away, and Alva seems to have forgotten about it.

When the two women did finally set sail for Europe in November 1920, Stevens acted as Alva's social secretary on board ship, contacting other prominent passengers—such as the wealthy socialite Nancy Biddle; the president of National Cash Register Company, John Patterson; and Senator Medill McCormick—to arrange meetings to discuss the state of world affairs and the prospects for advancing the cause of women.[58] All went well until they arrived in Paris and Belmont was forced to confront the fact that Stevens had a personal life of her own.

It turned out that Stevens was involved with Dudley Field Malone. A wealthy and politically well-connected attorney, Malone had helped to manage Woodrow Wilson's presidential campaign in 1912.[59] In return for his efforts, he was appointed Collector of Customs for the Port of New York, a position he held until September, 1917, when he resigned in protest over the government order to imprison suffrage supporters who were picketing in front of the White House. "The present policy of the Administration, in permitting splendid American women to be sent to jail in Washington, not for carrying offensive banners, nor for picketing, but on the technical charge of obstructing traffic, is a denial even of their constitutional right to petition for, and demand the passage of, the federal suffrage amendment," he told the president. "I think it is high time that the men in this generation, at some cost to themselves, stood up to battle for the national enfranchisement of American women."[60] Subsequently, he acted as defense attorney for the demonstrating suffragists, filed damage suits against the officials of the District of Columbia on their behalf, made speeches in support of NWP efforts, donated money to support their picketing campaign, and offered to serve as counsel for an appeal of their convictions, an effort that proved unnecessary once the president pardoned the jailed protesters.[61] In his role as champion of the besieged militants, he visited Alice Paul in jail. When he discovered that the warden had ordered that her windows be boarded up, he demanded that they be removed. They were.[62]

Stevens had known Malone for some time. Indeed, Alva may have been the one to introduce them when she included both of them in her yachting party in the summer of 1916.[63] Whatever the case, by the summer of 1917, they were very much a couple.[64] And in 1920 they were appearing together at society functions in New York.[65]

Alva was unenthusiastic about Stevens's relationship with Malone and jealous of the time she spent with him. So before they left for Europe, she extracted a promise from Stevens that the two of them would spend the first two months without Malone, thus guaranteeing that she would have Stevens's undivided attention. When Malone unexpectedly appeared before the agreed-upon deadline, Alva was furious. "As you will remember, when I invited you in New York to come to Europe with me for two months, it was perfectly understood by Mr. Malone and yourself that Mr. Malone was not to join us until the two months were over," she wrote in a note to Stevens. "I even explained to you both that I would not have you with me if this was not perfectly agreed upon." As far as she was concerned, Stevens had reneged on her part of the bargain. "I did not ask you to come to Europe as my guest to be annoyed," she declared in a huff. "I have decided to go South Sunday without you. I will give you the necessary amount for your expenses until Jan 31st which will be the end of your two month visit, also the money for your return passage. I am sure you will enjoy Paris much more than the south of France and at least I shall not have any more worry as regards our daily lives." She ended her letter expressing regret at being "obliged to take this decision."[66]

Forced to choose between Belmont and Malone, Stevens chose Malone and married him on December 5, 1921. She lived with her new husband in Europe for two years. After she returned to the United States in 1923, she resumed her work with the NWP and Alva, this time as a volunteer.[67]

Alva returned to the United States at about the same time, full of plans to initiate a number of ambitious projects which she expected someone else to help her carry out. In between speaking engagements, she sponsored a three-day conference in Seneca Falls, New York, in July to celebrate the seventy-fifth anniversary of the first American woman's rights convention held there on July 19 and 20, 1848, and to announce the inauguration of an equal rights campaign. Once again Alva indulged in her love of spectacle. NWP staff decorated three miles of streets in Seneca Falls with purple, white, and gold banners. Fifty women and children performed a dance drama in honor of the struggle for woman's rights. And the organizers raised an estimated $9000 to support NWP activities. Susan B. Anthony had not even been involved with the woman's rights movement in 1848 and did not attend the original Seneca Falls convention. Nevertheless, according to the *New York Times,* five thousand people watched while woman's rights advocates marched from Seneca Falls to Rochester to pay tribute to her. At the conference that followed, the NWP endorsed the wording of an equal rights amendment.[68]

Because of Stevens's marriage, Belmont could not depend on her services and, therefore, began to rely more and more on Paul's help. In July 1923, Alva agreed to funnel the money she was paying to support Paul through the newly created Woman's Research Foundation, a nonprofit unit of the NWP intended to serve as the headquarters for doing the research needed to assess the status of women in the United States.[69] Thereby assured of both a tax deduction and Paul's continuing involvement in NWP affairs, Alva took on the role of visionary and proposed the establishment of a world parliament of women. Men had been in charge of world affairs since the beginning of time, she said. It was now time for women to take their place as political activists on an international scale. The idea was a half-baked one. As Stevens put it later, it was never clear to anyone whether Alva really wanted to set up a government run by women or whether she merely wanted enough women elected to Congress so that they could run the U.S. government. Whatever the case, she successfully solicited Paul's help in convincing the NWP to endorse the idea. And after agreeing to chair the planning committee, Alva dropped the project in Paul's lap and sailed off to Europe in November.[70] She was not there when Senator Curtis, Republican of Kansas, introduced the Equal Rights Amendment to Congress on December 10, 1923.[71]

In early 1924, Paul resigned the vice presidency of the NWP to spend more time on graduate work.[72] Arguing that she was growing old, was unable to spend much time in the United States, and therefore could not direct the work that needed to be done, Alva persuaded Stevens to take charge of a "Women for Congress campaign" prior to the 1924 general election in order to create a women's bloc in the House of Representatives. With little money and no political organization behind her, Stevens faced the seemingly impossible challenge of ensuring the victory of women who had no broad base of support. Despite her best efforts, the campaign was a failure.[73]

When the election was over, Belmont insisted that Paul interrupt her studies and come to Europe to begin work on the international campaign. Paul left for France in December. They spent the better part of 1925 recruiting feminists from Britain, France, Germany, Holland, Hungary, Norway, Sweden, Romania, the Soviet Union, and Switzerland to serve on a yet-to-be-created NWP international advisory committee. Its purpose was to serve as an international feminist lobbying group whose job it would be to coordinate an international equal rights crusade.[74]

Belmont was also determined to see the NWP affiliate with the International Woman Suffrage Alliance (IWSA), one of the few international feminist organizations then in existence.[75] She persuaded Stevens to lead the NWP delegation to the IWSA conference to be held at the Sorbonne in Paris in mid-May 1926. Their purpose was to convince the delegates of the alliance to admit the NWP to membership. Despite the support of British feminists under the leadership of Lady Rhondda and her Six Point Group, the delegates rejected the NWP's application by a vote of 123 to 48. Alva responded by calling reporters to her Paris residence and issuing a statement blaming Carrie Chapman Catt, a former president of the IWSA who had not even attended the convention, for the NWP's failure to gain membership. There were long-standing personal and ideological animosities between the two. Catt had been critical of suffrage militancy during the American suffrage campaign and was no supporter of equal rights. In order to induce IWSA delegates to admit the NWP, Alva had offered 50,000 francs to help support its work. But Catt had a substantial legacy from Mrs. Frank Leslie at her disposal, so the IWSA did not necessarily need Alva's money.[76] Alva's second response was to express her disappointment by temporarily suspending her contributions to the NWP. Writing to Paul, she said "Please don't ask me for any more for this work. I do not think I should bear all this work anymore. If we do not carry it on otherwise, it had better stop for the present."[77]

Her testiness may have had to do with the fact that Consuelo was again involved in an effort to clarify her marital status. She was happily married to Jacques Balsan, but his devoutly religious family refused to recognize their marriage because it had not been sanctified by the Catholic Church. A solution to that problem was to have Consuelo's first marriage annulled by the Rota, the Catholic court in Rome, on the grounds that Alva had forced her daughter to marry the duke. After she was assured that the proceedings would be private, Alva testified to that effect.[78]

The proceedings did not stay private for long. In order to assert its right to annul a marriage performed in an American Episcopal church, the Rota released a transcript of the proceedings. What ensued was a media frenzy.[79] The news broke on November 25, 1926, when the *New York Times* and other newspapers ran front-page headlines announcing that Belmont had forced her daughter to marry. Under the banner "Rutherford Named as Man Ex-Duchess Wanted to Marry," the *Times* republished segments of the Rota's nine-page decree, quoting the testimony of various witnesses, including that of Consuelo, her ex-husband, and her governess. The paper quoted Belmont as having told the tribunal that she viewed Consuelo's infatuation with Rutherford as "merely a whim of a young inexperienced girl" and felt perfectly justified in forcing her daughter to marry the duke. "I have always had absolute control over my daughter," she told the Catholic clerics in charge of the case. She was the one who ruled the roost. "When I issued an order nobody discussed it," she is reputed to have said.[80]

Both Consuelo and her mother were deeply distressed about the publicity. Consuelo made every effort to avoid the press, and Belmont, aboard the SS *Berengaria* on her way to Europe, refused to comment on the matter.[81] Consuelo's propensity to hold herself responsible for maintaining the equilibrium in her relationship with her mother appears to have persisted into adulthood. "My mother, with her usual courage, remained undaunted," she wrote with begrudging admiration of her mother's stoicism in the face of adverse publicity. "But I suffered," she said, "to see her in so unfavorable a light, knowing that she had hoped to ensure my happiness with the marriage she had forced upon me."[82]

As soon as the annulment was granted, Consuelo remarried her husband according to the rites of the Catholic Church. Shortly thereafter, they traveled to Châteauroux, where Jacques's family welcomed her.[83]

While Consuelo was regularizing her marital status, Alva watched the Stevens-Malone marriage collapse. Historians Mary Trigg and Leila Rupp assert that Malone was abusive and that he drank excessively, spent time with other women, and, on at least a few occasions, physically abused Stevens.[84] But Alva's continuing demands on Stevens's time also caused friction. Even before he married, Malone resented Belmont's power to run Stevens's life and Stevens's apparent willingness to let her do so. He had every reason to expect that when Stevens married him, that situation would change. When it did not, their relationship deteriorated. "Hostility to the demands she made upon my time and my response to them were a constant source of friction between him and me before and during our marriage," Stevens commented later. Her trip to the International Woman Suffrage Alliance meeting and extended stay in France afterward did nothing to help the situation.[85]

When it became clear that the marriage was doomed, Alva encouraged Stevens, who by that time had taken Jonathan Mitchell, a writer for the *National Review,* as her lover, to file for divorce.[86] "I do hope something sensible is being arranged with Dudley," she wrote. "Do write me about it and don't do anything in the way of letting sentiment or feelings dictate the new life, they are all very well in their way but life founded on them can not continue and men will sacrifice any woman (any man not one) at any moment if he tires or if it is for his own interest to do so." She suggested that Stevens would be better off dedicating her life to advancing the cause of women than to saving her marriage. Experience had taught her, she explained, that a woman must depend only on herself. "No man *loves* a woman, he loves himself and woman must learn to love *herself* or else the continual fall of her air castles *will crush her* in the end. Take them as they take us, and all will end well, the old training must go, we are coming into our own . . . to walk alone is divinely great and the very man who would take this from you, later *will* leave you. Learn your lessons and be brave." She signed herself, "Your Friend, Alva Belmont."[87]

Stevens filed for divorce in July 1927, charging that Malone had abandoned her. According to the *New York Mirror,* the final straw was Malone's refusal to admit her to a party he was giving at his villa on the Riviera.[88]

Finding herself without a means of support, Stevens hoped to make a living as a writer and had started preparing drafts of two books, one a satire and the other a history of women and labor from 1830 to 1930. But neither manuscript was finished, so she could not expect to make money on royalties anytime in the near future. Given her financial circumstances, she must have been grateful for the hospitality that Alva extended when she invited her to stay at her chateau.[89]

That is where Stevens was when she received a cable from the officers of the NWP asking her to accept the chairmanship of their National Council. The position came with a salary. So Stevens took the letter to Alva to discuss the offer. With Paul distracted by her studies in the United States and an International Advisory Committee for the NWP in need of leadership, Alva saw this as a perfect opportunity to formalize her working relationship with Stevens.

"Mrs. Belmont begged me to refuse this [offer] in order to do international work for her," Stevens remembered. "She said she was too old to do active work any more and relied on me to help her on both Continents. She stressed her failing strength and added that whatever she could do herself would have to be done mostly in Europe from now on." Stevens explained to Belmont that having just filed for divorce she needed some way to support herself. Belmont suggested that Stevens raise capital by selling her six-room Croton-on-Hudson cottage in Westchester County, New York, and come to live abroad near her. Stevens demurred, saying that her cottage was not worth enough to provide for her support, that there were more employment opportunities in the United States than in France, and that she had no desire to become an expatriate. Belmont persisted, assuring Stevens that her work in the woman's movement was "invaluable" and that if she were willing to continue to work with her as a team, they could accomplish even greater things for women all over the world. When it was clear that her arguments were not convincing Stevens to give up an opportunity for paid employment, Belmont offered to include a bequest to Stevens in her will so that she could look forward to some degree of financial security.[90] Thus assured, Stevens declined the offer from the NWP, gave up her work on behalf of working women, and agreed to give her undivided attention to what she called Belmont's "orphan child."[91]

Stevens returned to the United States in August. Alva followed in November but returned to France almost immediately, leaving Stevens in charge of organizing the International Advisory Committee.[92] Before Stevens could make much headway on the project, however, she realized that an opportunity existed to act on Alva's behalf and press the case of woman's citizenship rights before the Sixth Pan-American Conference to be held in Havana, Cuba.[93]

Alva had made it clear that she wanted to find a way for women to exert more political power throughout the world but had outlined no concrete plan to accomplish that goal. Stevens was politically astute enough to realize that women had no base upon which to build their power on the international stage. The only international organization with any influence in world affairs was the newly created League of Nations, but the United States was not a member. And European women, whose countries belonged to the League, exerted no influence whatever over its policies or activities.[94]

An alternative to organizing women in Europe was to work through Latin America as a way to gain political influence over international affairs related to the status of women. That idea had emerged from a conversation between Alva and the director general of the Pan-

American Union at the woman's rights convention held in Seneca Falls in 1923. According to Stevens, Alva came away from their meeting quite "enthusiastic over the plan of trying to enlist the governments of Latin America to support [NWP programs to promote equality] and through these Latin American countries trying to bring pressure on the League of which these Latin-American countries were members."[95]

Attending the Havana conference and discussing the demand for equal nationality rights with its delegates was a good way to begin. Unable to communicate with Alva, who was on board a ship headed for Europe, Stevens solicited a $5000 contribution from her son, William K. Vanderbilt Jr., to cover the expense of sending American feminists to the meeting.[96]

Stevens and her associates left for Havana the first of January 1928 to solicit support for the adoption of an equal rights treaty. When they arrived, they set up their headquarters in the Sevilla Biltmore Hotel, contacted various women's organizations in Cuba to ask for their help, and organized a street procession to promote their proposal. Alva provided moral support from afar.

The conference did not adopt the treaty that Stevens and other female lobbyists proposed but did establish an Inter-American Commission of Women (IACW) to study the legal and civil condition of women in the Western Hemisphere. The group, composed of one woman representing each of the twenty-one American republics, was instructed to report its findings to the Seventh Pan-American Conference to be held in Montevideo in 1933. When Secretary of State Frank Kellogg appointed Stevens to represent the United States on the commission and the governing board of the Pan-American Union appointed her to be the commission's chairperson, Alva was ecstatic. Comparing the newly created commission to the first American woman's rights convention, she sent a check for $5000 to the NWP to support the commission's work.[97]

Stevens was gratified by her appointment but uncomfortably aware that she was in no position to undertake a task of this sort. She had neither the expertise to do the research which her new position demanded nor the financial resources to justify having been given the position. However important and prestigious, the chairmanship was a volunteer position intended for someone who had the money to pay people to carry out the work that needed to be done. The commission did not have a budget to cover travel and research expenses. So the ever-resourceful Stevens was forced to raise the money she needed.[98] Serving as Alva's lieutenant was turning out to be an even more expensive enterprise than she had anticipated.

Stevens was very much aware that she was a stand-in for Belmont. She acknowledged that "it was the power of Mrs. B and her money which I was translating into concrete proposals to carry out her policy."[99] And she was not entirely pleased with what she considered to be her extremely awkward position. Even though Stevens was by this time a well-connected, international activist in her own right, Alva often insisted on providing her with letters of introduction to people who she thought might be useful to the cause of equal rights. Stevens found having to present such letters to people she already knew both awkward and humiliating since it implied that Alva regarded her as some sort of employee whose job it was to represent her interests. "Sometimes I used to think she gave that impression unnecessarily pointedly," she said. The problem was, as Stevens put it, that she didn't know what sort of representative she was supposed to be. Alva would write to someone such as Lady Astor saying, "I cannot come to London; she is coming to see you." When the reply came, it came from a woman who identified herself as Lady Astor's "'political secretary.'" The position of Lady Astor's secretary was clear while Stevens's position vis-à-vis Belmont was ambiguous. And to make things worse, Alva sent such patronizing letters over and over again.[100]

The creation of the Inter-American Commission gave Alva and her lieutenant the venue they needed to pursue their international campaign. Since the NWP had no international standing and their failure to gain entry into the International Woman Suffrage Alliance had deprived them of an international affiliation, Belmont, working through Stevens, simply appropriated the Inter-American Commission and expanded its mission to suit her needs.

This potential conflict of interest made Stevens, the governing board of the NWP, and the Latin American commissioners uneasy. As Stevens pointed out, Belmont was clearly less interested in seeing that the commission's research work got done than she was in using the commission as "an instrument for carrying out her wishes."[101] A problem also arose as to how to direct the gifts that Belmont sent to the NWP for international work, as the following incident, detailed by Stevens, illustrates. "In February, 1929, Mrs. Belmont sent a contribution [to the NWP], saying it was for Latin-American work. Funds for international work, as I say, went through the National Treasury of the N.W.P. and as an example of the sometimes lukewarm enthusiasm of the staff at the N.W. P. headquarters; this money, intended by her for Inter-American work by the Commission, was subsequently transferred to national use. The Chairman of the Council did get Mrs. Belmont's subsequent authorization for the transfer of a part at least, but Mrs. Belmont never ceased to be upset by this as long as she remembered it."[102] When the Latin American commissioners realized that Stevens was taking orders from Belmont, there were murmurs of protest.[103] Oblivious to how her interference in commission affairs might appear to others, Alva continued to use Stevens to set the agenda for the Inter-American Commission.

Despite the fact that Stevens was now obliged to begin the research she had agreed to supervise for the Inter-American Commission, she and Alva made preparations to set up a headquarters at The Hague in anticipation of the World Conference for the Codification of International Law, which was scheduled to take place in 1930.[104] Alva considered the Hague conference very important. Under the auspices of the League of Nations and the Permanent Court of International Justice, delegates were charged with codifying laws affecting international relations. Alva was convinced that this was a unique opportunity for women to successfully plead their case for legal equality. According to Stevens, Alva believed that "the whole future status of women . . . in the world system was in the balance" since "the status accorded [women] in the proposed nationality code would tend to fix the status of women in all future world law."[105]

Before they immersed themselves in preparations for the Hague conference, however, Belmont insisted that Stevens go to Paris to place an equal rights treaty before the delegates of the Kellogg-Briand Peace Conference which was scheduled to meet in the summer of 1928. Stevens opened a headquarters, as Alva had instructed her to do, at the Hôtel Metropolitan, so that they would have some place to confer with the conference's delegates. Alva came to Paris from her chateau every few days to give Stevens instructions, to issue press statements, and to pressure the American ambassador to France into arranging a meeting between Stevens and French Foreign Minister Aristide Briand. Despite Alva's influence and the ambassador's efforts on her behalf, the meeting never took place. So Stevens and a group of equal rights supporters decided to present their petition to the conference delegates as they arrived for lunch at the president of France's summer home at Rambouillet. As they stood at the gate of the chateau, gendarmes placed them under arrest, roughed them up, and held them in a local jail all afternoon. An Associated Press correspondent broke the news to the world. But the local papers elaborated on his story by dramatizing the incident beyond recognition, claiming, among other things, that Stevens and those who had accompanied her had jumped onto the running boards of the guests' cars as they arrived for their meal.[106]

When she heard the news, Alva was furious. When Stevens returned to Alva's chateau, she met the full force of her anger. Alva accused her of exceeding her authority and of behaving inappropriately. So Stevens offered her resignation and went upstairs to pack her trunk. Alva, realizing that Stevens was about to leave and that, if she did, there would be no one to carry out the work that needed to be done in preparation for the Hague conference, sent a note of reconciliation up to her bedroom. Stevens came down. They kissed and made up.[107]

What Stevens did not realize is that between the time that Alva had read the newspaper coverage of what became known as the Rambouillet Affair and Stevens's arrival at her chateau, Alva had sent a letter and a memorandum to NWP headquarters in Washington denouncing Stevens's actions and demanding that the governing board make it clear to everyone in the organization that she, not Stevens, was in charge of international work and that she, not Stevens, would decide what tactics would be used to advance the cause. "I refuse absolutely from now on ever to work with Doris Stevens," she said. By using "hoodlum methods" in their attempt to present their demands to the convention delegates, Stevens and those who had accompanied her had embarrassed both her and the NWP.[108] "As President of the organization, I have always understood that I was the head of international as well as national work—in fact especially of international work, since I am living in Europe and the National Council functions in the United States," Alva wrote in her memo.[109]

In response, the board of the NWP, knowing that Belmont was paying most of the expenses incurred by those working to promote international equality, passed a resolution at their October 1928 board meeting acquiescing to Belmont's demands for clarification on her status within the organization: "The National Council wishes to express to Mrs. Belmont its desire that her wishes shall always be followed and assures her that every effort will be made to carry out her instructions. The council further assures Mrs. Belmont that it fully recognizes her authority as President of the organization and has complete confidence in her judgment regarding national and international policies." The members of the council expressed their "deep appreciation" of her "wise leadership" and assured her of their "loyal support."[110]

Alva wrote back to assure Paul that Stevens had apologized for having acted without her approval and that they had reconciled. "The whole matter is over and we are the very best of friends," Alva said.[111] NWP staff members were clearly relieved that Alva seemed to be able to put the past behind her. Jane Norman Smith, chair of the National Council, sent a letter to Belmont intended to smooth over whatever ill feeling might still remain. "Dear Mrs. Belmont," she wrote, "every organization makes mistakes. The Woman's Party has made very few. You are convinced that the Rambouillet affair was a mistake, and your letters state that Doris admitted it was. The fact that you forgave her shows the beautiful spirit behind the Woman's Party work. We are all working for a cause bigger than ourselves and we can be forgiven if we sometimes make mistakes for the right cause."[112]

That, Smith no doubt hoped, would be the end of it. Unfortunately, it was not—partly because Alva was inclined to hold grudges and partly because her absence complicated efforts to communicate with her. Smith found it necessary to continue her efforts on behalf of the NWP to salvage what was left of Alva's goodwill and ensure her continuing financial support. When Alva's private secretary, Mary Gertrude Fendall, wrote to say that Belmont still felt that the leaders of the NWP were exploiting her influence and name and spending her money but considered her a figurehead, Smith vehemently denied that such was the case.[113] In order to nurture a reconciliation between Belmont and the NWP, Smith invited Fendall, who was in the United States, to a National Council meeting in Washington to represent Alva's interests and present her concerns about leadership to the board.[114] Alva remained obstinately resistant to Smith's gestures of appeasement. Her response was to write to Smith to say in no uncertain terms that she deeply resented having her advice ignored and being placed in the position of financing a campaign that she did not control.[115]

However angry she might have been and whatever she may have said to Smith, Alva had no intention of withdrawing from international work. Having failed to get the delegates of the Kellogg-Briand Conference to consider the position of women in their deliberations, she and Stevens continued to make plans for the Hague Conference.[116] Considering herself too old to actively participate in making the preconference arrangements, Alva remained at her chateau, supervising Stevens from afar and insisting that public relations efforts be made to assure the reading public that she was still in charge. It was clear to Stevens that despite Alva's alleged incapacity, "She did not want to release her grasp which could no longer be backed by her physical presence."[117]

Stevens returned to Washington in November 1928 to resume her Latin American research at the offices of the Pan-American Union, enroll in morning and evening classes on international affairs, and prepare for the Hague Conference by trying to coordinate her efforts on behalf of women's nationality rights with those of the Latin Americans.[118]

On behalf of Belmont, who was determined to press her plan for using the Hague Conference as an excuse for assembling a congress of women, Stevens returned to Europe in June 1929 to represent the NWP in Berlin at the Open Door International Conference to discuss the plight of working women and to confer with feminists attending the Congress of the International Alliance for Equal Suffrage.[119] After the conferences, she returned home in order to enroll in a summer course on international law at Columbia University to prepare herself for the debate that was to take place at The Hague over the question of citizenship and nationality.[120]

Alva was seventy-six years old in 1929 and in increasingly poor health. Her awareness of her increasing fragility made her fearful and morose. In a letter to Stevens she wrote, "I indeed want to be with you all. During the long hours of the night when I do not sleep, I realize what I am unable to do out here, it is dreadful to grow old, to know that the body stops the will, I never expected this. I *have been* so strong. I am timid about overdoing myself. I want to stay a little longer, so much is still to be done. Perhaps witnessing so many funerals of noted men, this last few days, may have made me blue, forgive."[121] Alva had always been able to overcome anything that stood in her way. Now she had found an enemy that would be impossible to defeat.

Alva continued to send checks to NWP headquarters but was less direct about how the money was to be used. "I am sending you the check for five thousand dollars," she wrote to Smith. "I thought from what you had written me, you would care to use this money for speakers to South America. I understand better now from your letter that it would be more useful to use a part of this money to send speakers throughout the United States. I want you to do what you think best with this amount. I do not wish to restrict you in any way."[122] Smith was grateful for the unrestricted gift. Stevens had only $100 in her account, so the National Council voted to give her half of the five thousand to spend on work being done for the Inter-American Commission.[123]

As much as she may have wanted to, Alva was not able to participate actively in preparations for the Hague Conference. But she donated $2000 to cover any expenses that the NWP delegation might incur.[124] After conferring with Belmont in Paris, Stevens proceeded to The Hague where she set up a NWP-IACW headquarters, began a publicity campaign, and arranged interviews with as many delegates as possible in order to explain the terms of the equal nationality treaty that she and Belmont were proposing.[125]

Unfortunately, their efforts were unsuccessful. The international agreement on nationality drawn up by the delegates discriminated against women. So Stevens, knowing that the treaty could not succeed without the support of the United States, lobbied the U.S. delegation to reject the agreement and wrote to President Herbert Hoover warning him that the treaty's provisions inadequately protected women. When Hoover instructed the U.S. representatives to vote against it, they were the only delegation to do so.[126] Failure to gain equal nationality rights for women was disappointing to those who cared about the issue. In response, Viscountess Rhondda of Great Britain and Paul organized Equal Rights International to continue their lobbying efforts. Belmont sent them $5000 to cover the expenses of setting up headquarters for the organization in Geneva.[127]

Stevens continued to immerse herself in international feminist activities, but raising enough money to do so continued to be a problem.[128] Since 1927, when Stevens accepted Belmont's proposal that they work together on a permanent basis on the international equal rights campaign, Belmont had sent her gifts, payments for services rendered, and reimbursement checks to cover some of her expenses. But Alva's generosity was sporadic at best. In 1927, for example, Belmont sent Stevens a check for 1000 francs for having written an article for her. She instructed Stevens to give 100 francs to the person who had translated it and to spend the rest of it on herself.[129] In 1928, Stevens received a friendly note from Belmont accompanied by a check for 5000 francs intended to cover her hotel bill as well as money for meals, tips, and taxis.[130] At about the same time, Alva sent a letter to Emma Wold, NWP treasurer, telling her that she had paid all of Stevens's expenses in Europe and asking that the amount be entered in NWP as a donation.[131] In 1929, Stevens received a check from Belmont as an Easter gift.[132]

In late December 1930, Belmont sent Stevens a check for $2000 from Paris. The money was for Stevens's personal use, she told her. "Take it and go on a spree," she said.[133] Stevens was surprised by the gift and enormously grateful. "I scarcely know how to thank you," she wrote. "Nothing ever happened to me which lifted so wonderfully a feeling of despair as to how I was to go on with the coming months of work." She noted that she had been paying for incidentals like phone calls and telegrams herself. "As a matter of fact no one in their right senses would go on as I do spending the tiny capital that I have. But there seems no way out so I try to manage somehow." She admitted having fantasized about taking a vacation or buying a new car with the money. She also mentioned to Alva that she needed an operation to repair a hernia on her thigh and that the money could be used to get a nicer hospital room. "Maybe I'll compromise on at least getting a new dress. I am almost seedy in clothes." Having considered all her options, she told Belmont that in the end, she had decided to "use it on Washington expenses."[134]

There is no record of how Stevens actually used the money.[135] But her thank-you note was clearly intended to convince Alva that she was still the committed, self-denying feminist that she had always claimed to be.

After the failure of feminists to get an equal nationality rights treaty passed by the Hague Conference, Stevens returned to the United States to continue her studies in international law while Paul worked in Geneva to try convince the League of Nations to organize a European woman's rights committee modeled on the Inter-American Commission of Women. Paul succeeded. In January 1931, the delegates to the League voted to establish a Women's Consultative Committee on Nationality and designated the Inter-American Commission of Women, which was headed by Stevens, as one of its constituent members.[136] In order to support Stevens's efforts and improve public awareness of the need for equal nationality rights and the struggle facing those who were working to ensure it, Alva wrote an article for *Good Housekeeping* noting how easy it was for a woman to lose her citizenship and calling on Americans to "gather their forces" and join the "vanguard in the march toward the complete freedom of women."[137]

Just as the League of Nations was establishing its Women's Consultative Committee, the leaders of the NWP were dedicating their new headquarters at 144 Constitution Avenue NE. In 1928 the federal government had condemned the original NWP headquarters, purchased by Belmont in 1921, so that a new home for the U.S. Supreme Court could be built.[138] Hoping to get as much money as possible from their property, the leaders of the NWP had monitored the condemnation process carefully.[139] With the $299,200 they received in the settlement, they were able to purchase and furnish a new headquarters and had about $183,000 left over to establish an endowment fund. U.S. financial markets were in turmoil in 1928 and 1929 as speculators poured borrowed money into the purchase of stock and bonds. Prices rose precipitously as a result, making it harder and harder for amateurs and professionals alike to make wise investment decisions. Determined to control how the money was spent, Alva appointed herself as well as Maud Younger, Eunice Dana Brannan, Marion May, and Jane Norman Smith to serve on an investment committee, but she never attended any of their meetings.[140] When Smith wrote to her in May 1929 asking whether she wanted the committee to send their list of investment opportunities to her son or wait to consult with her when she came back to the United States in the fall, Alva answered that she trusted the judgment of the committee and that they should proceed without her.[141]

Working around Alva's schedule meant that planning the dedication ceremony for their new headquarters took almost two years and involved a great deal of negotiation. Alva had specific ideas about how the ceremony should be conducted. Ever sensitive to the public relations value of such an event, she wrote to Paul in February 1929 suggesting they move to their new headquarters by processing down the street with banners flying accompanied by a band and carts holding their bulletin boards and furniture.[142]

In March, Smith wrote to her suggesting that the newly purchased building be called Belmont House in her honor. Under normal circumstances, Alva would have jumped at the chance to be thrust into the limelight and receive the recognition she thought she deserved. But in this case, she seems to have been hesitant to accept the proposal. Perhaps it was because she had no way to gauge whether the offer was an indication of how much the leaders of the NWP appreciated her efforts on behalf of woman's rights or whether they simply wanted to guarantee her continued financial support. Whatever her concerns, she asked Smith to get the approval of all those who had served as prominent suffragists, saying with uncharacteristic humility, "Individually, I do not think that any of us amount to very much. It is the Party. The union of our mentality and great understanding of the work we are doing, that is what counts." She protested that just because she had the means to provide the party with their headquarters did not in and of itself make her more deserving than others.[143] By June, she had reconciled herself to the idea but still had reservations. She wrote that she appreciated the gesture and that a small plaque could be placed just inside the entry but was afraid that dedicating the house to her might "belittle" the efforts of others who could not afford to give as much to the cause as she had given.[144]

Unfortunately, such generosity of spirit was short-lived. The opening of the new headquarters had originally been planned for October, and Alva had rearranged her schedule so that she would be able to attend the event.[145] When the NWP staff rescheduled the dedication for December without consulting her, she was hurt and angry. "I think there is no excuse for treating me in the way I have been treated," she complained. It indicated a lack of "consideration and respect" on their part, she said. As president of the organization, she felt "greatly grieved" at not having been consulted.[146] Smith offered to postpone the dedication until it was clear that Alva could attend.[147] But Alva would have none of it. She told Smith that she did not know when she would be able to cross the ocean and ordered Smith to dedicate the building as soon as possible.[148] In anticipation of that ceremony, she wrote in July 1930 suggesting that since the building was to be called the Alva Belmont house that the organization's letterhead should carry that name.[149] It was not until January 4, 1931, however, that the dedication of Belmont House took place. Alva did not attend, but she did send a check for $10,000 to cover the cost of constructing an equal rights auditorium on the grounds.[150]

That spring, Alva made it clear to Paul that she wanted to see Stevens. So Paul wrote to Stevens, "Perhaps it might be worth while for you to come in order to try to get her to give more money to the [Inter-American] Commission." Paul was willing to make the appeal but thought that Stevens would be able to persuade her to give more. Paul had convinced Alva to contribute $5000 to the NWP in December, but a check specifically for the benefit of the commission had not been forthcoming.[151]

Stevens complied. In the summer of 1931, she joined Belmont and Paul in Europe in order to attend the first meeting of the Women's Consultative Committee in Geneva. Belmont sent her 2500 francs (about $100) to help pay for her expenses.[152] When the meeting was over, Stevens and Paul went to Belmont's chateau to relax and consult with their benefactor.[153]

The atmosphere was strained from the beginning. They found Belmont suffering from high blood pressure, distracted by various domestic problems, miffed that they had not arrived earlier, and resentful that she seemed to be carrying so much of the financial burden related to the party's international work.[154] She had indeed been the equal rights campaign's most generous supporter. Besides paying Paul's salary, she donated $200,620 to the National Woman's Party between February 25, 1921, and April 30, 1926. Other contributions and revenue from membership fees only amounted to $171,385 during that period.[155] Between mid-1923 and mid-1927, she donated $27,500 (worth over $300,000 in today's currency) to the National Woman's Party's tax-exempt Woman's Research Foundation whose purpose was to conduct research on the legal status of American women.[156]

For reasons that are unclear, Belmont stopped giving money to the foundation in 1927. Paul and her colleagues convinced the Carnegie Endowment for International Peace and a small group of donors to support the foundation, but the amount of money they had to work with dwindled dramatically without Belmont's support. The NWP Foundation raised only $6,048 from June 2, 1927 to December 31, 1933. Of that amount, the Carnegie Endowment gave $2000 and Paul gave $1260.[157]

The financial statements for the National Woman's Party's Committee on International Action Fund confirm the importance of Belmont's donations to international work. In 1928–1929 Belmont gave $8500 to the fund and persuaded her son to give another $5000. Their combined gift of $13,500 made up the majority of the income of $13,996 received by the committee that year.[158]

Alva may have been a generous donor, but she periodically expressed concern that her contributions were underappreciated. She had always been determined to get credit for what she had done. But her insistence on having her generosity acknowledged seemed to take on a new urgency in the summer of 1931. When she found out that Carrie Chapman Catt had written to a British feminist congratulating her on her role in bringing about the creation of the new League women's committee, for example, she was irate. The British had little to do with it, she argued. As far as she was concerned, if it had not been for her money and Paul's work, the committee would never have been formed.[159] When she discovered that the Inter-American Commission of Women had acknowledged Carnegie Foundation's donation to them but not hers, she complained to Stevens that no one seemed to appreciate the extent of her support.[160] So in August 1931, she wrote to NWP headquarters asking that her generosity be acknowledged at the next Executive Council meeting. "Few people in any way realize the interest that I have taken in this [international] work and the contributions that I have made toward it," she said, complaining that she seemed to be single-handedly supporting the whole campaign. What had others contributed? she asked.[161] In her reply, the chairwoman of the Executive Council pointed to Alice Paul, Doris Stevens, and Muna Lee, as "the unusual, courageous, and capable individuals who have been able to transmute your lavish gifts into a changed program and outlook for women, not only in the United States, but all over the world."[162]

Alva's sensitivity about money issues meant that when Paul and Stevens arrived at her chateau following the conference in Geneva, the three women spent their first morning together settling their accounts.[163] As the day progressed, the atmosphere became increasingly strained. Belmont insisted that the two women bowl in her new bowling alley while she watched from the sidelines. Neither Paul nor Stevens knew how to bowl, and Paul kept dropping the heavy ball. Belmont, perhaps concerned that Paul's ineptitude might damage her newly finished floor, began, in Stevens's words, "yelling and screaming," which, of course, did nothing to improve Paul's score. When Stevens won the game, Belmont gave her a trinket as a prize.[164]

That evening Alva demanded that Stevens and Paul play cards while she watched. Again, according to Stevens, Belmont began shouting at Paul, demanding that she watch how Stevens played and play the same way, insisting that she "drop her cards when she made a play," and criticizing her for taking so much time. Ignoring what Stevens described as Belmont's "petty criticisms," both she and Paul pleaded with their hostess to join them. But Alva refused, and according to Stevens, seemed "to be in a frenzy of delight at being able to run the game without taking part." The game continued until almost midnight. Not surprisingly, Stevens found Belmont's behavior peculiar and the whole incident extremely embarrassing. It is hard to say how Paul felt about it. Paul, though no doubt exasperated at Belmont's treatment of her, apparently endured her bullying without protest. She did, however, leave the chateau earlier than she had planned.[165]

When Stevens left the chateau in early August, she was aware that Belmont was gravely ill.[166] But she could not have known that Belmont was so angry with her that she had decided to change her will. Shortly after Stevens's departure, Belmont called her lawyer to the house and, before three witnesses, signed a codicil which rescinded the bequest she had intended for Stevens.[167]

During the period that Belmont, Stevens, and Paul worked together to promote international efforts to protect women's citizenship rights, NWP staff members continued their lobbying efforts to force Congress to address that issue at home. Hearings on immigration restriction and the naturalization process, held in 1926, illustrate the kind of resistance they had to overcome. During those meetings, congressmen discussed what it meant to be an American citizen and expressed some hostility toward American heiresses such as Consuelo Vanderbilt who, they claimed, valued their citizenship so little that they willingly sacrificed it in order to marry European aristocrats. "It is a well-known fact," said one congressman, "that no American farmer's daughter, no American laborer's daughter, no small businessman's daughter marries a foreigner. It is only the daughter of the so-called wealthy, the profiteer class, who marries a foreigner—those who coin American citizenship into gold which they use to purchase some Count No Account, some degenerate from over the seas."[168] Another congressman, pointing out that there were plenty of American men available to serve as husbands, expressed his dismay at women who married "foreign dukes and counts," concluding that they deserved the loss of their citizenship.[169]

Members of the Senate were no more sympathetic. Senator Frank Willis of Ohio impugned the motives of American women who willingly married foreigners and then complained about their loss of citizenship. It was, he implied, not a matter of equal rights but rather a matter of wanting your cake and eating it too. He suggested that their high regard for their American citizenship stemmed from the fact that they wanted to assure themselves the protection of the American government while they, as he put it, went "wandering about." Guaranteeing such protection, he believed, put an unnecessary burden on the resources of the U.S. government.[170]

By 1930, American women had demonstrated their willingness to participate in both domestic and international politics. The NWP had spent almost ten years lobbying for the passage of laws and treaties guaranteeing equal nationality rights for women. And in the midst of the Great Depression, concern about the American economy replaced concern about immigration issues. That being the case, Congress passed a law in July of that year which allowed American women to keep their citizenship when they married foreigners and those women who had lost it under previous legislation to recover it in most cases. Alva called reporters to her Paris house to express her satisfaction.[171]

But she did not live long enough to enjoy the final resolution of the equal nationality rights campaign, a crusade that she helped initiate, direct, and finance. Even as she became more and more incapacitated, she remained committed to the cause and her willingness to donate funds to support international work never wavered. NWP financial records show that between September 1930 and her death, Belmont gave $14,780 out of the $22,846 raised to finance international work, far more than any other single donor.[172] After she died in 1933, the NWP's fund-raising efforts continued. But with the world in the midst of a depression and political instability threatening the peace of Europe, there was no one willing to commit the kind of money that Belmont had given to continue a woman's equal rights campaign.[173]

By the time she died, however, sufficient groundwork had been laid for the ultimate success of the international campaign. The delegates to the December 1933 Pan-American Conference in Montevideo, including those from the United States, signed a nationality treaty guaranteeing women equal nationality rights before they adjourned.[174] It was a great personal victory for Stevens. After the vote had been counted, delegates to the conference gave her a standing ovation in the lobby of Uruguay's legislative palace. Secretary of State Cordell Hull paid tribute to her lobbying ability by playfully warning her that if he was "ever in trouble" he intended to ask her to get him out of it.[175]

On May 24, 1934, President Franklin Delano Roosevelt signed the Equal Nationality Act which confirmed the principle that marriage had no effect whatsoever on the nationality of either American men or American women and the Senate ratified the Montevideo Conference's Equal Nationality Treaty.[176]

Consuelo was little more than a passive participant in the struggle to ensure married women's nationality rights. She claimed to have regretted the loss of her American citizenship, describing it as "a citizenship I would never have resigned had the law of my day permitted me to retain it."[177] But she did not protest its loss at the time of her marriage and did not suffer much inconvenience because she was no longer an American citizen. While she did publish an article supporting international efforts to guarantee women's nationality rights, she remained in France and did not actively lobby either in the United States or at international conferences for the cause.[178]

# 6 The Last Word

AS SHE APPROACHED the age of eighty, Alva continued to be concerned about her image and legacy. Neither of her previous efforts at dictating a memoir seems to have satisfied her. So sometime between 1928 and 1932, she repeated the process once more by sharing her life story with her then secretary and companion Mary Young.[1] Fiercely determined to be remembered, Alva through Young was free to make herself yet one more time. This would be her final attempt to reflect in any systematic way on her life and its meaning.

We know almost nothing about Young or the nature of her relationship with her employer.[2] She was apparently efficient, attentive, and compliant enough to bear the brunt of Alva's volatility with some degree of equanimity for the five years of their association. The 173-page manuscript that Young produced describes Alva's life up until the death of her second husband. There is no evidence that Young took the same kinds of liberties in writing the text that Sara Bard Field clearly did. Young seems to have accepted Alva on her own terms. For her, Alva was who she appeared to be and the meaning of her life was what she said it was.

The narrative that emerged from Alva's conversations with Young is in some ways very similar to the one that she dictated to Field in 1917. In it, we find a description of Belmont's pedigree, childhood, and early interest in architecture. Alva again described herself as a willful and insubordinate child. She remained convinced that she had had a profound influence on the development of American architecture and interior design. She reiterated her belief that she had been a good mother. "I have always considered that motherhood involved a great responsibility as well as a great happiness," she told Young. She took pride in the way she had educated her three children and the opportunities for self-expression that she had provided them.[3]

Alva's anger over her husband's infidelity was in no way diminished by the passage of time. She still believed that she deserved recognition for having made herself a pioneer in efforts to provide women with what she considered to be an appropriate response to their husbands' illicit affairs. She was convinced that she was central to efforts to free her contemporaries from what she called the terror of "the bogy of social ostracism" for having demanded a divorce.[4] "It was more than a personal matter to me," she told Young. "It was a question of social justice not only to myself but other women situated as I was."[5]

Indeed, male privilege appears to be the only social issue that concerned her as she reflected on her life before her entry into the woman's rights movement. She, her friends, and her daughter had all been subjected to what she considered to be disgraceful behavior on the part of their husbands. A proud woman, she continued to feel the pain of the humiliation she suffered because of her first husband's adultery. She believed that she had been the victim of a system that gave men the power to denigrate women: "For years I had witnessed the putting aside of wives of wealthy and prominent men. . . . Not by divorce. They did not want or need divorces. . . . They left their wives to maintain the dignity of their position in the world, such as it was, and to take care of their children while they amused themselves elsewhere." Her memories of women in her social circle who were "practically deserted by their husbands who not only neglected them but insulted them by their open and flagrant and vulgar infidelities" were still vivid. "It was a time when men of wealth seemed to think they could do anything they liked; have anything, or any woman, they, for the moment wanted," she said. Men with immense fortunes and secure social positions were notorious for their philandering, she told Young. She remembered that they were particularly inclined to flaunt their illicit behavior in Monte Carlo. There, she remembered, they appeared on the casino floor, not with their wives but with their mistresses, upon whom they "lavished" expensive clothes and sparkling jewelry.[6]

There, however, the similarities between the Field manuscript and the one produced by Young end. On the whole, the memoir that Alva dictated to Young is a detailed, somewhat gossipy description of Alva's life as a wealthy socialite. Under Alva's direction, Young dedicated page after page to discussions of Alva's philanthropic activities, trips taken on her first husband's yacht, and lavish parties organized for her very narrow circle of friends.

As was typical for members of the upper class, noblesse oblige motivated Alva's pre-feminist philanthropy. And like others in her set, she gave to causes in which she had a personal interest and from which she could derive substantial personal benefit.[7] When she lived at Idlehour, her home on Long Island, for example, she attended an Episcopalian church in nearby Islip. She remembered her shock at the willingness of her rich neighbors to worship in what she considered to be a "dilapidated," shed-like structure. To make things worse, they seemed perfectly oblivious to the discomfort of the minister and his family, who lived in a drafty shanty of a house. So she built a new church with the help of architect Richard Morris Hunt and hired Lewis Tiffany to construct the stained glass windows. Once she had an aesthetically pleasing place to worship, she convinced her fellow parishioners to raise their minister's salary and build him a new rectory.[8]

What is so striking about the manuscript produced by Young in comparison to that written by Field is the absence of introspection or any sense of feminist consciousness, any sustained discussion of gender discrimination beyond that of complaining about male prerogatives, or any real awareness of the world outside that inhabited by New York's smart set. It portrays a self-absorbed woman whose most serious concerns were to enjoy herself and get what she wanted. What Young described in her text was what Field called "the grinning spectacle of unlovely living, selfish ease in the presence of want."[9]

To be fair, the period Alva was describing in the manuscript was characterized by the process of growing up, getting married, social climbing, rearing children, and establishing her social celebrity rather than by efforts to change the social and political landscape of the United States. She had yet to have her feminist epiphany. Until the death of her second husband in 1908, she was more or less oblivious to the larger feminist social, economic, and political issues that eventually became important to her. Nevertheless, had Field read Young's manuscript, her worst prejudices regarding the upper class in general and Alva in particular would have been confirmed once more.

Alva would not have understood Field's disdain. What Field thought of as self-indulgent frivolity, Alva considered serious business. She was proud of her accomplishments as a socialite. "Women of position" who "spent their time and energy in winning and holding social leadership" might seem like "butterflies" to outsiders, she once told a *New York Times* reporter. "But it requires infinitely more brains to shine and soar than to drudge like an ant. I know of no profession, art, or trade, that women are working in to-day as taxing in mental resources as being a leader in society, where you have all sorts of complex personalities to manipulate, where you occupy a position so that a mistake unnoticed in a lesser light would be fatal to you, and where opposition is as constant as it is subtle and difficult to locate."[10] One needed to be competitive, clever, and hardworking as well as very rich to work one's way into the highest echelons of New York society. And remaining there was a continuous challenge to one's financial resources and diplomatic skills, not to mention administrative ability. Every social event or fund-raiser had to be more imaginative, extravagant, and memorable than the last. Guest lists had to be carefully scrutinized. Every detail of a public event had to be carefully overseen. Social celebrity may have been satisfying, but it also had its downside. Everything one did was always on display. Every error of judgment was likely to be noticed and commented upon. Every misstep had the potential for undermining one's position. It was testimony to Alva's social skills as well as her wealth and her connection to a titled aristocrat in England that she was able to preserve her social position despite her divorce of William Kissam Vanderbilt, her marriage to Oliver Belmont, and her adoption of suffrage as her life's work, all of which alienated her from those whom she had previously called friends.

It is not clear whether Alva intended the manuscript that she dictated to Young to include a discussion of her eventual career as a woman's rights advocate. But once she had her first stroke on May 12, 1932, there was little likelihood this last version of her life would ever be revised or expanded upon to include more substantive issues.[11] She eventually recovered her ability to speak but had little energy for work. And she was more or less cut off from the rest of the world and the feminist activists that had been so much a part of her later life.[12]

Young's sister Matilda, who came to France to visit her sister, wrote to their mother describing Alva's condition three months after her stroke: "Poor thing, she really is so valiant. I took hold of her paralyzed hand, which has feeling in it now and really looks as well as the other. It had quite a grasp in it, but when I started to go, it was difficult to free my hand. She said: 'Now that's a funny hand. It can take hold of things but it won't let go.'—which brought tears to my eyes."[13]

Alva's children visited periodically. The most attentive appears to have been her youngest son, Harold. He proposed teaching his mother dominos because the game could be played with one hand, and he ordered a projector to be sent to the chateau so she could watch movies. Edmund Gros, one of Alva's attending physicians, was impressed that Harold had gone to the trouble of learning something about strokes and paralysis, which gave him the impression that Harold was more interested in his mother's physical and mental health than were her other children.[14]

Alva spent most of her time recuperating in her room at the chateau. Mary visited her in the morning before tending to the mail and conferring with the chef and then again at lunchtime and in the late afternoon. Four nurses attended her around the clock. There was a doctor on call at all times.[15] Despite her illness, she continued to try to run the household and control the lives of those who lived in it. One afternoon after Harold arrived, for example, he asked Dr. Gros to dine with him. So Alva ordered the kitchen staff to prepare an elaborate meal accompanied by wine and champagne served in huge, oversized glasses and sent two valets to the formal dining room to serve dinner and drinks. Gros enjoyed both the dinner and Harold's company. After dinner, the two of them entertained themselves by wheeling each other around the chateau in Alva's wheelchair.

Gros returned Harold's hospitality by inviting Harold to eat dinner with him, his wife, and the Youngs. Harold, no doubt grateful for the invitation and the company, was a charming guest, and everyone apparently had a good time. What to do about Harold thereafter, however, remained a problem, according to Matilda. She found it "amusing" that the most important topic of conversation during the next few days was whether the staff should ask the "poor little rich boy" to dine again, as she put it, or whether he should be left to dine all alone at the chateau.[16]

Despite her condition, Alva did get out of the house occasionally. When the weather was nice, someone on her staff took her for a stroll in a wheelchair down to the bowling alley or along the paths near the chateau. Occasionally, they wheeled her to a school located on the estate where she watched while the doctor taught the students the principles of personal hygiene and passed out toothbrushes and toothpaste.[17]

Disability did not diminish her determination to control her physical environment or order people around. Matilda wrote to her mother that Alva was "hell bent" on rejecting her doctor's orders that she be attended by four nurses. So when she could not convince Dr. Gros to release two of them, she bullied one of her other doctors into dismissing them.[18] Her friend Elsa Maxwell remembered that after Alva suffered her stroke, she became distraught at the idea that the gray in her hair was beginning to show. Always vain about her appearance, she demanded that her nurses bring a hairdresser to her room so she could have it dyed "titian red." She did not intend to go to her death with "white hair," she said. She found the idea "depressing."[19]

A second stroke on November 3 left her paralyzed and mute.[20] She died in Paris on January 26, 1933, a few days after her eightieth birthday.[21]

As obsessed with self-making in old age as she had been earlier, Alva was equally determined to stage-manage how she was remembered in death. From the beginning of her campaign to make herself a household name, she seems to have intuitively understood that maintaining one's social celebrity required image control and a constant infusion of theatricality. Toward that end, she left very specific instructions about how her funeral was to be conducted.[22] It was her wish that she be surrounded in death, as she had during the latter part of her life, by feminist activists and the symbols of women's struggle for equal rights.[23]

After a funeral at the American Cathedral Church of the Holy Trinity in Paris, her children brought her body to New York.[24] The spectacle that ensued stood as testimony to Alva's sense of self-importance and the celebrity status that she had spent her lifetime nurturing. After the ship that had carried her home docked at Pier 54 in New York's harbor, eight sailors carried her coffin down the gangway. As newspaper reporters and an honor guard from the NWP looked on, they placed it in a hearse which took her to the Chapel of the Resurrection in St. Thomas Episcopal Church on Fifth Avenue where she was to lie in state until her funeral. In the chapel, leaders of the NWP, holding the purple, gold, and white banners of their party, stood as sentinels guarding the casket.[25]

At her funeral, twenty honorary pallbearers including such feminist notables as Alice Paul, Doris Stevens, Christabel Pankhurst, Millicent Wilson Hearst, Harriot Stanton Blatch, Margaret Sanger, and Jane Norman Smith preceded her casket as it was moved into the crowded sanctuary and placed before the altar. As 1500 mourners looked on, representatives of the NWP processed down the main aisle carrying an American flag, the banner of the NWP, and a purple banner that had been held by White House picketers emblazoned with the words "Failure is Impossible" inscribed in gold. At the same time, feminist activists took up their vigil along the side aisles where they stood at attention throughout the service, bearing purple, gold, and white banners. During the funeral, the choir sang an anthem written for the English suffragettes as well as a hymn written by Alva and put to music by St. Thomas's organist and choir director. When the service was over, three buses transported representatives of various women's organizations to Woodlawn Cemetery, where they trudged through the snow to escort her body from the hearse into the chapel where she was to be buried. Alice Paul entered the vault with the members of Alva's family and laid a purple, white, and gold banner on the casket. The playing of taps was the final tribute to her memory.[26]

Once she was gone, Alva had to depend upon journalists to write her obituary. She had every reason to believe that they would write nothing that would contradict the image she had worked so hard to establish for herself and that they would describe her rise to social prominence and portray her as a social activist who was willing to sacrifice herself, her reputation, and her fortune to promote the cause of woman's equality. And so they did. But in the process they contributed to her reputation by adding a bit of urban legend to her story. According to the *Chicago Tribune* and the *New York Times,* Alva forced the Astors into publicly accepting the Vanderbilts into their inner circle during the early years of her marriage by masterfully manipulating social protocol. She sent out over a thousand invitations to her famous ball in 1883, they reported, but did not send one to Caroline Schermerhorn Astor, the widely acknowledged leader of

New York society. When inquiries were made on Mrs. Astor's behalf, Alva explained that since Mrs. Astor had not deigned to call upon her, she was not in a position to presume that she was interested in attending. Mrs. Astor paid her call, thus recognizing the Vanderbilts as members of the social elite, and promptly received her invitation.[27] The story may or may not have been true. It was the sort of thing Alva would have been proud of, but she never mentioned it in her memoirs. The fact that the story was published long after the event took place testifies to the strength of her reputation for outsmarting those who tried to prevent her from getting what she wanted.

In her two wills (one French and one American), filed with the Surrogate's Court of New York, she named her two sons as her executors and left most of her property to her daughter. The NWP received $100,000 out of an estate appraised at $1,326,765, most of it invested in securities. A codicil filed with the will revoked a $50,000 bequest originally made to Doris Stevens.[28]

Although Alva was reputed to have been a very rich woman, the total amount of her estate was little more than the amount she had inherited from her second husband. She had not hesitated to spend money to guarantee herself a life of luxurious comfort and was generous in her support of the activities of the NWP. The stock market crash in 1929 no doubt took its toll on her investments. The $100,000 that she left to the NWP represented almost ten percent of her net worth, but it was a paltry sum compared to the legacies left to worthy causes by other philanthropic women in the twentieth century. Olivia Sage, the wife of Russell Sage, who died in 1918, for example, left an estate of about $49 million and bequeathed a great deal of it to female-centered institutions including Troy Female Seminary, Barnard, Bryn Mawr, Vassar, and Smith as well as the Women's Hospital in the state of New York.[29] Katharine Dexter McCormick, who died some years later, left an estate of $35 million. Among her bequests were $5 million to the Planned Parenthood Federation and another $5 million to Stanford University to fund scholarships for women who wanted to become doctors.[30]

On July 8, 1933, six months after Alva's funeral, the NWP held a nationally broadcast memorial service in Washington, D.C., at the National Amphitheater near the Washington Monument intended to pay tribute to Alva as well as Elizabeth Cady Stanton, Lucy Stone,

Susan B. Anthony, and Julia Ward Howe, all of whom had played an important role in efforts to advance the cause of women.[31] The cost for this extravaganza, held during one of the worst years of the Great Depression, exceeded $4500. To help pay for it, Alva's son Harold advanced the NWP $3000.[32]

In front of a cheering crowd standing amidst banners demanding equal rights for women, Doris Stevens delivered Alva's eulogy. She was a "gallant leader and beloved comrade," Stevens told her audience. Describing Alva as a vital, willful, and impatient woman, she pointed out that Alva's "sometimes ruthless leadership" was characterized by "a relentless determination to see her plans carried out" that was less than endearing to others. The result, she noted, was that "hers was a lonely road which more compassion, more loving approval would have made less lonely." Nevertheless, Stevens described Alva as a woman who dreamt "of a world in which men and women [could] live and work together in loving harmony . . . a world in which the capacities of women [would] not [be] handicapped by any man-made restrictions."[33]

When she gave that eulogy, Stevens not only knew that Alva had reneged on her promise to provide for her but had also suffered the humiliation of having that fact mentioned in the *New York Times*.[34] She may have been generous in her words of praise for Alva, but she was also angry and hurt. Believing that she had earned the money Alva had promised her, she hired Frank P. Walsh, a lawyer who had been an active supporter of the NWP through the years, to begin the process of contesting Alva's will. A few days after the terms of the will were made public, George Battle, the attorney whose job it was to settle Alva's affairs, sent Stevens a letter. Acknowledging that she had a right to contest the will, he asked her to sign a waiver if she had no intention of doing so. Stevens met with Battle in early March 1933, but they came to no resolution of the matter.[35]

That summer, Stevens began collecting evidence testifying to the personal services that she had performed for Belmont. Lawyers in charge of the case called Mary Young, Elsa Maxwell, and Marcelle Alice Gay, all of whom had witnessed the codicil that Belmont had added to her will removing Stevens as a beneficiary, to testify. Dudley Field Malone, Anna Kelton Wiley, chairman of the National Council of the NWP, and Emma Wold, its treasurer, appeared as well.[36]

Under Walsh's supervision, Stevens spent weeks preparing to give her deposition. Going through her records, she meticulously outlined on dozens of 5×7-inch note cards the services she had performed between 1914 and 1931 for a woman she claimed to have considered a surrogate mother.[37] It was an exercise designed to help her remember not only what she had done for Alva but also how she felt about it. And it also offered her the opportunity to practice giving her testimony. From those cards she prepared a "General Statement" summarizing the basis of her claim.[38]

Then she wrote a confidential memorandum for her lawyer which, as she put it, "refers to incidents which happened during the year 1931 which may be related to Mrs. Belmont's revocation of the legacy." She hoped it would be useful to Walsh as he questioned her at the deposition. It may also have provided her with a way of coming to some understanding of why she had been written out of Belmont's will.[39]

Beginning with a misunderstanding over the tax deductibility of Alva's contributions to the NWP and the Inter-American Commission of Women, the memorandum described various examples of miscommunication between Stevens and Belmont. It also dwelt on Paul's puzzling lack of collegiality toward Stevens during the time they spent together in Geneva and, after their arrival at Alva's chateau, Paul's bewildering efforts to manipulate what Belmont was and was not told about the work that they had done under her direction. Stevens maintained that, at the time, she dismissed the incidents she was describing as unrelated and only began to understand their significance when she was shown a letter from Belmont, written after her visit to the chateau, complaining about her. She claims to have immediately asked Paul's help in clearing up whatever misunderstandings existed between herself and Belmont. But, she said, Paul rebuffed her, commenting that she should have known better than to have asked for orange juice for breakfast and that Belmont had come to believe that she had spent a good deal of her time in Europe socializing with men instead of tending to her duties. In the document, Stevens denied that she had ever betrayed Belmont's trust, insisted that she had always been willing to sacrifice herself and her own interests to help Belmont pursue her feminist goals, and argued that there was no justification for her having been disinherited.

Meanwhile, friends wrote to express their dismay that Stevens had been denied her legacy. "Your services to Mrs. Belmont were legion," one wrote; "I remember I could not see how you could bear being at her beck and call at all hours of the day and night."[40] And Max Eastman wrote, "Entirely apart your work for the Woman's Party, you were functioning almost continually throughout those years as an unofficial personal and political secretary for Mrs. Belmont. . . . She spoke of you, and regarded you, and used you as an *alter ego* in an infinite number of literary, intellectual, and social matters."[41]

Thus confirmed in her conviction that she deserved what she had been promised and armed with the documentation necessary to substantiate her claim, she walked through the doors of the Wall Street law firm of Battle, Levy, Van Tine, & Fowler in New York City on the morning of August 23, 1933. At 10:30 AM, Battle and Walsh began taking a deposition intended to serve as the basis for Stevens's claim against the Belmont estate for personal services rendered to Belmont from 1914 to 1931 as an unpaid private secretary and companion. She considered the $50,000 that had originally been intended for her to be inadequate. She wanted $75,000 in compensation.[42]

The story that Stevens told was certainly self-interested and says as much about her as it does about Alva. At the same time, however, it provides an alternative frame of reference for understanding who Alva was and how she went about constructing her public persona. In giving her testimony, Stevens challenged the image that Alva had so carefully constructed of herself as outgoing, self-assured, and in control. Because it suited her purposes, Stevens depicted Alva as a shy, emotionally needy, socially insecure woman who was excessively dependent upon others to make her into the strong feminist leader she appeared to be.

Besides keeping Alva company, Stevens claimed to have played a role in establishing Alva's reputation as a suffragist by serving as her publicist. "One of the first things I had to do when I took charge of that office [in New York City] was to publicize her in a way that she had not been publicized before," she said. Doing so was difficult, she continued. "I found that the New York press, in spite of the work she had done up to this time, was still hostile. They still regarded her as a rich woman who had a hobby, and those antagonisms within the old suffrage group had left their mark," she noted. She found that Alva had not yet been able to convince New York's journalists that she was seriously committed to working to improve the lives of other women. "Being a trained [field-]worker and knowing what she [Alva] wanted, I set about to change that tone," she said.[43] Toward that end, Stevens wrote Alva's speeches, letters, and articles, arranged for press conferences and photography sessions, and made appointments for meetings with prominent people who Alva thought might be useful in the woman's rights campaign.[44] It was her job, she believed, to create an image for Belmont that portrayed her as a "farsighted, determined, powerful leader of women."[45]

It also fell to Stevens to act as Belmont's social secretary. Belmont may have been a socialite but that did not necessarily mean that she felt comfortable meeting strangers. Since her children did not live close by and she had few friends who shared her interest in woman's rights, Stevens believed her to be extremely lonely. Indeed, Stevens discovered that Alva was suspicious of people she did not know, a condition that manifested itself in ambivalence about planning and executing social events.[46] Thus, it fell to Stevens to act as an intermediary between Alva and those whose attention, friendship, and affection she craved. "Mrs. Belmont was very timid about crowds and ten people seemed to her like a mob," she said. "She wanted crowds and was deeply disappointed if they were not assembled, but she had to have someone with her to act as buffer. She was afraid that people would be unkind to her. She wanted to be sure people appreciated her and I would say this person is all right and that one is all right."[47] For example, prior to Alva's arrival at the Panama-Pacific Exposition in 1915, Stevens claimed to have prepared her way by "making friends with the officials of the Exposition so they would treat her with all the courtesy and respect due her when she came."[48] She took responsibility for making sure that the only people Alva associated with were those with whom she felt comfortable and those whom she might exploit in some way. For example, Alva demanded that Stevens prepare guest lists for dinner and theater parties including invitations to "men of political and social importance" who she believed could be persuaded to be of use to the suffrage movement.[49] Stevens's job was to identify such individuals and make sure that they were included in Alva's social circle.

It was also common for Belmont to demand that Stevens accompany her to dinner parties. Stevens testified that Alva "was often afraid to go alone with her chauffeur at the wheel, to a friend's house, for example, for dinner. She would ask permission to bring me along. She was afraid, she said, she might be robbed of her jewels."[50] Stevens admitted that she had no idea "what good [she] could have done if [Alva] had been attacked," but she did as she was asked.[51] Accompanying Alva to dinner parties and other social gatherings apparently became routine. Like Field, she felt excruciatingly awkward attending social events with Alva. She claims to have struggled, unsuccessfully for the most part, to find strategies that would spare her the embarrassment of accompanying Belmont to social events to which she had not been invited given by people she did not know, did not like, and with whom she had little in common.[52]

According to Stevens, Alva's need for attention and sympathy was endless. She remembered having spent a great deal of time listening to Alva's personal problems, many of which focused on "difficulties about lack of filial love and what to do about the whole family problem and whether children really loved their parents." Stevens claims to have tried to reassure Belmont that just because her children had lives of their own and were preoccupied with their own concerns did not mean that they had ceased to love her or to be concerned about her welfare. In retrospect, Stevens concluded that Alva was a lonely and "wretchedly unhappy" woman who had what she described as an "almost tragic desire to be approved of."[53]

Stevens's Belmont also needed constant confirmation of her associates' loyalty and affection. When she was with Stevens, Alva demanded Stevens's undivided attention and affection. She was jealous of anyone who she thought might take her place in Stevens's life. Early in their relationship, Alva had done what she could to prevent Stevens from spending too much time with Dudley Malone. Alva responded in much the same way to the budding friendship between Stevens and Margaret Haig Thomas Mackworth, Lady Rhondda, a militant British suffragette and equal rights feminist. Stevens met Lady Rhondda in Paris in 1926 when the NWP was petitioning for membership in the International Woman's Suffrage Alliance. Rhondda was an impressive figure, a young, attractive businesswoman who sat on the boards of thirty-three companies. She also financed and edited *Time and*

*Tide,* a forum for the discussion of feminist issues, and was founding director of Britain's Six Point Group, a nonpartisan pressure group dedicated to social reform and equal rights.[54] In her deposition, Stevens described Rhondda as "a very glamorous and important figure in England" and claimed to have convinced Rhondda to support the NWP's petition for membership in the international suffrage organization and to have introduced her to Belmont in the hope that they might work together on the international equal rights campaign.[55]

As a matter of fact, Rhondda and Belmont had a great deal in common. Both used their inherited wealth to advance the cause of women, divorced their husbands, recognized the benefits to be derived from using militant tactics when all other strategies failed, exploited journalism to promote discussion of women's issues, were deeply committed to international feminism, and looked to other women for emotional support and intellectual stimulation. But it was Stevens, acting as Alva's lieutenant, who was able to develop both a personal and working relationship with the English feminist. Once they got to know each other, Rhondda and Stevens became friends, and Rhondda invited Stevens to spend time at her home and to travel with her.

According to Stevens, when it became apparent that her relationship with Rhondda was becoming something more than a professional one, Alva became quite critical of the English activist, denigrating her social status and her work in the international equal rights campaign. When Rhondda invited Stevens to go skiing over the Christmas holidays in 1927, Alva was upset. Alva had made her own holiday plans and had not invited Stevens to accompany her, Stevens told the lawyers. So she concluded that Alva was jealous and simply did not want her to spend so much time with Rhondda.[56]

In the end, according to Stevens, all of the fuss over Rhondda was about Alva's determination to discourage anyone from challenging her leadership of the international movement. She wanted the support of British feminists for her program, but she wanted to be in charge of the program and was suspicious of anyone who might be in a position to challenge her power.[57]

That sort of suspicion was not confined to feminists from abroad. According to Stevens, while Alva had a great deal of respect for Alice Paul, their relationship was fraught with tension because Belmont saw Paul as a competitor. Stevens recalled that after Paul began receiving a salary from Belmont in 1921, Paul increased her contributions to the NWP. Under normal circumstances, Paul's generosity would have posed no problem. But, according to Stevens, Alva saw Paul's donations not as evidence of her commitment to the advancement of women but as a way to augment and consolidate the power she already had in the organization. Alva found the situation both infuriating and frustrating since there was nothing she could do to prevent Paul from donating money to the NWP.[58]

By describing Alva as a self-absorbed, unhappy woman riddled with anxieties, insecurities, loneliness, and jealousy, Stevens deconstructed the image Alva so carefully created for herself and made her into the sort of person that Alva struggled unsuccessfully to hide from those around her. As Stevens would have it, Alva's forcefulness was a veil for her timidity. And her need to be the center of attention served to mask a serious lack of self-confidence. Her possessiveness, characterized by jealous outbursts of emotion and the tendency to exploit others, was an effort to compensate for her feelings of aloneness. And, as Stevens pointed out, her reform efforts served her needs as much as they served the needs of those around her.[59]

Stevens's description of Alva may have been insightful, but it had little influence on the public persona that Alva spent years so carefully shaping. After the deposition was taken, the Vanderbilt children settled Stevens's claim out of court, thus ensuring that the press would not get wind of the controversy or any documents associated with it.[60]

Alva Vanderbilt Belmont was an unlikely feminist. Yet as she looked back to the period of her childhood, she was able to identify an early sensitivity to women's subordination made particularly acute by her father's perceived indifference to her and expressed by her resentment of social conventions that denied girls the prerogatives enjoyed by boys. Her marriage to William Kissam Vanderbilt and the sexual double standard that encouraged him to be unfaithful only exacerbated her anger at the way women were treated in a society that privileged the interests of men. Suffrage provided Alva with a frame of reference that could help her understand and articulate her latent feminism and act upon the anger she had been harboring for years. At loose ends after the death of Oliver, she was bored with her life as a leader of New York society and tired of associating with rich women for whom she had considerable contempt. She needed to meet new people and find something to occupy her time. The English suffragettes' militancy, observed during her trip to Europe in 1909, inspired her to return home and dedicate her time and money to advancing the cause of woman's rights. Frustrated by the internal dissension that plagued the NAWSA, by their unwillingness to adopt the militant tactics she found so appealing, and by their hesitancy to give her a leadership position in the organization, she accepted an invitation from Alice Paul and the other leaders of the CU to join their advisory board in return for her financial support. From that position, she did what she could to create and finance an organization that would promote woman suffrage. And when her efforts were rewarded in 1921 by being elected to the presidency of the NWP, she took the opportunity to focus her energy and resources on efforts to guarantee gender equity for women both at home and abroad.

Alva's social celebrity provided American feminists with the mechanism they needed to gain access to the popular press. When her name was associated with their activities, they were certain to attract attention. When she wanted to talk to reporters, she sent for them, and they came. And when she wanted to say something in print, she sent an article or a letter to the editor, certain that it would be taken seriously. She was savvy and successful when it came to fund-raising and rich enough to provide funds to her feminist co-workers when they needed them. She was able to successfully work with Paul because they supported the same principles when it came to implementing strategies such as organizing public demonstrations and bullying politicians into supporting the idea of woman suffrage. The result was that with a promise of financial support, she was able to strong-arm Paul and her associates into engaging in a two-front battle for equal rights after women won the vote. Her efforts and financial resources were crucial to the success of the early twentieth-century woman's rights movement.

Alva was a woman with many shortcomings. Strong-willed, domineering, opinionated, and determined to be the center of attention, she was clearly difficult to work with. But suffrage and equal rights advocates worked out ways to exploit her enthusiasm, administrative expertise, and financial resources. The tensions that characterized her relationships with others in the woman's movement often had a positive outcome. Like the leaders of the NAWSA before her,

Paul turned Belmont into a special projects manager. When Belmont had one of her temper tantrums, as was the case after the feminist demonstration at Rambouillet, the NWP's executive council and its chair offered sincere if somewhat obsequious apologies to smooth her ruffled feathers and assure her that they appreciated her efforts on their behalf, thus guaranteeing her continuing support. With Paul's blessing, Stevens served as Alva's unpaid secretary and companion, attempting to coordinate the NWP's activities with those of Belmont and doing the legwork that was required to promote suffrage before 1920 and international gender equity after ratification of the Nineteenth Amendment. Backed by Belmont's money, she was able to negotiate the passage of an international equal nationality treaty.

Alva was no intellectual, but she was most certainly a visionary. She believed that ordinary philanthropy and support of humanitarian causes were futile misdirections of time and energy. From her point of view, what society needed was a complete overhaul. Toward that end, she envisioned a world where men and women could work together to promote gender equity and where women would take their rightful place as power brokers in the political life of the nation and the world. She looked forward to the day when women's issues would receive the attention they deserved. And she fantasized about the benefits to be derived both from turning the NWP into a regular political party whose sponsorship would make it possible for women to run successfully for public office and from creating a World Parliament of Women to represent their interests.[61] She was convinced that women could control the world through public opinion if not through laws. And she insisted that Americans take an interest in the welfare of women throughout the world.[62] Her sort of feminism could not be bound by narrow nationalisms and artificial geographical boundaries. She was, according to her friend Elsa Maxwell, at least "twenty years ahead of her generation."[63]

As it turned out, she was more than twenty years ahead of her time. The sort of sea change that marked the privileging of women's issues in American politics did not come until the 1960s. After President John F. Kenney's Commission on the Status of Women issued its report in 1963, Congress began to pass legislation intended to address issues of gender inequality outlined therein. Betty Friedan helped to organize the National Organization for Women in 1966. In

1968, feminists in Cleveland established the Women's Equity Action League, an association dedicated to improving the status of women through education, legislation, and litigation.[64]

Women all over the country participated in what was called a "Women's Strike for Equality" at the end of August in 1970. On August 26, the fiftieth anniversary of the passage of the Nineteenth Amendment, they took to the streets carrying posters that read "I Am Not a Barbie Doll," "Male Chauvinists Better Start Shakin—Today's Pig Is Tomorrow's Bacon," and "Don't Iron while the Strike Is Hot." One demonstrator wore pots on her back. Another chained herself to a typewriter. The mayors of New York, Pittsburgh, and Syracuse as well as the governor of New York declared the day Woman's Rights Day. President Richard Nixon issued a statement demanding "a wider role for women in political, economic, and social life."[65]

In 1971, feminist activists founded the National Women's Political Caucus, a national bipartisan organization dedicated to increasing women's participation in politics and getting more women elected to political office.[66] Four years later the United Nations declared 1975 as International Women's Year. Congress appropriated the money to hold a National Women's Conference in Houston in 1977. There, a cross section of women from all over the country debated and passed a public policy agenda intended to address every sort of feminist issue from child care and reproductive freedom to violence against women and anti-discrimination legislation.[67] More recently, the *New York Times* identified the effort to end the subjugation of women throughout the world as "the cause of our time."[68]

Had she lived, Alva would have been in her element. And she would, no doubt, have written checks to cover expenses and taken credit for it all.

# Postscript: My Turn

FOLLOWING THE EXAMPLE of those who have come before me, I have written this biography in an effort to make something of Alva Smith Vanderbilt Belmont. In the process, I have been very much aware that I am in some ways saying as much about myself as I am about her. For in writing about Alva, I, like all historians whether they want to admit it or not, write from a personal perspective. Or to revert back to the metaphor I used in the introduction, I have turned the kaleidoscope one more time and the Alva Belmont that appears this time is both similar to and different from the one who appeared before. It is the twist of my hand at a particular moment in time that has made her this way.

My goal as a historian is to be objective, always knowing that doing so is not really possible. So instead of ignoring the problem, I have embraced it. And in doing so, I have found myself engaged in both an autobiographical and a biographical exercise. I have interpreted her life through my own personal lens. So in my narrative, the line between autobiography and biography is obscured just as it was in the other texts that I have discussed. And I assert my authority as the teller of Belmont's story in contestation with those who have come before me. I have built upon what they have written, and in doing so, I have engaged in a negotiation process with them, a process in which our reconstructions of the past compete with each other for validity. We all want to claim that we are telling the "truth."

Writing about Alva has been a tricky enterprise. I am not just the inhabitant of the academic world dedicated to the discovery and production of new knowledge. By virtue of my marriage, I also occupy a place in the world of nonprofit fund-raising. Generally speaking, I have great regard for those whose wealth allows them to engage in philanthropic, humanitarian enterprises. But I have also known those who, like Belmont, cared as much about the power and recognition they received from their gestures of generosity as they did about the good their money was likely to do. And through the years, I have watched as Fortune 500 companies and their CEOs have turned philanthropy and civic responsibility into an expensive form of advertising. The result is that I am sensitive to and sometimes suspicious of the motivations that induce philanthropists to give away their money and have a particularly high regard for those who anonymously give large gifts to deserving causes. In my experience, it does not happen very often. But memories of those occasions have made a powerful impression on me and, therefore, color my approach to charitable giving and those who engage in it.

Like Alva, I came to feminism later than some. A product of the 1940s and 1950s, I experienced discrimination because I was female. I remember applying to be a congressional page without realizing that the only people accepted into the program were boys. I remember my disgust at being forced to play half-court basketball in gym class because, as our teacher explained it, girls could not stand the physical stress inherent in playing by boys' rules. Apparently, she thought that all our strength would be consumed by bouncing the ball three times in succession and then passing it off to one of our teammates. And I remember my outrage when my first graduate school professor looked around the room during the first day of class and remarked in passing: "A woman's mind, if there is such a thing." Like Alva, I was angry when I came face-to-face with evidence of what we now call sexism, but there was no way to direct my anger because, at the time, I did not have a frame of reference for understanding that I was being treated unfairly not because I was inadequate but rather because I had a particular set of physical characteristics. Busy being a teacher and then wife, mother, and graduate student, I had little time before my thirties to pay much attention to gender discrimination let alone search for an explanation for it. But when I found that explanation, it made perfect sense to me. So I found Alva's search for the origins of her feminism credible and could identify with her desire to give her repressed anger expression in some sort of positive way. Like Alva, I took enormous pleasure in the sisterhood of like minds and social/political activism that I found in the feminist community that I eventually became a part of.

I am by nature a romantic. As such, I prefer my feminist heroines to be likable, collaborative, brave, generous, and self-sacrificing in the face of resistance to efforts on the part of women to ensure themselves equal treatment. Sara Bard Field may have been correct when she portrayed Belmont as a woman with feminist sensibilities before she became involved in the suffrage movement. But there is little evidence that Alva had any interest in progressive reform or any real concern about the lives of women outside her own narrow circle of friends before she began attending NAWSA meetings in New York City. Her "aha!" moment seems to have come when she confronted the militant suffragettes in England in 1909. After that, she was generous with her time, money, and administrative expertise in an effort to advance women's quest for gender equity. She allowed the woman's rights movement to exploit her celebrity to focus the attention of the press on their demand for the vote and then for equal nationality rights. There is no reason to doubt that she was sincere in her determination that women no longer be subordinated to men. And she had the imagination and initiative to use her resources to construct a feminist program designed to change that situation. It seems fair to say that if it had not been for her insistence on both a domestic and international equal rights campaign and her willingness to pay for a good deal of it, women would have had to wait much longer to see their social, economic, legal, and political position improved. I have a great deal of respect for her work on behalf of women. It was as noteworthy in its own way as that of Susan B. Anthony, Elizabeth Cady Stanton, Carrie Chapman Catt, and Alice Paul.

But from my perspective, the historical Belmont has some serious flaws as a feminist heroine.[1] She was arrogant, imperious, and self-absorbed. She was obsessed with being in the limelight. She was generous but only when it required no personal sacrifice of ease or comfort on her part. She did her best to control the lives of those around her by using her money and her social status as a weapon to guarantee their submission to her will. Her relationships with other women were characterized more by attempts to gain the upper hand in order to demonstrate her power over them than they were on establishing relationships based on equality, mutual concern, and respect.

I find myself agreeing with Field that Belmont's feminist sensibilities derived more from her resentment of the tyranny of men than it did from her concern about women. The result was, as Field pointed out, that Belmont was most forceful in her feminism when she thought of women in the abstract rather than as individual people.[2] That abstraction allowed her to overcome class prejudices and racism to collaborate with working-class and black women to try to advance the cause of suffrage and to work with international feminists to promote the idea of equal rights. And it was Consuelo as an abstraction rather than as a vulnerable, impressionable little girl that encouraged Alva to approach the job of mothering as if it were a construction project designed to provide her the opportunity to create a young woman who would find satisfaction living the sort of life her mother defined as fulfilling and meaningful.

So I have found making something of Alva Belmont more difficult that it might have been had she been a more personally appealing subject. Elizabeth Minnich has said of writing a biography of another woman that it "requires some of the same qualities or conditions as a good conversation with a friend: mutuality, as interdependence risked, respected, and enjoyed; equality, guaranteeing the grounds for and so allowing the celebration of difference; familiarity, knowing enough about each other in the various worlds we inhabit to hear what is said and to comprehend what is meant."[3] If I have failed to exhibit those qualities or recreate those conditions, it is not for want of trying. A feeling of mutuality was difficult for me to establish with someone for whom I had so little personal sympathy. And I find it hard to imagine that if we had known each other, we would have regarded each other as equals let alone friends. But if I could not always sympathize with Alva, I tried to be empathetic—which is to say that I tried to appreciate how we are different from each other, to be sensitive to how those differences might affect my narrative, and to listen carefully to what she had to say in an effort to understand what she meant.

While I willingly acknowledge that all biographies have a psychological component, I do not consider myself a practitioner of psychohistory. Nor am I particularly sympathetic with that approach to explaining the past.[4] But the more time I spent with Belmont, the more I found her narcissism off-putting in the extreme. My exasperation with her hit a high point just as I finished up my research in Newport, Rhode Island, in the fall of 2009. I was going through a file of documents held by the Preservation Society of Newport County when I picked up a handwritten note scrawled on the outside of one of the society's envelopes. On August 18, 1997, Paul Miller, the archivist of the society, had interviewed a woman identified as Elsie T. Power of Newport. Her parents, John and Ruth Townsend, had been Alva's housekeepers at Marble House from 1914 to 1915. This is what it said: "asked to leave when baby Elsie was to be born. 'Mrs. Belmont didn't want baby in house' 'give her up for adoption or leave' Replaced by Mr. and Mrs. James Nolan. Elsie born on Thames St. 'Old Mother Belmont' known as such to servants."[5]

I was, to put it mildly, stunned. What kind of woman, I wondered, could actually believe that expectant parents would give up their baby in order to continue to serve the needs of their employer? The text of the note haunted me on the trip back home. There was something going on here that went far beyond the self-centeredness of a rich and willful woman. So I went to the library where I consulted the American Psychiatric Association's *Diagnostic and Statistical Manual of Mental Disorders*. Having done so, I became convinced that Belmont exhibited many of the symptoms common to what clinical psychologists call "narcissistic personality disorder"—the need for constant attention and admiration, lack of empathy, a sense of entitlement, an inability to accept criticism, a grandiose sense of self-importance, and the tendency to take advantage of others in order to achieve one's ends.[6]

As a child, Alva believed it was perfectly within her right to disobey any rule that interfered with her ability to do as she pleased. She spent her adult life trying to establish and then to maintain her celebrity status. The leather-bound volumes of carefully preserved press clippings at the Sewall-Belmont House in Washington, D.C., stand as testimony to the value she placed on the attention she received. Doris Stevens and Sara Bard Field both described her obsessive desire for love, affection, and gratitude. When she was subjected to criticism, she responded with childlike anger and obstructionism. The leaders of the NAWSA discovered that failing to privilege Alva's ideas about how to promote suffrage prompted her to withdraw her support from their organization. And much to her dismay, Caroline Reilly experienced one of Alva's famous temper tantrums when she had the audacity to ask her to rewrite a pro-suffrage letter to the editor. As she grew older, Alva was convinced that she was bearing most of the burden for financing the activities of the NWP and displayed a compulsive need to have her efforts publicly acknowledged.

Alva's relationship with her feminist allies tended to be patronizing. I am not suggesting that she felt no affection for those who worked closely with her. Nor am I saying that she thought their work in the woman's rights movement in any way inferior to her own. But she was more than willing to exploit the work of others and take credit for it herself. She also seemed unwilling or unable to really understand how what she did or did not do as well as what she said or failed to say influenced the way her associates felt about themselves, about her, and about their relationship with her. Her efforts on behalf of women less fortunate than herself were laudable. But they could also be exploitive and opportunistic. She may have been concerned about improving their circumstances, but trying to do so gave her the chance to toot her own horn.

In all fairness, it should be pointed out that the possession of great wealth encourages some degree of narcissism. The rich both in her day and ours can demand and elicit attention from others not only because they can afford to do things that are exceptional and, therefore, noteworthy but also because they can afford to pay to have attention bestowed on them. A sense of entitlement often goes hand in hand with possessing enough money to buy oneself out of "sticky situations." With a lawyer on retainer and only a phone call or text message away, it is easy to believe that one need not obey the rules that presumably apply to everyone else. It is easy for those with wealth and power to believe that they are beyond criticism, particularly when they are surrounded by people who are likely to find it in their interest to be agreeable. In a society that places great value on making and having money, it is not surprising that those who have a great deal of it tend to be impressed, even consumed, by a sense of their own importance. And for those who appreciate how much power their money gives them, there is sometimes a fine line between acts of philanthropy designed to provide others with opportunities and those that exploit them.

So I have made Alva Vanderbilt Belmont one more time. What you have read is my representation of the truth. In that sense, this version of Belmont's story, like those that have come before it, is both biography and autobiography. I admit to having approached the telling of her life from a particular historical context, one in which my attitude toward philanthropy and commitment to a feminism ideally expressed by collaboration rather than competition and generosity of spirit rather than self-aggrandizement provided the parameters for my interpretation of how she lived her life.

Each of Alva's life narratives—told in bits and pieces, from various perspectives, at various times and in various places, by a wide variety of people—is fictive to one degree or other. Each of our stories is a little bit different. But while we emphasize various aspects of her life, we all agree that, whatever her many shortcomings, she was an important figure in the woman's rights movement in the early twentieth century. Her support of the suffrage movement was critical to its success. Without her, the leaders of the NWP might never have initiated an international equal rights campaign. Without her, they certainly would have had trouble paying for it.

# APPENDIX

## *Belmont's Financial Contributions to Woman's Rights*

It is difficult to determine the exact value of Alva Belmont's contributions to the woman's rights movement between 1909 and her death in 1933. There is no way to accurately estimate the value of her time, energy, and administrative activities. Nor is there a systematic way to trace the amount she solicited from her friends and acquaintances. The financial records of the NAWSA and the NWP are incomplete. Those that do exist are to be found in a number of widely scattered collections. Not only do those records often overlap, making it impossible to get a clear picture of the total amount given, but they do not usually list individual contributors by name. Then there is the matter of "in kind" contributions such as furnishings, insurance payments, and lawyer's fees as well as expenses paid out of pocket to individuals as reimbursements or for services rendered. All are difficult to account for precisely. For example, Belmont kept attorney George Gordon Battle on retainer for $1000 a month and then paid him to take care of the legal work for the NWP on a case-by-case basis. He drew up the deeds when she bought property for the NWP and prepared briefs when the NWP needed them for their presentations to Congress.[1] But we do not know how often he did so or how long he was on retainer for such purposes.

Belmont also paid for fund-raising events out of her own pocket. According to Alice Paul, there seemed to be no limit to the amount of money that Belmont was willing to spend. For example, early in her association with the CU, Belmont decided to give a dinner to benefit the organization at the Willard Hotel in order to attract members of Washington society to the cause. After she had made the necessary arrangements, she told Paul to invite whomever she wanted—the entire NWP national board, all of the state chairmen, and anyone who had made a significant contribution to the suffrage campaign. Paul estimated that the NWP entertained from 600 to 1000 guests that night.[2]

It should also be noted that information about how much money the NWP raised through fund-raisers was reported to the newspapers by people who had every reason to exaggerate the amount. Furthermore, it remains unclear whether the figures that appeared in print were gross figures or net figures. Since fund-raisers cost a great deal to put on, this distinction is important. Thus, what follows are examples of Belmont's generosity rather than a tally of her total contributions to the cause of woman's rights.

*Belmont's Financial Contributions to the Suffrage Campaign (1909–1919)*

(PEA, NAWSA, and NWP)
Contributions for 1909–1910—$41,107[3]
1911 (purchased and furnished new PEA headquarters)—$320,000[4]
Contributions for 1914—$6100[5]
Contributions for 1915—$6015[6]
Contributions for 1916—$20,650[7]
Contributions for 1917—$19,900[8]
Contributions for 1918—$3830[9]
Contributions for 1919—$2000[10]

*Belmont's Financial Contributions to the NWP after 1920*

Contributions from February 25, 1921, to October 25, 1922—$179,557[11]
Additional contributions listed separately for that period:[12]
- Furniture—$668
- Purchased lease from tenants—$8000
- Purchased headquarters property—$101,504
- Paid taxes on property—$635
- Paid insurance on property—$663
- Additional payments on headquarters property paid by Belmont which did not pass through NWP treasury—$47,317
- Executive salaries—$3246
- Legal research salaries—$4600
- Staff salaries—$400
- Organization Department salaries—$2550
- Treasury Department salaries—$220

Contributions from October 26, 1922, to November 1, 1923[13]
- Paid salaries in advance for legal research staff—$4200
- Money for headquarters that did not pass through the treasury—$13,313

Contributions from July 1, 1921, to January 25, 1923—$192,377[14]
Bills paid by Belmont directly from October 1, 1921, to January 15, 1923—$61,152[15]

Contributions from July 1, 1921, to November 17, 1926—$209,518[16]
Salary paid to Alice Paul from October 15, 1921, to March 1927—$30,000[17]
Contributions for 1927—$6680[18]
Contributions for 1928—$7532[19]
Contributions for 1929—$6937[20]
Contributions from January 16, 1930, to December 3, 1931—$23,500[21]

*Belmont's Contributions to the Woman's Research Fund (Foundation)*[22]

Contributions from August 6, 1923, to December 9, 1926—$27,500

*Belmont's Contributions to the NWP International Fund*

Contributions from January 1928 to September 26, 1929—$8500[23]
Contributions from September 6, 1930, to October 28, 1933—$14,240[24]

*Belmont's Contributions to the Inter-American Commission on Women*

Contributions Total—$23,242[25]

*Examples of Belmont's Miscellaneous Gifts*

November and December 1925 donated royalties to NWP—$130[26]
December 1930 Renovation of Assembly Hall in Belmont House—$10,000[27]

*Belmont's Legacy to the NWP*

$100,000[28]

*Examples of Belmont's Children's Donations to the Woman's Rights Movement*

William K. Vanderbilt Jr., January 1928 to September 26, 1929 (International Fund)—$5000[29]
William K. Vanderbilt Jr., October 1933—$1000[30]
Harold S. Vanderbilt, October 1933—$1000[31]
Consuelo Vanderbilt Balsan, July 1933—$1014[32]

*Examples of the Amount of Money Raised by Belmont from Friends and Acquaintances*

1912–1913—$1600[33]
1914—$500[34]

*Examples of the Amount of Money Raised by Belmont from Fund-Raising Events*

Thé Desant at Marble House, Newport, Rhode Island, July 1915—$3000[35]
Suffrage Operetta in New York City, February 1916—$8000[36]

*Example of In-Kind Donations by Belmont*[37]

Furnishings insured for $65,000

*Examples of Cash Given to Cover Expenses*

$2109—money spent on international work[38]
$1000—check given to Doris Stevens for international work[39]
$2000—check given to Doris Stevens for work in The Hague[40]
$200—check given to Doris Stevens for travel[41]

# NOTES

**INTRODUCTION**

1. Paul John Eakin, *Fictions in Autobiography: Studies in the Art of Self-Invention* (Princeton, N.J.: Princeton University Press, 1985), 5.

2. Sara Alpern et al., eds. *The Challenge of Feminist Biography: Writing the Lives of Modern American Women* (Urbana: University of Illinois Press, 1992), 10–11.

3. Paul Murray Kendall, *The Art of Biography* (New York: W. W. Norton, 1965), x.

4. The scholarly literature on autobiography and memoir as a genre is vast. In addition to Eakin's study listed above, see Roy Pascal, *Design and Truth in Autobiography* (Cambridge, Mass.: Harvard University Press, 1960); Timothy Dow Adams, *Telling Lies in Modern American Autobiography* (Chapel Hill: University of North Carolina Press, 1990); James Olney, ed., *Autobiography: Essays Theoretical and Critical* (Princeton, N.J.: Princeton University Press, 1980); Estelle C. Jelinek, ed., *Women's Autobiography: Essays in Criticism* (Bloomington: Indiana University Press, 1980); Estelle C. Jelinek, *The Tradition of Women's Autobiography: From Antiquity to the Present* (Boston: Twayne, 1986); Sidonie Smith, *A Poetics of Women's Autobiography: Marginality and the Fictions of Self-Representation* (Bloomington: Indiana University Press, 1987); Shari Benstock, ed., *The Private Self: Theory and Practice of Women's Autobiographical Writings* (Chapel Hill: University of North Carolina Press, 1988); Bella Brodzki and Celeste Schenck, eds., *Life/Lines: Theorizing Women's Autobiography* (Ithaca, N.Y.: Cornell University Press, 1988); Personal Narrative Group [Joy Webster Barbre et al.], ed., *Interpreting Women's Lives: Feminist Theory and Personal Narrative* (Bloomington: Indiana University Press, 1989); Sidonie Smith and Julia Watson, eds., *De/Colonizing the Subject: The Politics of Gender in Women's Autobiography* (Minneapolis: University of Minnesota Press, 1992); Margo Culley, ed., *American Women's Autobiography: Fea(s)ts of Memory* (Madison: University of Wisconsin Press,

1992); William Zinsser, ed., *Inventing the Truth: The Art and Craft of Memoir* (Boston: Houghton, Mifflin, 1987); Carolyn A. Barros, *Autobiography: Narrative of Transformation* (Ann Arbor: University of Michigan Press, 1998); G. Thomas Couser, *Altered Egos: Authority in American Autobiography* (New York: Oxford University Press, 1989). These authors approach autobiographies and memoirs as literary texts. The most authoritative discussion of autobiography as a historical tool is to be found in Jennifer Jensen Wallach, *"Closer to the Truth Than Any Fact": Memoir, Memory, and Jim Crow* (Athens: University of Georgia Press, 2008), 13–56. Although literary scholars try to distinguish among recollections, reminiscences, autobiography, memoir, and life-writing, I will be using these terms interchangeably. For discussion of this issue, see Marcus Billson, "The Memoir: New Perspectives on a Forgotten Genre," *Genre* 10 (1977): 359–82; Philippe Lejeune, *On Autobiography,* ed. Paul John Eakin, trans. Katherine Leary (Minneapolis: University of Minnesota Press, 1989).

5. Jo Burr Margadant, *The New Biography: Performing Femininity in Nineteenth-Century France* (Berkeley: University of California Press, 2000), 2–3.

6. Alva E. Belmont Memoir typescript, Sara Bard Field Papers in the Charles Erskine Scott Wood Papers, Huntington Library, San Marino, Calif. (hereafter cited as Field-Belmont Memoir).

7. Alva E. Belmont Memoir typescript, Box 9, Folder 291, Doris Stevens Papers, Schlesinger Library, Radcliffe Institute for Advanced Study, Harvard University, Cambridge, Mass. (hereafter cited as Stevens-Belmont Memoir).

8. Alva E. Belmont Memoir typescript, Matilda Young Papers, Rare Book, Manuscript and Special Collections Library, Duke University, Durham, N.C. (hereafter cited as Young-Belmont Memoir).

9. Sara Bard Field to Charles Erskine Scott Wood, July 27, 1917, Field Papers.

10. "In the Matter of the Estate of Alva E. Belmont: Statement of Doris Stevens Taken in Support of Her Claim Filed against the Said Estate, at the Office of Battle, Levy, Van Tine & Fowler, 37 Wall Street, New York City, on August 23, 1933, at 10:30 AM, " Box 9, Stevens Papers (hereafter cited as Stevens Deposition).

11. Consuelo Vanderbilt Balsan, *The Glitter and the Gold* (New York: Harper & Bros., 1952).

12. Amelia Fry interviewed Field during the period from 1959 to 1963. She interviewed Paul in 1972 and 1973. Amelia R. Fry, "Sara Bard Field: Poet and Suffragist," 1979; Amelia R. Fry, "Conversations with Alice Paul: Woman Suffrage and the Equal Rights Amendment," 1976 (hereafter cited as Field Interview and Paul Interview, respectively). http://bancroft.berkeley.edu/ROHO/projects/suffragist (accessed April 24, 2008).

13. Maureen Fastenau, "Alva Vanderbilt Belmont: Social Arbiter and Militant Feminist" (MA thesis, San Jose State University, 1976); Rebecca T. Keeler, "Alva Belmont: Exacting Benefactor for Women's Rights" (MA thesis, University of South Alabama, 1987); Kris Ann Cappelluti, "The Confines of

Class: Alva Belmont and the Politics of Woman Suffrage" (MA thesis, Sarah Lawrence College, 1995); Ann H. Jaime, "Alva Smith Vanderbilt Belmont: Radical Socialite Suffragist" (MA thesis, Sonoma State University, 2002). Well researched and over 800 pages long, Peter Geidel's unpublished dissertation "Alva E. Belmont: A Forgotten Feminist" (PhD diss., Columbia University, 1993) is the most complete and dependable study of her life. Amanda Mackenzie Stuart has written a full-length book about Belmont, but her discussion focuses on the relationship between Alva and her daughter, Consuelo. *Consuelo and Alva Vanderbilt: The Story of a Daughter and a Mother in the Gilded Age* (New York: HarperCollins, 2005). Other published sources include John Sledge, "Alva Smith Vanderbilt Belmont: Alabama's 'Bengal Tiger,'" *Alabama Heritage* 44 (1997): 6–17; Raymond E. Spinzia, "In Her Wake: The Story of Alva Smith Vanderbilt Belmont," *Long Island Historical Journal* 6 (1993): 96–105; Janet W. Buell, "Alva Belmont: From Socialite to Feminist," *Historian* 52 (1990): 219–41; Rebecca T. Keeler, "Alva Belmont: Exacting Benefactor for Women's Suffrage," *Alabama Review* 41 (1988): 132–45. Margaret Hayden Rector's *Alva: That Vanderbilt-Belmont Woman: Her Story as She Might Have Told It* (n.p.: Dutch Island Press, 1992) is an imaginative account of her life complete with dialogue.

14. Steven Pinker, "My Genome, My Self," *New York Times Magazine*, Jan. 11, 2009, p. 26.

15. Field-Belmont Memoir, 48. Since these observations do not appear in the notes that Field took and upon which she based her narrative, it is impossible to tell if Belmont actually said this.

16. This issue of truth versus falsehood has dominated discussions of the genre. See Eakin, Pascal, Adams, and Zinsser.

17. For discussion of that negotiation, see Couser, 253.

## 1. AN IMPOSSIBLE CHILD

1. Field-Belmont Memoir, 9; and Field Notes, [86], Field Papers. The pages in the notes that Field took during her conversations with Belmont are not numbered. For the sake of convenience, I have numbered them in order as they appear in the Huntington Library microfilm. The numbers appear in brackets.

2. Young-Belmont Memoir, 37a, Young Papers.

3. Field-Belmont Memoir, 2. For the date of her birth, see Geidel, 2. Four of her siblings died before they reached adulthood, so Alva grew up with three sisters and a brother. For a list of her siblings, see Geidel, 48–50, notes 2 and 3.

4. Field-Belmont Memoir, [1]; Young-Belmont Memoir, 5–6. For Phoebe's birth date, see Geidel, 48, note 2.

5. "Robert Desha," *Biographical Dictionary of the United States Congress*, http://bioguide.congress.gov (accessed Sept. 18, 2009). For a discussion of his

role in the Eaton Affair, see John F. Marszalek, *The Petticoat Affair: Manners, Mutiny, and Sex in Andrew Jackson's White House* (Baton Rouge: Louisiana State University Press, 1997), 47, 146–48, 177.

6. Robert Greenhalgh Albion, *The Rise of New York Port* (New York: Charles Scribner's Sons, 1939), 103–104.

7. Hiram Fuller, *Belle Brittan on a Tour, at Newport, and Here and There* (New York: Derby and Jackson, 1858), 112.

8. The date of their marriage can be found at www.familysearch.org (accessed Aug. 23, 2008). Field-Belmont Memoir, 2; Young-Belmont Memoir, 6.

9. Sledge, 8; Harriet E. Amos, *Cotton City: Urban Development in Antebellum Mobile* (University: University of Alabama Press, 1985), 99.

10. Young-Belmont Memoir, 6, 9–10, 11; Field-Belmont Memoir, 2.

11. Young-Belmont Memoir, 2.

12. Young-Belmont Memoir, 2, 5.

13. Field-Belmont Memoir, 1; Young-Belmont Memoir, 2–5. For a short biography of James Erskine, Lord Alva and Barjarg, and his wife, Jean Stirling Erskine, see [Arthur Collins], *Collins's Peerage of England; Genealogical, Biographical, and Historical,* 9 vols. (London: F. C. and J. Rivington et al., 1812), 5:443.

14. Geidel, 2 and 49, note 3.

15. Field-Belmont Memoir, 10; Young-Belmont Memoir, 6–7.

16. Elizabeth Cady Stanton, *Eighty Years and More (1815–1897): Reminiscences of Elizabeth Cady Stanton* (London: T. Fisher Unwin, 1898), 20–23.

17. Field-Belmont Memoir, 6.

18. Field-Belmont Memoir, 27, 7–8.

19. Field-Belmont Memoir, 7.

20. Field-Belmont Memoir, 6–7, 23–24, quotation on 24.

21. Field-Belmont Memoir, 25.

22. Field-Belmont Memoir, 21.

23. Field-Belmont Memoir, 23.

24. Field-Belmont Memoir, 7.

25. Field-Belmont Memoir, 24–25.

26. Field-Belmont Memoir, 7.

27. Field-Belmont Memoir, 29.

28. Field-Belmont Memoir, 7.

29. Field-Belmont Memoir, 8, 26.

30. Young-Belmont Memoir, 37a.

31. Field-Belmont Memoir, 2–3; Young-Belmont Memoir, 13.

32. Young-Belmont Memoir, 19.

33. T. C. DeLeon, *Belles, Beaux and Brains of the 60s* (New York: G. W. Dillingham, 1909), 181–82.

34. Albion, 96, 116.

35. Field-Belmont Memoir, 9; Young-Belmont Memoir, 10, 33.

36. Field-Belmont Memoir, 25½.

37. Field-Belmont Memoir, 15.

38. Field-Belmont Memoir, 26–27.

39. Field-Belmont Memoir, 12.

40. U.S. Census, Manuscript Slave Census, 1850, Mobile, Alabama. The U.S. Census, Manuscript Slave Census, 1860, Mobile, Alabama, indicates that in 1860, Smith registered two slaves in Mobile, one black female aged sixty and one mulatto male aged thirty-five.

41. Edgar J. McManus, *History of Negro Slavery in New York* (Syracuse, N.Y.: Syracuse University Press, 1966), 174, 178–79. For a discussion of slavery in New York City during the revolution and early republic, see Shane White, *Somewhat More Independent: The End of Slavery in New York City, 1770–1810* (Athens: University of Georgia Press, 1991).

42. Don Edward Fehrenbacker, *The Dred Scott Case: Its Significance in American Law and Politics* (New York: Oxford University Press, 1978), 432–34.

43. Young-Belmont Memoir, 35.

44. Field-Belmont Memoir, 12.

45. Field-Belmont Memoir, 12.

46. Ernest A. McKay, *The Civil War and New York City* (Syracuse, N.Y.: Syracuse University Press, 1990), 13–14; Edwin G. Burrows and Mike Wallace, *Gotham: A History of New York City to 1898* (New York: Oxford University Press, 1999), 860–61.

47. McKay, 308.

48. McKay, 306–308.

49. Young-Belmont Memoir, 47.

50. Young-Belmont Memoir, 48.

51. Desmond Seward, *Eugenie: The Empress and Her Empire* (Stroud, Gloucestershire: Sutton, 2004), 127–29.

52. Seward, 51, 54, 56. Young-Belmont Memoir, 49; Field-Belmont Memoir, 19; Field Notes, [93, 95].

53. Young-Belmont Memoir, 50, 55, 57–62.

54. Seward, 94–98.

55. Seward, 99–106.

56. Field-Belmont Memoir, 15.

57. Field-Belmont Memoir, 15, 69.

58. Field-Belmont Memoir, [14½].

59. Field-Belmont Memoir, 15.

60. Field-Belmont Memoir, 18; Young-Belmont Memoir, 70.

61. Young-Belmont Memoir, 17.

62. Field-Belmont Memoir, 75.

63. Field Notes, [92]; Young-Belmont Memoir, 67–68.

64. Young-Belmont Memoir, 68–69.

65. Field-Belmont Memoir, 16; Field Notes, [92].

66. Field-Belmont Memoir, 18½.

67. Young-Belmont Memoir, 78.

68. Field-Belmont Memoir, 16–17.

69. Field-Belmont Memoir, 19.

70. Field-Belmont Memoir, 68.

71. Seward, 190–97.

72. Young-Belmont Memoir, 74, says "14 East 33rd St"; Field-Belmont Memoir, 29, says "West 33rd St."

73. Young-Belmont Memoir, 74–75; Geidel 13 and 48, note 2.

74. Young-Belmont Memoir, 75–76; Field-Belmont Memoir, 29–31; Field Notes, [101].

75. Field-Belmont Memoir, 29

76. Field-Belmont Memoir, 29.

77. Field-Belmont Memoir, 30.

78. Field-Belmont Memoir, 30–31; Young-Belmont Memoir, 75–76; Field Notes, [101].

79. Young-Belmont Memoir, 76–80.

80. Young-Belmont Memoir, 76.

81. Edward J. Renehan Jr., *Commodore: The Life of Cornelius Vanderbilt* (New York: Basic, 2007).

82. Edwin Palmer Hoyt, *The Vanderbilts and Their Fortunes* (London: Frederick Muller, 1926), 232; "Against W. K. Vanderbilt: His Wife Gets a Divorce," *New York Tribune,* March 6, 1895, pp. 1, 2.

83. Field-Belmont Memoir, 31–32.

84. Field-Belmont Memoir, 32.

85. Burrows and Wallace, 1020–1023. For a detailed account of the demise of Jay Cooke and Associates, see M. John Lubetkin, *Jay Cooke's Gamble: The Northern Pacific Railroad, the Sioux, and the Panic of 1873* (Norman: University of Oklahoma Press, 2006).

86. Field-Belmont Memoir, 32–33; Field Notes, [102].

87. Edward J. Balleisen, *Navigating Failure: Bankruptcy and Commercial Society in Antebellum America* (Chapel Hill: University of North Carolina Press, 2001); Scott A. Sandage, *Born Losers: A History of Failure in America* (Cambridge, Mass.: Harvard University Press, 2005).

88. Young-Belmont Memoir, 82–83.

89. Young-Belmont Memoir, 84–85

90. Young-Belmont Memoir, 85–88.

91. For an analysis of their social status, see Stuart, 35–38; Geidel, 12–13.

92. Field-Belmont Memoir, 33.

93. Field-Belmont Memoir, 34.

94. Murray Forbes Smith died on May 4, 1875. Geidel, 17.

95. Geidel, 57, note 35. In her memoirs, Belmont did not mention her brother Desha or what became of him.

96. Stuart, 109, 304.

97. Field-Belmont Memoir, 35.

98. Field-Belmont Memoir, 35; Young-Belmont Memoir, 89–90.

### 2. EVERY INCH A GENERAL

1. In addition to Idlehour near Islip on Long Island, her Fifth Avenue mansion in New York City, Marble House in Newport, Rhode Island, and Brookholt near Hempstead, Long Island, all discussed in this chapter, she built a mansion at 477 Madison Avenue in 1909, a Chinese tea house on the grounds of Marble House in 1914, and Beacon Towers near Sands Point, Long Island, in 1915. See Stuart, 53–54, 57–59, 78–79, 89–92, 294, 342, 365; "The Belmont Armory as a Suffragist Hall," *New York Times*, Aug. 22, 1909, p. SM8.

2. Field-Belmont Memoir, 11, [81], [86], Field Papers.

3. Field-Belmont Memoir, 11.

4. Field-Belmont Memoir, 2.

5. Field-Belmont Memoir, 14.

6. Field-Belmont Memoir, 22–23.

7. Stuart, 50–52.

8. Stuart, 53–54.

9. Field-Belmont Memoir, 37–39, quotation on 38.

10. Young-Belmont Memoir, 92, Young Papers.

11. Field-Belmont Memoir, 36.

12. Field-Belmont Memoir, 37; Young-Belmont Memoir, 111.

13. Field-Belmont Memoir, 39–40.

14. Joshua Gamson, *Claims to Fame: Celebrity in Contemporary America* (Berkeley: University of California Press, 1994), 17–23; Richard Schickel, *Intimate Strangers: The Culture of Celebrity* (Garden City, N.Y.: Doubleday, 1985), 28; Charles L. Ponce de Leon, *Self-Exposure: Human Interest Journalism and the Emergence of Celebrity in America, 1890–1940* (Chapel Hill: University of North Carolina Press, 2002), 4–5, 18–30, 42–75, 81; Leo Braudy, *The Frenzy of Renown: Fame and Its History* (New York: Oxford University Press, 1986), 13. It should be noted that celebrity was not a new phenomenon in American life. While George Washington was well known in the early republic, it took the efforts of Parson Weems to make him a celebrity. And it was with the help of P. T. Barnum that the "Swedish nightingale" Jenny Lind attained celebrity status in the early nineteenth century. See Lewis Gaston Leary, *The Book-Peddling Parson* (Chapel Hill: Algonquin Books, 1984); Neil Harris, *Humbug: The Art of P. T. Barnum* (Boston: Little, Brown, [1973]); Bluford Adams, *E. Pluribus Barnum: The Great Showman and the Making of U.S. Popular Culture* (Minneapolis: University of Minnesota Press, 1997).

15. Sven Beckert, *The Monied Metropolis: New York City and the Consolidation of the American Bourgeoisie, 1850–1896* (New York: Cambridge University Press, 2001), 156.

16. Ishbel Ross, *Ladies of the Press* (New York: Arno Press, 1974 [1936]), 441.

17. Beckert, 156; Eric Homberger, *Mrs. Astor's New York: Money and Power in a Gilded Age* (New Haven, Conn.: Yale University Press, 2002), xii; Maureen E. Montgomery, *Displaying Women: Spectacles of Leisure in Edith Wharton's*

*New York* (New York: Routledge, 1998), 9, 62–65, 86, 147–50, 151; Jackson Lears, "The Managerial Revitalization of the Rich," in *Ruling America: A History of Wealth and Power in a Democracy,* ed. Steve Fraser and Gary Gerstle (Cambridge, Mass.: Harvard University Press, 2005), 181–214.

18. Thomas N. Baker, *Sentiment and Celebrity: Nathaniel Parker Willis and the Trials of Literary Fame* (New York: Oxford University Press, 1999), 189–90; Warren Susman, "Personality and the Making of Twentieth-Century Culture," in *Culture as History: The Transformation of American Society in the Twentieth Century* (New York: Pantheon, 1984), 271–85.

19. Schickel, viii–ix; Ponce de Leon, 82; Baker, 12.

20. Schickel, 28–29; James Monaco, "Celebration" in *Celebrity: The Media as Image Makers,* ed. James Monaco (New York: Dell, 1978), 6, 14. For other discussions of celebrity, see P. David Marshall, *Celebrity of Power: Fame in Contemporary Culture* (Minneapolis: University of Minnesota Press, 1997); Leonard J. Leff, *Hemingway and His Conspirators: Hollywood, Scribners and the Making of American Celebrity Culture* (Lantham, Md.: Rowman & Littlefield, 1997); Daniel J. Boorstin, "From Hero to Celebrity: The Human Pseudo-Event," in *The Image: A Guide to Pseudo-Events in America* (New York: Harper and Row, 1961), 45–76; Joy Kasson, *Buffalo Bill's Wild West: Celebrity, Memory, and Popular History* (New York: Hill and Wang, 2000).

21. Ross, 449.

22. Ross, 443–44, 445, 448; Beatrice Fairfax (Marie Manning), *Ladies Now and Then* (New York: E. P. Dutton, 1944), 9, 146–47; Baker, 189.

23. George Juergens, *Joseph Pulitzer and the* New York World (Princeton, N.J.: Princeton University Press, 1966), 3–63, 175–209.

24. The *World*'s approach to reporting about the upper class was apparently typical in the late nineteenth century. Ponce de Leon, 142–50.

25. The *Times* society column was titled "Society Topics of the Week." By 1892, the paper ran a second society column called "In the Social World."

26. Meyer Berger, *The Story of the* New York Times, *1851–1951* (New York: Simon & Schuster, 1951), 105, 107, 110–11.

27. The *Times* announced their marriage along with that of other New Yorkers in their "Married" column. *New York Times,* April 26, 1875, p. 5.

28. "All Society in Costume," *New York Times,* March 27, 1883, pp. 1–2; see also "The Vanderbilt Ball," *New York Tribune,* March 27, 1883, p. 5. Stories about society events typically had no bylines.

29. "Social Dynamite: A Conspiracy of Wallflowers, Bores, and 'Dudes' against the Vanderbilt Ball," *New York World,* March 24, 1883, p. 1. According to http://westegg.com/inflation/, $250,000 in 1883 would have been worth approximately $5,681,349 in 2009 (accessed Sept. 30, 2010) (hereafter referred to as inflation calculator). This website is updated frequently. In the process, the figures change slightly so the amount given is approximate.

30. *New York World,* March 25, 1883, p. 5.

31. "Mrs. Vanderbilt's Ball," *New York World,* March 27, 1883, p. 1.

32. "World of Society," *New York World,* April 1, 1883, p. 5.

33. *Boston Globe,* March 26, 1883, p. 1, and March 27, 1883, p. 1; *Atlanta Constitution,* March 27, 1883, p. 1; *Baltimore Sun,* March 27, 1883, p. 1; *Los Angeles Times,* March 25, 1883, p. 1; *St. Louis Post-Dispatch,* March 28, 1883, p. 1.

34. The *Chicago Daily Tribune* published two stories on March 25 (p. 12), three stories on March 27 (p. 3), and one story on March 28 (p. 5). For reference to the *World's* "Dude" story, see "Bombs," *Chicago Daily Tribune,* March 27, 1883, p. 3.

35. "Balshazzar's Feast," *St. Louis Post-Dispatch,* March 24, 1883, p. 4.

36. Young-Belmont Memoir, 108, 110.

37. Geidel, 23. In 2009, his inheritance would have been worth approximately $1,532,314,076. See inflation calculator (accessed Sept. 30, 2010).

38. Field-Belmont Memoir, 40–44; quotation on 40.

39. Field-Belmont Memoir, 11.

40. Field-Belmont Memoir, 6, 10–11, quotation on 10.

41. Field-Belmont Memoir, 48–49.

42. Field-Belmont Memoir, 49.

43. Field-Belmont Memoir, 56; Nancy M. Theriot, *Mothers and Daughters in Nineteenth-Century America: The Biosocial Construction of Femininity* (Lexington: University of Kentucky Press, 1996), 114.

44. Field-Belmont Memoir, 4; Young-Belmont Memoir, 11.

45. Young-Belmont Memoir, 15–18, quotations on 17–18.

46. Field-Belmont Memoir, 29.

47. Consuelo was born on March 2, 1877. William Kissam Jr., was born on Oct. 26, 1878. Harold Stirling was born on July 6, 1884. Geidel, 25.

48. Field-Belmont Memoir, 53–56.

49. Field-Belmont Memoir, 11.

50. Field-Belmont Memoir, 52–53, 55. For another reference to the Trinity Seaside Home, see Young-Belmont Memoir, 93–94.

51. Field-Belmont Memoir, 54.

52. Field-Belmont Memoir, 54–55.

53. Field-Belmont Memoir, 52; Field Notes, [107], Field Papers.

54. Young-Belmont Memoir, 97–98.

55. Field-Belmont Memoir, 55–56; Field Notes [107].

56. Field-Belmont Memoir, 56. Both William Kissam Jr. and his brother served in the armed forces during World War I. After the war, William became a yachtsman with an interest in marine biology. As a member of the board of directors of the New York Central Railroad, Harold helped to ease the transition from steam engines to diesel. He was also a master bridge player and yachtsman. Stuart, 377, 450–51; Elsa Maxwell, *R.S.V.P.: Elsa Maxwell's Own Story* (Boston: Little, Brown, 1954), 106.

57. Dorothy Kelly MacDowell, *Commodore Vanderbilt and His Family: A Biographical Account of the Descendants of Cornelius and Sophia Vanderbilt* (Hendersonville, N.C.: privately printed, 1989), 210–15.

58. Field-Belmont Memoir, [79].

59. Balsan, *The Glitter and the Gold.* Evidence in the Harper & Row papers indicates that Balsan did not use a ghost writer to write her memoirs; Stuart, 486–87.

60. Linda W. Rosenzweig, *The Anchor of My Life: Middle-American Mothers and Daughters, 1880–1920* (New York: New York University Press, 1993), 29, 68, 88; Theriot, 114.

61. Balsan, 1.

62. My approach to analyzing Consuelo's autobiography derives in part from ideas to be found in Joan Gould, *Spinning Straw into Gold: What Fairy Tales Reveal about the Transformations in a Woman's Life* (New York: Random House, 2005); and Elizabeth Wanning Harries, "The Mirror Broken: Women's Autobiography and Fairy Tales," in *Fairy Tales and Feminism: New Approaches,* ed. Donald Haase (Detroit: Wayne State University Press, 2004), 99–111.

63. Balsan, 1–2.

64. Balsan, 5, 6, 11.

65. Balsan, 11.

66. Balsan, 6, 7.

67. Balsan, 25.

68. Balsan 2.

69. Balsan, 9.

70. Balsan, 6, 33.

71. Balsan, 9.

72. Balsan, 6.

73. Balsan, 6.

74. Balsan, 11–12.

75. Balsan, 8. She claims that her mother also forced her to wear a steel rod against her spine during her adolescence in order to ensure that she had good posture. Balsan, 13. Literary critic Luann Walther has argued that autobiographers, particularly those who grew up in the nineteenth century, often depicted their childhoods as being full of adversity and hardship. Consuelo seems to have been no exception. But while the autobiographers that Walther refers to do so in order to "implicate without accusing" those at whose hands they suffered, Consuelo did not hesitate to accuse. Luann Walther, "The Invention of Childhood in Victorian Autobiography," in *Approaches to Victorian Autobiography,* ed. George P. Landow (Athens: Ohio University Press, 1979), 64–83, quotation on p. 80.

76. Balsan, 26–27.

77. Balsan, 25, 26.

78. Jane H. Hunter, *How Young Ladies Became Girls: The Victorian Origins of American Girlhood* (New Haven, Conn.: Yale University Press, 2002), 4–5.

79. Balsan, 9, 20–23, 25–26, 29; Field-Belmont Memoir, 55, [85]. Consuelo's home schooling was thorough enough to allow her to pass the entrance exams for admission to Oxford. Young-Belmont Memoir, 98.

80. Field-Belmont Memoir, [81]; Field Notes, [64]. For a description of Consuelo, see "Marlborough and Wife, Daughter of Vanderbilt, Part," *St. Louis Post-Dispatch,* Oct. 21, 1906, A1.

81. Field-Belmont Memoir, 61, 58.

82. Young-Belmont Memoir, 77.

83. Field-Belmont Memoir, 57–59; Young-Belmont Memoir, 152–54.

84. Field-Belmont Memoir, 60.

85. Young-Belmont Memoir, 153.

86. Field Interview, 389.

87. "Against Mr. Vanderbilt: His Wife Gets a Divorce," *New York Tribune,* March 6, 1895, pp. 1, 2. Alva even told Sara Bard Field that he brought his mistress into their home. Field Interview, 370.

88. Balsan, 5.

89. Balsan, 34–40. Gossipy stories in the *New York World* and the *Boston Globe* suggested that his mistress was Alva's best friend, Consuelo Yznaga, the widowed Duchess of Manchester. "Mrs. Vanderbilt Free," *New York World,* March 6, 1895, p. 2 and "May Marry the Duchess," *Boston Globe,* March 7, 1895, p. 5. The two women had been friends since childhood. They had spent summers together in Newport. Field-Belmont Memoir, 22. Consuelo was one of Alva's bridesmaids. Young-Belmont Memoir, 86. And when Alva gave birth to her daughter in 1877, she named the baby after her friend and asked the duchess to be her child's godmother. Stuart, 50, 109. Alva's sister Jenny married Consuelo's brother, Fernando Yznaga. Young-Belmont Memoir, 87. Though, as Stuart points out (p. 109), no one denied the story, it is unlikely that it was true. In her last memoir, written shortly before she died, Alva, who was not prone to forgive, referred to Consuelo Yznaga as "my dear friend." Young-Belmont Memoir, 86. According to the visitor's book at Blenheim, Yznaga visited her goddaughter twice in 1897. Stuart, 522, note 74.

90. William Gilmour Diary, Dec. 5, 1894–March 13, 1895, William Gilmour Papers, Preservation Society of Newport County, Newport, R.I.

91. The other two lawyers were William Jay and William Duer. Young-Belmont Memoir, 142; Gilmour Diary, Dec. 22, 1894.

92. Field-Belmont Memoir, 63.

93. Young-Belmont Memoir, 156; "W. K. Vanderbilt Loses: His Wife Gets an Absolute Divorce and Custody of Children," *New York Times,* March 6, 1895, p. 1; "Her Divorce," *Los Angeles Times,* March 6, 1895, p. 1.

94. "W. K. Vanderbilt Loses," *New York Times,* March 6, 1895, p. 1; "Mrs. Vanderbilt Free," *New York World,* March 6, 1895, pp. 1–2. The *World* story was accompanied by pencil drawings of the litigants. See also "Against Mrs. Vanderbilt: His Wife Gets a Divorce," *New York Tribune,* March 6, 1895, pp. 1–2.

95. "Nellie Neustretter a Mother," *New York World,* Jan. 29, 1895, p. 1.

96. "Mrs. Vanderbilt Free," *New York World,* March 6, 1895, p. 2.

97. *Boston Globe,* March 6, 1895, p. 1; *Atlanta Constitution,* March 6, 1895, p. 1; *Chicago Tribune,* March 6, 1895, p. 1; *San Francisco Chronicle,* March 6, 1895, p. 1; *Los Angeles Times,* March 6, 1895, p. 1.

98. Field-Belmont Memoir, 64.

99. Young-Belmont Memoir, 151.

100. Field-Belmont Memoir, 61.

101. "Bought a New House," *San Francisco Chronicle,* March 7, 1895, p. 5.

102. Field-Belmont Memoir, 64–65.

103. Young-Belmont Memoir, 142.

104. Field-Belmont Memoir, [81].

105. Field-Belmont Memoir, [85].

106. Field-Belmont Memoir, [82].

107. Jessica Gerard, "Lady Bountiful: Women of the Landed Classes and Rural Philanthropy," *Victorian Studies* 30 (1987): 183–210.

108. Field-Belmont Memoir, [82].

109. Field-Belmont Memoir, [84]; Field Notes, [64].

110. Ruth Brandon, *The Dollar Princesses: Sagas of Upward Mobility, 1870–1914* (New York: Alfred A. Knopf, 1980), 2.

111. According to Maureen Montgomery, 102 American women married peers or the younger sons of peers between 1870 and 1914. Maureen E. Montgomery, *"Gilded Prostitution": Status, Money, and Transatlantic Marriages, 1870–1914* (London: Routledge, 1989), 43.

112. Anita Leslie, *Lady Randolph Churchill: The Story of Jennie Jerome* (New York: Charles Scribner's, 1969), 6.

113. Montgomery, *"Gilded Prostitution,"* 23.

114. Montgomery, *"Gilded Prostitution,"* 232–33. For other examples, see Burrows and Wallace, 1084.

115. Brandon, 3–4. This list was published from 1890 to 1915. Brandon, 204.

116. Beckert, 259–60.

117. Field-Belmont Memoir, [86].

118. Balsan, 37–38.

119. Balsan, 40.

120. Balsan, 41; Stuart, 112–13.

121. "The Valiant Off on Her Trip," *New York Times,* Nov. 24, 1893, p. 1.

122. Balsan, 41.

123. Balsan, 42–45.

124. Balsan, 46–50. In 1902, Rutherford married Alice Morton, the daughter of Levi P. Morton, who had been both vice president of the United States under Benjamin Harrison and governor of New York. After she died, he married Lucy Mercer, a woman destined to become Eleanor Roosevelt's social secretary and Franklin Delano Roosevelt's mistress.

125. Young-Belmont Memoir, 146; "Great Ball in Newport," *New York Times,* Aug. 29, 1895, p. 3; "Mrs. Vanderbilt's Ball," *New York World,* Aug. 29, 1895, p. 2.

126. Balsan, 50.

127. Balsan, 51–52.

128. "Millions for a Title," *Atlanta Constitution,* Nov. 3, 1895, p. 30.

129. Brandon, 58–59; Montgomery, *"Gilded Prostitution,"* 96.

130. Montgomery, *"Gilded Prostitution,"* 96, 167. For more on English married women's property law, see Mary Lyndon Shanley, *Feminism, Marriage, and the Law in Victorian England* (Princeton, N.J.: Princeton University Press, 1989), 103–130. The *New York Times* and other newspapers estimated the value of the stock at $5,000,000. "Millionaire's Gifts," *New York Times,* Nov. 17, 1895, p. 4; "Not $10,000,000," *Boston Globe,* Nov. 3, 1895, p. 4; "Gets Only $5,000,000," *Chicago Daily Tribune,* Nov. 3, 1895, p. 3, and "Sign All the Papers," *Chicago Daily Tribune,* Nov. 6, 1895, p. 4.

131. *New York World,* Sept. 29, 1985, p. 19; Oct. 6, 1895, p. 19; Oct. 12, 1895, p. 19; Oct. 27, 1895, p. 18; Nov. 1, 1895, p. 9; Nov. 2, 1895, p. 8; Nov. 3, 1895, pp. 7, 19, 29; Nov. 4, 1895, p. [14]; Nov. 5, 1895, pp. 1, 2; Nov. 6, 1895, pp. [8, 9]. *New York Times,* Oct. 6, 1895, p.16; Oct. 13, 1895, p. 12; Nov. 2, 1895, p. 2; Nov. 3, 1895, p. 16; Nov. 4, 1895, p. 5; Nov. 5, 1895, p. 1; Nov. 6, 1895, p. 3. *Chicago Daily Tribune,* Nov. 1, 1895, p. 5; Nov. 2, 1895, pp. 3, 16; Nov . 3, 1895, pp. 3; 49; Nov. 4, 1895, p. 8; Nov. 5, 1895, p. 4; Nov. 6, 1895, p. 4. *Atlanta Constitution,* Nov. 3, 1895, p. 30; and Nov. 6, 1895, p. 1. *Boston Globe,* Nov. 1, 1895, p. 2; Nov. 3, 1895, p. 4; Nov. 6, 1895, p. 7.

132. *New York World,* Nov. 3, 1895, pp. 28, 29.

133. "Wed in Regal Pomp," *Chicago Tribune,* Nov. 7, 1895, p. 1.

134. Balsan, 53.

135. "Married in St. Thomas's," *New York Tribune,* Nov. 7, 1895, p. 7.

136. Field-Belmont Memoir, [88–89].

137. "Now She Is a Duchess," *New York World,* Nov. 7, 1895, pp. 1–2; "She Is Now a Duchess," *New York Times,* Nov. 7, 1895, pp. 1–3, "Wed in Regal Pomp," *Chicago Daily Tribune,"* Nov. 7, 1895, p. 1. "Lives United," *Boston Globe,* Nov. 7, 1895, pp. 1, 5, 6; "She's a Duchess Now," *Atlanta Constitution,* Nov. 7, 1895, p. 1; "Miss Vanderbilt Becomes a Duchess," *San Francisco Chronicle,* Nov. 7, 1895, p. 1; "The Ducal Wedding," *Baltimore Sun,* Nov. 7, 1895, p. 1.

138. "To Spend $500,000 on the Wedding," *Chicago Daily Tribune,* Nov. 2, 1895, p. 3; "Wedding Costs Nearly a Million," ibid., Nov. 7, 1895, p. 2.

139. "Luxury and Society," *Chicago Daily Tribune,* Nov. 8, 1895, p. 6. See also "Wedding a Boom to Trade," *Boston Globe,* Nov. 1, 1895, p. 2.

140. "Oliver Belmont's Bride," *New York Times,* Jan. 12, 1896, p. 2; "Mayor Married Them," *New York World,* Jan. 12, 1896, p. 10; "O. H. P. Belmont's Bride," *New York Tribune,* Jan. 12, 1896, p. 7; Young-Belmont Memoir, 156–57. See also *Baltimore Sun,* Jan. 13, 1896, p. 7; *Atlanta Constitution,* Jan. 12, 1896, pp. 8, 12; *Boston Globe,* Jan. 12, 1896, pp. 6, 9; *Chicago Tribune,* Jan. 12, 1896, p. 1; *St Louis Post-Dispatch,* Jan. 12, 1896, p. 3; *San Francisco Chronicle,* Jan. 12, 1896, p. 19.

141. "Oliver Hazard Perry Belmont," *Biographical Dictionary of the United States Congress,* http://bioguide.congress.gov (accessed Sept. 18, 2009); Irving Katz, *August Belmont: A Political Biography* (New York: Columbia University Press, 1968), 3, 6.

142. David Black, *The King of Fifth Avenue: The Fortunes of August Belmont* (New York: Dial, 1981), 707.

143. Stuart, 94–95.

144. Field Notes, [73]; Belmont essay on marriage, Field Papers.

145. Young-Belmont Memoir, 165.

146. Young-Belmont Memoir, 162.

147. Young-Belmont Memoir, 166.

148. Young-Belmont Memoir, 158–61; Van Tassel Sutphen, "Newport's Automobile Parade," *Harper's Weekly*, Sept. 16, 1899, p. 922, describes the obstacles to be avoided as "flags" and "dummy figures."

149. Young-Belmont Memoir, 162–64, 166.

150. Stuart, 269–77.

151. "Ocean Travelers," *New York Times*, Nov. 3, 1906, p. 7; "Society at Home and Abroad," *New York Times*, Nov. 18, 1906, p. X7.

152. "Ocean Travelers," *New York Times*, Nov. 24, 1906, p. 8.

153. "Marlborough Conference," *New York Times*, Jan. 13, 1907, p. 6.

154. Phyllis Moir, *I Was Winston Churchill's Private Secretary* (New York: Wilfred Funk, 1941), 78–79. Amanda Mackenzie Stuart and Peter Geidel disagree as to when Churchill engaged in negotiations with Consuelo's family. Stuart says that Alva Belmont and Churchill negotiated a settlement preceding Consuelo's separation from the duke in 1906; Stuart, 273–77. Geidel says they did so prior to Consuelo's divorce in 1920; Geidel, 650–52. Moir does not provide a date for the Belmont-Churchill negotiations. Newspaper accounts suggest that such a negotiation did indeed take place in 1906, and the *St. Louis Post-Dispatch* specifically mentions Churchill's role in the matter; "Marlborough's Friends Say He Wants a Divorce," *St. Louis Post Dispatch*, Nov. 4, 1906, A2. There is no mention of meetings between the two families in 1920 in the press. It is possible, however, that there were two sets of negotiations, one before the separation and another before the divorce. Consuelo went to court in March 1920 to ask for a divorce. Her divorce petition was entered in November 1920. Her divorce became final in May 1921. Stuart, 390–91. Doris Stevens and Alva Belmont left for Europe in November 1920. Stevens, Deposition, 67, 75. Assuming that they stopped in England, there would have been plenty of time for Alva to negotiate a settlement before the divorce became final.

155. "Marlboroughs Agree on Separation Terms," *New York Times*, Jan. 20, 1907, p. 13. For a detailed discussion of the negotiations, see Stuart, 269–77.

156. Field-Belmont Memoir, [89–90].

157. Balsan, 86–89, 189–92, 196–99, 213–18; "An American Woman's Work in England," *Suffragist*, May 17, 1919, p. 7; Stuart, 283–94, 329–35, 383–84.

158. Young-Belmont Memoir, 167.

159. *New York Times*, June 4, 1908, p. 1; June 5, 1908, p. 1; June 6, 1908, p. 1; June 7, 1908, p. 9; June 9, 1908, p. 1; June 10, 1908, p. 7; June 11, 1908, p. 1; June 12, 1908, p. 7; June 13, 1908, p. 7. *New York World*, June 8, 1908, p. 2; June 9, 1908, p. 3; June 10, 1908, p. 18; June 11, 1908, p. 7; June 13, 1908, p. 10.

160. "Texan Says She Is Only Child of O. H. P. Belmont," *New York World*, June 12, 1908, p. 1; "Belmont Claimant Engages Lawyer," ibid., June 13, 1908, p. 3; "Offers to Assist Claimant," ibid., June 14, 1908, p. 10.

161. Gilmour Diary, June 18, 1908; Young-Belmont Memoir, 167.

162. Gilmour Diary, March 28, 1909; J. A. MacMahon to William Gilmour, June 12, 1909, Gilmour Papers.

163. Belmont inherited $1,094,995 from her husband. Geidel, 44, 126. That amount would have been worth about $25,923,843.44 in 2008 (inflation calculator, accessed August 27, 2009).

### 3. A SEX BATTLE

1. Young-Belmont Memoir, 93–94, 99–100.

2. Her sister Julia died on Aug. 4, 1905. Armide died on April 19, 1907. Geidel, 71–72. Sara Bard Field attributed Belmont's interest in suffrage to loneliness following the death of her husband combined with a real concern about the condition of women. Field Interview, 391.

3. Young-Belmont Memoir, 149–50; Stuart, 305; Ellen Carol Dubois, *Harriot Stanton Blatch and the Winning of Woman Suffrage* (New Haven, Conn.: Yale University Press, 1997), 107.

4. Ida Husted Harper, ed., *The History of Woman Suffrage,* vol. 6 (New York: National American Woman Suffrage Association, 1922), 6:444.

5. Her presence was reported in the press. See "Says Suffragettes Lean to Socialism," *New York Times,* April 1, 1908, p. 7.

6. Young-Belmont Memoir, 169.

7. Lori D. Ginzberg, *Untidy Origins: A Story of Woman's Rights in Antebellum New York* (Chapel Hill: University of North Carolina Press, 2005).

8. Judith Wellman, *The Road to Seneca Falls: Elizabeth Cady Stanton and the First Woman's Rights Convention* (Urbana: University of Illinois Press, 2004).

9. Eleanor Flexner, *Century of Struggle: The Woman's Rights Movement in the United States* (New York: Atheneum, 1972), 222, 248.

10. Quoted in Geidel, 78.

11. Young-Belmont Memoir, 169–70, quotation on 170; "Suffragists Ready for World Congress," *New York Times,* April 25, 1909, p. C3.

12. Andrew Rosen, *Rise Up Women! The Militant Campaign of the Women's Social and Political Union, 1903–1914* (London: Routledge & Kegan Paul, 1974), 25; Jill Liddington and Jill Norris, *One Hand Tied behind Us: The Rise of the Women's Suffrage Movement* (London: Rivers Oram Press, 2000), 70.

13. Liddington and Norris, 195–215; Rosen, xviii–xix, 30, 49–53; Martin Pugh, *The March of the Women: A Revisionist Analysis of the Campaign for Women's Suffrage, 1866–1914* (New York: Oxford University Press, 2000), 171–223. For a detailed description of suffragette activities with illustrations, see Midge Mackenzie, ed., *Shoulder to Shoulder: A Documentary* (New York: Alfred A. Knopf, 1975).

14. Rosen, 58–107, 118–21.

15. Stevens-Belmont Memoir, 1–3. A small band of American suffrage supporters had organized open air meetings and demonstrations as early as 1907 in New York. Dubois, 102–103.

16. Stevens-Belmont Memoir, 5.

17. Pugh, 217.

18. Pugh, 218–19.

19. Stevens-Belmont Memoir, 2.

20. Stevens-Belmont Memoir, 4.

21. Stevens-Belmont Memoir, 2.

22. Stevens-Belmont Memoir, 4.

23. "Mrs. Belmont, Suffragette," *New York Times,* June 1, 1909, p. 1; Stevens-Belmont Memoir, 4–5, quotation on p. 4.

24. Young-Belmont Memoir, 170.

25. "Active Suffragist Fight," *New York Times,* June 16, 1909, p. 5; Stevens-Belmont Memoir, 7.

26. Stevens-Belmont Memoir, 7–8; "Suffragettes at Newport," *New York Times,* Aug. 3, 1909, p. 6; "Lectures at Marble House," ibid., Aug. 8, 1909, p. 4. For extensive coverage of the events, see "Glories of Marble House Attract Many," ibid., Aug. 20, 1909, p. 7; "Suffragists Meet at Marble House," ibid., Aug. 25, 1909, pp. 1–2; "Winter Campaign in City for Suffrage," ibid., Aug. 29, 1909, p. 9. For criticism of the event, see "The Marble House Meeting," ibid., Aug. 26, 1909, p. 8.

27. "Suffragist Armory at Mrs. Belmont's," *New York Times,* Aug. 13, 1909, p. 7; "The Belmont Armory as a Suffragist Hall," ibid., Aug. 22, 1909, p. SM8.

28. Alva E. Belmont to Mrs. Harper, June 9, 1909, and Alva E. Belmont to Mrs. Harper, June 25, 1909, Field Papers; "To Have Suffrage Office," *New York Times,* Aug. 31, 1909, p. 1; "Luncheon for Suffragists," ibid., Sept. 14, 1909, p. 15; DuBois, 112; Harper, 5:276.

29. "Suffragist Armory at Mrs. Belmont's," *New York Times,* Aug. 13, 1909, p. 7.

30. "The Belmont Armory as a Suffragist Hall," ibid., Aug. 22, 1909, p. SM8.

31. Stevens-Belmont Memoir, 9–10; "Bannard Seeks to Calm Suffragists," *New York Times,* Oct. 10, 1909, p. 3.

32. "Kate Carew Asks Mrs. Belmont about the Baby and the Ballot," *New York World,* Dec. 12, 1909, p. E1. This is a theme that she returned to in 1912. See Mrs. O. H. P. Belmont, "A Son Loses Respect for His Mother the Day He Votes," *Chicago Sunday Tribune,* June 2, 1912, section 3, p. 1.

33. Mrs. Oliver H. P. Belmont, "Woman's Right to Govern Herself," *North American Review* 190 (Nov. 1909): 664–74, quotation on 665. She subsequently published the following articles: Mrs. Oliver H. P. Belmont, "Woman Suffrage As It Looks To-day," *Forum* 43 (March 1910): 264–68; Mrs. Oliver H. P. Belmont, "How Can Women Get the Suffrage," *Independent* 68 (March 31, 1910): 686–89; Mrs. O. H. P. Belmont, "Why I Am a Suffragist," *World To-Day* 21 (Oct. 1911): 1171–78; Mrs. O. H. P. Belmont, "The Liberation of Sex," *Hearst's Magazine* 23 (April 1913): 614–16.

34. Stevens-Belmont Memoir, 11.

35. For a more detailed discussion, see Philip S. Foner, *Women and the American Labor Movement* (New York: Free Press, 1979), 324–45; Meredith

Tax, *The Rising of the Women: Feminist Solidarity and Class Conflict, 1880–1917* (New York: Monthly Review Press, 1980), 205–240.

36. Geidel, 127.

37. Stevens-Belmont Memoir, 11–12. For discussion of her activities, see Geidel, 132–45; DuBois, 116–19. For newspaper coverage of her activities, see "Suffragists to Aid Girl Waist Strikers, *New York Times,* Dec. 2, 1909, p. 3; "Throng Cheers On the Girl Strikers," ibid., Dec. 6, 1909, p. 1; "More Funds for Strikers," ibid., Dec. 18, 1909, p. 9; "Mrs. Belmont Aids Arrested Strikers," ibid., Dec. 19, 1909, pp. 1, 2; "Police Break Up Strikers' Meeting," ibid., Dec. 22, 1909, p; 8; "More Aid for Girl Strikers," ibid., Dec. 29, 1909, p. 3; "The Rich Out to Aid Girl Waistmakers," ibid., Jan. 3, 1910, pp. 1, 2; "Plan to Call Out 3,000 More Strikers," ibid., Jan. 7, 1910, p. 6; "Mrs. Belmont Wants All-Woman Strike," ibid., Jan. 8, 1910, p. 5; "Mrs. Belmont Holds Stock in Union Shop," ibid., Jan. 25, 1910, p. 1; "Mrs. Belmont to Buy Only Union Waists," ibid., Feb. 8, 1910, p. 5.

38. "Suffragists to Aid Girl Waist Workers," *New York Times,* Dec. 2, 1909, p. 3; "Woman Socialists Rebuff Suffragists," ibid., Dec. 20, 1909, p. 5; Geidel, 144; Kathryn Kish Sklar, Thomas Dublin, and Diedre Doherty, "How Did the Perceived Threat of Socialism Shape the Relationship between Workers and Their Allies in the New York City Shirtwaist Strike, 1909–1910?" in *Women and Social Movements in the United States, 1600–2000,* ed. Kathryn Kish Sklar and Thomas Dublin. See documents 6, 7, 8, and 14. (Database accessed through Evans Library, Texas A&M University, accessed Feb. 12, 2008).

39. "Suffrage for Negresses," *New York Times,* Jan. 19, 1910, p. 5.

40. "Negro Women Join in Suffrage Fight," *New York Times,* Feb. 7, 1910, p. 4. For more on Fanny Garrison Villard, see Harriet Hyman Alonso, *Growing Up Abolitionist: The Story of the Garrison Children* (Amherst: University of Massachusetts Press, 2002).

41. "Settlement House for Suffragists," *New York Times,* Dec. 25, 1909, p. 1; "Mrs. Belmont's Club Opens," ibid., Jan. 13, 1910, p. 4; "Harlem Women Organize," ibid., Feb. 2, 1910, p. 18. She moved the facility in September. "Aids Colored Suffragettes," ibid., Sept. 28, 1910, p. 6.

42. Stevens-Belmont Memoir, 13–15. There were eleven in all—the Harlem League, the Wage Earners League, Negro Men and Women League, the East New York Branch, the Bronx Branch, the 14th Assembly District Club, the Brooklyn Physicians and Surgeons League, the New York Physicians and Surgeons League, the Trained Nurses League, the Artist League, and the Artists Musical League. She also established a branch office on Long Island near her Brookholt estate. "Mrs. Belmont's Club Opens," *New York Times,* Jan. 13, 1910, p. 4, lists the services to be provided. See also Geidel, 270–80.

43. "What Mrs. Belmont Has Done for Women," *New York Times,* March 9, 1910, pp. 1–2.

44. Geidel, 157–58.

45. "Mrs. Belmont Goes Abroad," *New York Times,* June 30, 1910, p. 3; Stevens-Belmont Memoir, 16. For more on Milholland, see Linda J. Lumsen,

*Inez: The Life and Times of Inez Milholland* (Bloomington: Indiana University Press, 2004).

46. "Chivalry Humbug, Says Mrs. Belmont," *New York Times,* July 12, 1910, p. 4.

47. Rosen, 136–37.

48. Stevens-Belmont Memoir, 17.

49. "Women Farmers Arrive," *New York Times,* March 5, 1911, p. 10; Geidel, 223–33.

50. The *New York Times,* for example, ran a story on how appreciative the farming students were and reported that Belmont had transported them all to Newport to introduce them to her friends there. "Farmerette Honors for Mrs. Belmont," *New York Times,* July 16, 1911, p. 9; "Mrs O. H. P. Belmont to Entertain Girl Farm Students of Hempstead at Her Newport Home," ibid., July 30, 1911, p. X5.

51. "Belmont's Lunch Moves," *New York Times,* Sept. 16, 1911, p. 12; "Suffragette Farm Untilled," ibid., April 24, 1912, p. 1.

52. Stevens-Belmont Memoir, 17–18; "Fair Miss Suffrage Waits on Strikers," *New York Times,* Nov. 26, 1911, p. 15.

53. Stevens-Belmont Memoir, 18. The press's practice of denigrating the appearance of woman's rights advocates dated back to the 1840s. See Sylvia D. Hoffert, *When Hens Crow: The Woman's Rights Movement in Antebellum America* (Bloomington: Indiana University Press, 1995), 97, 100–101.

54. Geidel, 273–74.

55. Fairfax, 101.

56. Geidel, 276–77, quotation on 277.

57. These articles appeared from April 28 to November 3, 1912.

58. Mrs. Oliver H. P. Belmont, "Do Not Let Women Vote—Slogan of Political Bosses," *Chicago Sunday Tribune,* July 14, 1912, section 2, [p. 3]; Mrs. Oliver H. P. Belmont, "Man Has Failed to Care for Women and Children," ibid., July 28, 1912, section 2, p. 3; Mrs. Oliver H. P. Belmont, "Men Will Forget the Rosenthal Murder, Women Will Remember It," ibid., Aug. 11, 1912, section 2, p. 7.

59. Mrs. Oliver H. P. Belmont, "We Have Gone Back to the Worship of the Golden Calf," *Chicago Sunday Tribune,* Sept. 29, 1912, section 8, p. 1.

60. Mrs. O. H. P. Belmont, "Why Women Need the Ballot," *Chicago Sunday Tribune,* May 12, 1912, Section 3, p. 1.

61. Mrs. O. H. P. Belmont, "How Suffrage Will Protect Women from Men Who 'Sow Wild Oats,'" *Chicago Sunday Tribune,* April 28, 1912, section 9, p. 1.

62. Mrs. O. H. P. Belmont, "Why I Am a Suffragist," *World To-Day,* Oct. 21, 1911, 1173–74; Mrs. O. H. P. Belmont, "How Votes for Women Will Improve Existing Conditions," *Chicago Sunday Tribune,* May 26, 1912, section 3, p. 1.

63. Mrs. Oliver H. P. Belmont, "In What Respect Do Women Differ from Slaves or Serfs?" *Chicago Sunday Tribune,* June 16, 1912, section 3, p. 1; Mrs. Oliver H. P. Belmont, "In Non-Voting States Women Are Classed with Lunatics," ibid., July 21, 1912, section 2, p. 3.

64. Mrs. Oliver H. P. Belmont, "Women Suffragists Ask for Progressive Constitution," *Chicago Sunday Tribune*, July 7, 1912, section 3, p. 1; Mrs. Oliver H. P. Belmont, "How Shall the Market Basket of America's Poor Be Filled?" ibid., Aug. 25, 1912, section 8, p. 1.

65. Mrs. O. H. P. Belmont, "How Votes for Women Will Improve Existing Conditions," *Chicago Sunday Tribune*, May 26, 1912, section 3, p. 1.

66. Mrs. Oliver H. P. Belmont, "Woman's Suffrage Raises the Quality of the Electorate," *Chicago Sunday Tribune*, June 30, 1912, section 3, p. 1.

67. Mrs. Oliver H. P. Belmont, "A Girl? What a Pity It Was Not a Boy," *Chicago Sunday Tribune*, June 9, 1912, section 3, p. 1; Mrs. Oliver H. P. Belmont, "We Read Signposts along the Road that Leads to Votes for Women," ibid., Sept. 8, 1912, section 8, p. 1.

68. Mrs. Oliver H. P. Belmont, "We Must Not Be Made the Laughing Stock of the Voters," *Chicago Sunday Tribune*, Oct. 27, 1912, section 8, p. 5.

69. Mrs. Oliver H. P. Belmont, "We Have to Take What We Can in the Company It Comes," *Chicago Sunday Tribune*, Sept. 22, 1912, section 8, p. 1; Mrs. Oliver H. P. Belmont, "Equal Suffrage Not a National Question?" ibid., Nov. 3, 1912, section 8, p. 5.

70. "Suffrage Army Out on Parade," *New York Times*, May 5, 1912, p. 1.

71. Balsan, 215.

72. Fairfax, 187.

73. "Newport Suffrage Quarters Opened," *New York Times*, July 19, 1912, p. 9.

74. "Strike to Have Aid of Mrs. Belmont," *New York Times*, Dec. 29, 1912, p. 10; "Women Rush Theatre, Despite Police Clubs," *New York Tribune*, Jan. 6, 1913, p. 14; "Women in Strike, Riot, Rout Police," *New York Tribune*, Jan. 7, 1913, pp. 1, 6; "Riot? Riot?—Mrs. Belmont," *New York Tribune*, Jan. 7, 1913, p. 6. For more on this strike, see Rose Schneiderman with Lucy Goldthwaite, *All for One* (New York: Paul S. Eriksson, 1967), 107–108.

75. "Suggest Remedies to Graft Inquirers," *New York Times*, March 6, 1913, p. 3.

76. Balsan, 216–17.

77. Stevens-Belmont Memoir, 20; "Women Must Fight, Says Mrs. Belmont," *New York Times*, April 22, 1913, p. 3.

78. Parliament dissolved on Nov. 28, 1910. Rosen, 138.

79. Rosen, 154, 183–84.

80. Rosen, 189.

81. Rosen, 192–93.

82. Stevens-Belmont Memoir, 20–21.

83. "Mrs. Belmont Calls Englishmen Brutes," *New York Times*, April 30, 1913, p. 3.

84. Rosen, 159.

85. Stevens-Belmont Memoir, 22–23.

86. Geidel, 379–81.

87. Stevens-Belmont Memoir, 23.

88. Stevens-Belmont Memoir, 23.

89. "Mrs. O. H. P. Belmont among Militants," *New York Times,* Sept. 19, 1913, p. 9.

90. Stevens-Belmont Memoir, 25.

91. "Mrs. O. H. P. Belmont among Militants," *New York Times,* Sept. 19, 1913, p. 9.

92. "Put on Daring Play to Upset Old Laws," *New York Times,* Sept. 29, 1913, p. 1.

93. "Police Confiscate White Slave Films," *New York Times,* Dec. 21, 1913, p. 5.

94. "Mrs. Pankhurst Is Barred Out," *New York Times,* Oct. 19, 1913, p. 1; "Wilson Takes Up Pankhurst Case," *New York Times,* Oct. 20, 1913, p. 1.

95. "What Will New York Do with Mrs. Pankhurst?" *New York Times,* Sept. 14, 1913, p. SM6.

96. Stevens-Belmont Memoir, 24–25.

97. Carroll Smith-Rosenberg, "The New Woman as Androgyne: Social Disorder and Gender Crisis, 1870–1936," in *Disorderly Conduct: Visions of Gender in Victorian America* (New York: Oxford University Press, 1985), 245–96.

98. Susan Ware, ed., *Notable American Women: A Biographical Dictionary Completing the Twentieth Century* (Cambridge, Mass.: Harvard University Press, 2004), 500–502; Katherine H. Adams and Michael L. Keene, *Alice Paul and the American Suffrage Campaign* (Urbana: University of Illinois Press, 2008), 1–20.

99. Stevens-Belmont Memoir, 24.

100. Inez Hayes [Irwin] Gilmore, *The Story of Alice Paul and the National Woman's Party* (Fairfax, Va.: Denlinger's, 1977), 14; Doris Stevens, *Jailed for Freedom,* (New York: Boni and Liveright, 1920), 10, 16.

101. Sarah Bard Field quoting Mabel Vernon in Field Interview, 249; "Chronology—Mabel Vernon," xviii, in Amelia Fry, "Speaker for Suffrage and Petitioner for Peace: An Interview by Amelia Fry," Suffragists Oral History Project, Regional Oral History Office, Bancroft Library, University of California—Berkeley, Berkeley, Calif., http://bancroft.berkeley.edu/ROHO/projects/suffragist/ (accessed April 24, 2008).

102. Field Interview, 302, 317.

103. Stevens, *Jailed,* 10–11, 12, 14; Fairfax, 184; Field Interview, 303.

104. Geidel, 438.

105. Sarah J. Moore, "Making a Spectacle of Suffrage: The National Woman Suffrage Pageant, 1913," *Journal of American Culture* 20 (1997): 89–103; Linda G. Ford, *Iron-Jawed Angels: The Suffrage Militancy of the National Woman's Party, 1912–1919* (Lanham, Md.: University Press of America, 1991), 46, 48; Christine A. Lunardini, *From Equal Suffrage to Equal Rights: Alice Paul and the National Woman's Party, 1910–1928* (New York: New York University Press, 1986), 25–31; Kimberly Jensen, *Mobilizing Minerva: American Women in the*

*First World War* (Urbana: University of Illinois Press, 2008), 1–10; Adams and Keene, 76–98; "File [CU] Annual Report, [1913]," Reel 87, Frame 8, *National Women's Party Papers, Part II: The Suffrage Years, 1913–1920* (Bethesda, Md.: University Press of America, 1981) (hereafter cited as *NWP Papers*).

106. Caroline I. Reilly to Miss [Lucy] Burns, January 28, 1913, Reel 1, Frame 493, *NWP Papers.*

107. Reilly to Burns, January 30, 1913, Reel 1, Frames 563–64, and Reilly to Burns, February 10, 1913, Reel 1, Frame 859, *NWP Papers.*

108. Handwritten note at the bottom of Reilly to Burns, January 30, 1913, Reel 1, Frames 563–64, *NWP Papers.*

109. Engraved Invitation, Reel 2, Frame 77, *NWP Papers.*

110. Alva E. Belmont to Glenna Smith Tinnen, Feb. 15, 1913, Reel 1, Frame 1042, *NWP Papers.*

111. Lisa Tetrault, "The Incorporation of American Feminism: Suffragists and the Postbellum Lyceum," *Journal of American History* 96 (2010): 1027–1056.

112. Ruth Crocker, *Mrs. Russell Sage: Women's Activism and Philanthropy in Gilded Age and Progressive Era America* (Bloomington: Indiana University Press, 2006); Kathleen Waters Sander, *Mary Elizabeth Garrett: Society and Philanthropy in the Gilded Age* (Baltimore, Md.: Johns Hopkins University Press, 2008); Dubois, *Blatch.*

113. "Oliver Hazard Perry Belmont," *Biographical Dictionary of the United States Congress,* http://bioguide.congress.gov (accessed Sept. 18, 2009).

114. Mary Ritter Beard to Alice Paul, Feb. 4, [1914], Reel 7, Frames 506–507, *NWP Papers.*

115. For examples of that bickering, see Geidel, 86–98, 175–83, 194–95, 203–207, 212–14, 242–56, 324–30.

116. This had been a problem from the beginning. Alva was prone to take umbrage when her ideas and suggestions were ignored. See "Mrs. Belmont Quits Bazaar," *New York Times,* Dec. 24, 1910, p. 16.

117. Harper, 5:381; Stevens-Belmont Memoir, 24–25.

118. Dubois, 187.

119. Anna Howard Shaw to the president and Executive Council, [Jan. 1914], Reel 7, Frames 438–440, *NWP Papers;* Ida Husted Harper, ed., *The History of Woman Suffrage,* vol. 5 (New York: National American Woman Suffrage Association, 1922), 5:380–81.

120. Harper, 5:675; Ford, 49; Lunardini, 22.

121. Mary Beard to Lucy Burns, Jan. 9, [1914], Reel 6, Frames 1173–74, *NWP Papers.*

122. Crystal Eastman Benedict to Alice Paul, [Jan. 1914], Reel 7, Frame 442, *NWP Papers.* See also Lucy Burns to Alice Paul, Jan. 15, 1914, Reel 6, Frame 1306, ibid.

123. Paul Interview, 321.

124. Crystal [Eastman Benedict] to Lucy [Burns], Jan. 9, [1914], Reel 6, Frames 1156–58, *NWP Papers.*

125. Mary Beard to Lucy Burns, Jan. 9, [1914], Reel 6, Frames 1173–74, NWP *Papers*.

126. Mary Beard to Lucy Burns, Jan. 18, [1914], Reel 7, Frames 49–50, NWP *Papers*.

127. Gail L. Kroepel, "Nettie Fowler McCormick: Her Philanthropy at Tusculum College," *American Educational History Journal* 30 (2003): 125–33, quotation on 127–28. For more on McCormick, see Charles O. Burgess, *Nettie Fowler McCormick: Profile of an American Philanthropist* (Madison: State Historical Society of Wisconsin, 1962).

128. Tax, 113, 115; Diane Kirkby, *Alice Henry: The Power of Pen and Voice: The Life of an Australian-American Labor Reformer* (New York: Cambridge University Press, 1991), 110, 121.

129. Elizabeth Payne, *Reform, Labor, and Feminism: Margaret Drier Robins and the Women's Trade Union League* (Urbana: University of Illinois Press, 1988), 71; quotation in Tax, 115–116.

130. Sander, 2, 160–90.

131. KHH [Katharine Houghton Hepburn] to Alice Paul, Jan. 15, 1914, Reel 6, Frame 1301, NWP *Papers*. Doris Stevens testified later that Hepburn's concern was well founded. Belmont, she noted, "never took part in anything she did not want to direct" and her "desire to run things" often created "antagonism" within the ranks of whatever organization she was involved with. Stevens Deposition, pp. 2–3.

132. KHH to Pid [Edith Houghton Hooker], Jan 15, 1914, Reel 6, Frame 1290, NWP *Papers*.

133. KHH to Pid, Jan. 15, 1914.

134. Mary Beard to L[ucy] B[urns], March 15, [1914], Reel 8, Frame 558, NWP *Papers*.

135. Stevens-Belmont Memoir, 5.

136. Quoted in Geidel, 113.

137. The treasurer's report that appeared in the Aug. 14, 1915, issue of the *Suffragist* on p. 8 illustrates the point. The small amount of individual donations continued throughout the campaign. See, for example, the "Treasurer's Reports," *Suffragist*, Dec. 28, 1918, p. 11; ibid., Sept. 20, 1919, p. 12.

138. For a particularly graphic description of the problem, see Rebecca Hourwich, "Money, Money Everywhere and Not a Cent to Spend." *Equal Rights*, March 27, 1926, p. 51.

139. Quoted in Geidel, 88. Upton was treasurer of NAWSA from 1894 to 1910 and ran NAWSA's headquarters from 1903 to 1909. Margaret Finnegan, *Selling Suffrage: Consumer Culture and Votes for Women* (New York: Columbia University Press, 1999), 15.

140. Stevens Deposition, p. 3.

141. Alice Paul to Mary Beard, Jan. 9, 1914, Reel 6, Frame 1175, NWP *Papers*.

142. Stevens-Belmont Memoir, 25. Stevens also acknowledged that Belmont "came with that clear understanding" that she would join the inner circle. Stevens Deposition, p. 3.

143. "Our New Committee Member," *Suffragist*, Feb. 21, 1914, 3.

144. Quoted in Geidel, 457.

145. Alva E. Belmont to Lucy Burns, Feb. 20, 1914, Reel 7, Frame 875, Alice Paul to Mrs. O. H. P. Belmont, March 23, 1914, Reel 8, Frame 821, and Caroline Reilly to [Lucy] Burns, Jan. 31, 1914, Reel 7, Frame 419, all in NWP *Papers*.

146. Treasurer's report and list of contributors in the annual report of the Congressional Union for Woman Suffrage for the Year 1914, Reel 87, Frames 77–82, NWP *Papers*.

147. "An Estimable Leader," *Washington Post*, Feb. 24, 1914, p. 6.

148. Armond Fields, *Katharine Dexter McCormick: Pioneer for Women's Rights* (Westport, Conn.: Praeger, 2003), 76, 101, 103, 107–108, 117; Madeleine B. Stern, *Purple Passage: The Life of Mrs. Frank Leslie* (Norman: University of Oklahoma Press, 1953), 182; Harper, 5:755.

149. Geidel, 103, note 37.

150. Geidel, 173–74. An increase in attention from New York papers was particularly impressive. In a survey of sixteen New York newspapers published in the five months before their 1910 convention, Harper's staff counted 3000 articles on the subject of suffrage.

151. Mary Beard to Alice Paul, January 3, [1913?], Reel 1, Frame 87, NWP *Papers*.

152. Caroline Reilly to [Lucy] Burns, Jan. 31, 1914, Reel 7, Frame 419, NWP *Papers*.

153. CIR [Caroline I. Reilly] to [Mary] Beard, no date [Feb. 1914], Reel 86, Frame 790, NWP *Papers*.

154. The text of the amendment can be found in Harper, 5:416.

155. The most complete discussion of the controversy surrounding the Shafroth-Palmer amendment can be found in Geidel, 472–84.

156. "Mrs. Belmont's Wire Stirs Suffragists," *New York Times*, March 8, 1914, p. C5; "Mrs. Belmont's Telegram," *Suffragist*, March 14, 1914, p. 5.

157. Geidel, 484.

158. Paul E. Fuller, *Laura Clay and the Woman's Rights Movement* (Lexington: University of Kentucky Press, 1975), 141–42. According to Ida Husted Harper, the NAWSA refused to support the SSWS financially. Harper, 5:672.

159. Harper, 5:672.

160. Lucy Burns to Alice Paul, Feb. 23, 1914, Reel 7, Frames 908–915, Alva E. Belmont to Lucy Burns, Feb. 27, 1914, Reel 7, Frame 1078, and Mrs. Oliver H. P. Belmont to Mrs. Sharp, Feb. 27, 1914, Reel 7, Frame 1078, all in NWP *Papers*; "Mrs. Belmont Cordially Greeted Here in Society and Woman's Suffrage Circles," *Washington Post*, April 16, 1914, p. 4; "Suffrage Ball Is Gay," *Washington Post*, April 22, 1914, p. 2.

161. Geidel, 494.

162. Doris Stevens, "General Statement," [2–3], Folder 292, Box 9, Stevens Papers; Stevens Deposition, 4–10.

163. "Mrs. H. Oelrichs Balks Camera Man," *New York Times*, July 8, 1914, p. 9; "Duchess Makes Plea to Newport Throng," ibid., July 9, 1914, p. 7; Balsan, 217–18; Geidel, 504–510.

164. Schneiderman, 123–24.

165. Mary Beard to Alice Paul, Aug. 15 [1914], in *A Woman Making History: Mary Ritter Beard through Her Letters,* ed. Nancy F. Cott (New Haven, Conn.: Yale University Press, 1991), p. 79.

166. Mary Beard to Alice Paul, Aug. 21, [1914] in Cott, *Woman Making History,* 79–80.

167. "Suffragists Vote to Oppose New Bill," *New York Times,* Aug. 30, 1914, p. 13; "Women in Council on Suffrage Fight Warn Politicians," *New York World,* Aug. 30, 1914, p. 12.

168. "War Threat by Suffrage Chiefs to Democrats," *New York World,* Aug. 31, 1914, p. 7; Stevens, *Jailed,* 30–31, 33–34; Paul Interview, 331.

169. Geidel, 523.

170. "Mrs. Belmont to Open Soup House," *New York Press,* Dec. 30, 1914, p. 5.

171. "Women Besiege Soup Kitchen," *New York Press,* Jan. 31, 1915, p. 9; "Mrs. Belmont Gives Needy Women Clothing," ibid., Feb. 7, 1915, p. 9.

172. Dubois, 184. The states were Wyoming, Utah, Colorado, Idaho, Washington, California, Oregon, Montana, Kansas, Arizona, and Nevada.

173. "Suffragists Harry President's Guards," *New York Times,* May 18, 1915, p. 8.

174. "Ask Suffragettes to Drop New York" and "Answers Mrs. Belmont," *New York Times,* May 23, 1915, C4. On the New York referendum campaign, see Dubois, 148–81.

175. "Women Host on March," *Washington Post,* Dec. 5, 1915, p. 11; "March for Suffrage," ibid., Dec. 6, 1915, pp. 1, 4.

176. The CU placed display ads in the *Washington Post* on Dec. 2, 1915, p. 16, Dec. 3, 1915, p. 7, Dec. 4, 1915, p. 3, Dec. 5, 1915, p. E14, and Dec. 6, 1915, p. 12; "Vote Plea Scene Gay," *Washington Post,* Dec. 7, 1915, pp. 1, 3.

177. "Clash of Suffragists," *Washington Post,* Dec. 8, 1915, p. 2.

178. "Women Envoys Guests," *Washington Post,* Dec. 8, 1915, p. 11.

179. Geidel, 600. Havermeyer was a wealthy New York art collector whose husband was in the sugar business. Dubois, 111, 200. Rogers was the sister-in law of Henry L. Stimson. Dubois, 120, 189. Brannan was the daughter of newspaper editor Charles Dana and the wife of John Brannan, head of the board of trustees at Bellevue Hospital. Dubois, 119, 189.

180. "Suffrage Opera Tonight," *New York Times,* Feb. 18, 1916, p. 11; "Society Satirized in Suffrage Opera," ibid., Feb. 19, 1918, p. 11; "Suffrage Operetta Gives Cause $8000," ibid., Feb. 20, 1916, p. 15; "Suffrage Opera Scores Immediate Success," *Suffragist,* Feb. 26, 1916, p. 6. For the libretto of the opera, see "Melinda and Her Sisters," in *On To Victory: Propaganda Plays of the Woman Suffrage Movement,* ed. Bettina Friedl (Boston: Northeastern University Press, 1987), 343–61.

181. Geidel, 612–16.

182. "Finance," *Suffragist,* Jan. 10, 1917, p. 8, announced that the CU raised over $111,000 in 1916. "Suffragists Will Picket White House," *New York Times,*

Jan. 10, 1917, p. 1; "Picket White House," *Washington Post,* 10 Jan. 10, 1917, pp. 1, 3. For the most recent discussion of that campaign, see Adams and Keene, 157–90.

183. "Picket Line of 3,000," *Washington Post,* Jan. 11, 1917, pp. 1, 5; "President Ignores Suffrage Pickets," *New York Times,* Jan. 11, 1917, p. 13.

184. "President Ignores Suffrage Pickets," *New York Times,* Jan 11, 1917, p. 13.

185. "Suffragists Will Picket White House," *New York Times,* Jan. 10, 1917, p. 1.

186. Geidel, 621; "Suffragists Pledge to Aid the Nation," *New York Times,* Feb. 26, 1917, p. 8; Field Interview, 374.

187. *New York World,* Feb. 26, 1917, p. 1.

188. "Wilson Shocked at Jailing Militants," *New York Times,* July 19, 1917, pp. 1–2; "Militants to Picket Today," ibid., July 23, 1917, p. 9; Geidel, 628; Stevens, *Jailed,* 355–56, 361, 364.

189. Stevens, *Jailed,* 108–109.

190. "Excuses for White House Picketing," *New York Times,* July 9, 1917, p. 7; "Pickets Defended by Mrs. Belmont," *New York World,* July 9, 1917, p. 9.

## 4. IMMORTALIZING THE LADY IN AFFECTING PROSE

1. Eakin, 5.

2. "Hints for Mothers from Mrs. Belmont," *New York Times,* Oct. 21, 1909, p. 9; "Mrs. Belmont Sees Danger," ibid., July 14, 1912, p. 11; "Prominent Women Stand by Wilson," ibid., May 15, 1915, p. 4. See Linda H. Peterson, "Audience and the Autobiographer's Art: An Approach to the Autobiography of Mrs. M. O. W. Oliphant," in *Approaches to Victorian Autobiography,* ed. George P. Landow (Athens: Ohio University Press, 1979), 171, for a discussion about the uses of autobiographical incidents and anecdotes as a way to satisfy public interest in the lives of prominent people.

3. See Barros, *Autobiography: Narrative of Transformation,* for a discussion of autobiography as a description of personal transformation.

4. Sara Bard Field to Charles Erskine Scott Wood, [Aug. 15, 1915], Field Papers.

5. Field knew both Stevens and Belmont, having met and worked with them organizing woman's rights activities at the Panama-Pacific Exposition held in San Francisco in the summer of 1915. Stevens stayed with Field while she set up a suffrage booth in the Educational Building on the fairgrounds, recruited members for the CU, and engaged in fund-raising activities. Belmont made a special trip to the West Coast to participate in the suffrage festivities held at the exposition. Field Interview, 287–88, 294, 300, 301, 368.

6. Field to Wood, [Aug. 15, 1915].

7. Catherine M. Scholten, "Sara Bard Field: Her Place in History," xii–xiv, and Sara Bard Field Chronology, xv–xviii, both in the introduction to Field Interview; Field Interview, 204, 221, 246–249, 287; Glenda Riley, "Sara Bard

Field, Charles Erskine Scott Wood, and the Phenomenon of Migratory Divorce," *California History* 69 (1990): 251–59.

8. Field to Wood, [Aug. 15, 1915 and Aug. 16, 1915]; Field Interview, 288, 369.
9. Field to Wood, Aug. 21, 1915.
10. Field to Wood, July 27, 1917.
11. Field to Wood, Aug. 21, 1915.
12. Field to Wood, Dec. 18, [1915].
13. Field to Wood, Jan. 19, [1916].
14. Field to Wood, Jan. 22, [1916]; Field Interview, 373.
15. Alva E. Belmont to Field, June 13, 1917, Field Papers.
16. Belmont to Field, [July 2, 1917], Field papers.
17. Field-Belmont Memoir, [35a], Field Papers.
18. Field Notes, [67–69], quotations on [41] and [76], Field Papers.
19. When the United States declared war on Germany on April 6, 1917, Field allied herself with Eastman, Reed, and Beard to help establish the short-lived People's Council of America for Democracy and Peace. Organized in May, the group was disintegrating by December. C. Roland Marchand, *The American Peace Movement and Social Reform, 1898–1918* (Princeton, N.J.: Princeton University Press, 1973), 266, 295–96, 321.
20. For more on "new women," see June Sochen, *The New Woman: Feminism in Greenwich Village, 1910–1920* (New York: Quadrangle Books, 1972); Smith-Rosenberg, 245–96; Patricia Marks, *Bicycles, Bangs, and Bloomers: The New Woman in the Popular Press* (Lexington: University Press of Kentucky, 1990); Martha H. Patterson, *Beyond the Gibson Girl: Reimagining the American New Woman, 1895–1915* (Urbana: University of Illinois Press, 2005); Lois Palken Rudnick, *Mabel Dodge Luhan: New Woman, New Worlds* (Albuquerque: University of New Mexico Press, 1984); Ruth Bordin, *Alice Freeman Palmer: The Evolution of a New Woman* (Ann Arbor: University of Michigan Press, 1993); Judith N. McArthur, *Creating the New Woman: The Rise of Southern Women's Progressive Culture in Texas, 1893–1918* (Urbana: University of Illinois Press, 1998).
21. Field to Wood, [Nov. 21, 1917].
22. Field to Wood, [August 15, 1915] and Field to Wood, July 29, 1917.
23. Field to Wood, July 29, 1917.
24. Field to Wood, Aug. 16, [1917].
25. Field to Wood, July 27, 1917.
26. Field to Wood, Aug. 14, [1917].
27. Field to Wood, Aug. 15 [1917].
28. Field to Wood, Aug. 24 [1917].
29. Field to Wood, July 27, 1917.
30. Kathryn Hughes, *The Victorian Governess* (London: Hambledon Press, 1993); Mary Poovey, "The Anathematized Race: The Governess and Jane Eyre," in *Uneven Developments: The Ideological Work of Gender in Mid-Victorian England* (Chicago: University of Chicago Press, 1988), 126–63; Teresa McBride, "'As the Twig Is Bent': The Victorian Nanny," in *The Victorian Family: Structure*

*and Stresses,* ed. Anthony S. Wohl (New York: St. Martin's Press, 1978), 44–58; M. Jeanne Peterson, "The Victorian Governess: Status Incongruence in Family and Society," *Victorian Studies* 14 (1970): 7–26.

31. The demands made on them were similar to private secretaries in the business world. See Margery W. Davies, *Woman's Place Is at the Typewriter: Office Work and Office Workers, 1870–1930* (Philadelphia: Temple University Press, 1982), 129–62. For other discussions of office workers, see Ileen A. DeVault, *Sons and Daughters of Labor: Class and Clerical Work in Turn-of-the-Century Pittsburgh* (Ithaca, N.Y.: Cornell University Press, 1990); Sharon Hartman Strom, *Beyond the Typewriter: Gender, Class, and the Origins of Modern Office Work, 1900–1930* (Urbana: University of Illinois Press, 1992); Jerome P. Bjelopera, *City of Clerks: Office and Sales Workers in Philadelphia, 1870–1920* (Urbana: University of Illinois Press, 2005); Cindy Sondik Aron, *Ladies and Gentlemen of the Civil Service: Middle-Class Workers in Victorian America* (New York: Oxford University Press, 1987).

32. Employers used these strategies on other domestic servants as well. See David M. Katzman, *Seven Days a Week: Women and Domestic Service in Industrializing America* (New York: Oxford University Press, 1978), 146–83, 188; and Judith Rollins, *Between Women: Domestics and Their Employers* (Philadelphia: Temple University Press, 1985), 155–203. For a discussion of such relationships in the nineteenth century, see Faye E. Dudden, *Serving Women: Household Service in Nineteenth-Century America* (Middletown, Conn.: Wesleyan University Press, 1983).

33. For more on private secretaries who also served as companions, see Sylvia D. Hoffert, "Private Secretaries in Early Twentieth-Century America," *Labor: Studies in Working Class History in the Americas* 7 (2010): 45–65.

34. Field Interview, 370.

35. Field Interview, 370.

36. Field to Wood, July 29, 1917.

37. Field to Wood, July 31, 1917.

38. Field to Wood, July 27, [1917]

39. Field to Wood, July 29, [1917].

40. Field to Wood, July 27, 1917 and July 29, [1917]; Field to Wood, July 31, 1917; Field to Wood, Aug. 2, 1917.

41. Field to Wood, July 31, 1917; Field to Wood, Aug. 2, 1917.

42. Field to Wood, Aug. 16, 1917.

43. Field to Wood, Aug. 2, 1917.

44. Field to Wood, Aug. 4, 1917.

45. Field to Wood, Aug. 6, 1917.

46. Field to Wood, July 29, 1917. For some reason Field believed that Belmont had first married at the age of seventeen. Belmont was twenty-two when she married.

47. Field Interview, 372; Field to Wood, July 25, [1917].

48. Field to Wood, July 29, 1917.

49. Field Interview, 370.
50. Field to Wood, Aug. 13 [1917].
51. Field to Wood, July 29, 1917.
52. Field to Wood, Aug. 13, [1917].
53. Field Interview, 370–71.
54. Field to Wood, July 31, 1917.
55. Stuart, 370–71.
56. Field to Wood, Aug. 2, [1917].
57. Field to Wood, Aug. 13, [1917] and Field to Wood, Aug. 16, [1917].
58. Field Interview, 371.
59. Field Interview, 370.
60. Field Interview, 371–72.
61. Field to Wood, July 27, [1917] and July 29, 1917.
62. Field to Wood, July 27, 1917.
63. Field to Wood, Aug. 14, [1917].
64. Field to Wood, Aug. 8, [1917].
65. Penny Summerfield, "Dis/composing the Subject: Intersubjectivities in Oral History," in *Feminism and Autobiography: Texts, Theories, Methods*, ed. Tess Cosslett, Celia Lury, and Penny Summerfield (London: Routledge, 2000), 102.
66. Her notes read like those of a student whose goal is to write down some of what she hears in order to prompt memory of what is "important," that which resonates or connects with previous knowledge or experience either by confirming or challenging its accuracy or legitimacy.
67. Field-Belmont Memoir, 57–67, discusses Alva's divorce.
68. Field Notes, [5–8].
69. Field to Wood, Aug. 15, [1917]
70. Field Notes, [8].
71. Field-Belmont Memoir, 61.
72. Field-Belmont Memoir, 65.
73. Field Notes, [7].
74. Field-Belmont Memoir, 63.
75. Field-Belmont Memoir, 68–77, discusses Alva's travel experiences.
76. Field to Wood, Aug. 15, [1917].
77. Field-Belmont Memoir, 69–70, 73–74, 75–76.
78. Field-Belmont Memoir, 72; Field Notes, [16].
79. Field-Belmont Memoir, 71–72. Visiting the Oracle at Delphi prompted similar feminist reflection on Alva's part. She remembered being particularly impressed by the fact the oracle was a woman and that "every class came to consult her," a practice that had the potential for giving at least one woman considerable political power. See also Field Notes, [17–19].
80. Field-Belmont Memoir, 36–47, discusses Alva's interest in architecture.
81. Field Notes, [126].

82. Field-Belmont Memoir, 43.

83. Field Notes, [81].

84. Field-Belmont Memoir, [78–91], discusses Consuelo's wedding.

85. Field-Belmont Memoir, [78]

86. Field-Belmont Memoir, [78]-[79]

87. Alva E. Belmont, [untitled essay on marriage and divorce], Field Papers.

88. Field Notes, [9].

89. Belmont, [essay on marriage and divorce]. Belmont clearly discussed this issue with Field, see Field Notes, [70–72].

90. Field-Belmont Memoir, [78–79]

91. Field to Wood, Jan. 19, [1916]. Belmont apparently had expressed the concern that Field might come to work with her and then leave because she was homesick for her children.

92. Field-Belmont Memoir, 48–56, discusses Alva's attitude toward motherhood.

93. Field-Belmont Memoir, 49.

94. Field Notes, [108–109].

95. Field-Belmont Memoir, 48–48 ½.

96. Field-Belmont Memoir, 65.

97. Field-Belmont Memoir, 49–50.

98. Field-Belmont Memoir, 51–52.

99. Field-Belmont Memoir, 50. For a discussion of the use of such evocative metaphoric language in autobiography, see Wallach, 41–44.

100. Dubois, 67; Charlotte Perkins Gilman, *The Living of Charlotte Perkins Gilman: An Autobiography* (Madison: University of Wisconsin Press, 1990), 162–63.

101. Field-Belmont Memoir, 13.

102. Field Interview, 372–73.

103. Field to Wood, July 29, 1917.

104. Field to Wood, July 31, 1917.

105. Field to Wood, July 31, 1917. In this letter, Field commented that she should have charged Belmont at least a thousand dollars and expenses a month. This statement is puzzling since she remembered having earned $2000 for the summer. See Field Interview, 373.

106. Field to Wood, July 31, 1917.

107. Field to Wood, Aug. 16, [1917].

108. Field to Wood, (sometime after Aug. 28, 1917).

109. Belmont to Field, Nov. 16, 1917, Field Papers.

110. Field to Wood, Aug. 2, 1917.

111. Field to Wood, Aug. 27, [1917].

112. Belmont to Field, Nov. 16, 1917 and Field to Wood, [Nov. 21, 1917], Field Papers.

113. Field to Wood, [Nov. 21, 1917].

114. Field to Wood, (sometime after Aug. 28, 1917).

115. Belmont to Field, Feb. 14, 1918, Field Papers.

116. Belmont to Field, Oct. 4, 1918, Field Papers.

117. Albert died on October 12, 1918. See Field Chronology, xvii.

118. Belmont to Dear Friend, Jan. 5, 1919, Field Papers.

119. Field Interview, 373.

120. Brenda Ueland to Field, Feb. 19, 1925 and March 3, 1925, Field Papers.

121. Field Interview, 372–73.

122. Scholten, xiv.

123. Field Interview, [404–407].

124. She published two other books: *Barabbas* in 1932 and *Darkling Plain* in 1936.

125. Riley, 259.

126. Field Chronology, xviii.

## 5. BELMONT'S ORPHAN CHILD

1. In 1916 at the CU convention in Chicago, enfranchised members of the CU formed a sister organization called the Woman's Party to campaign against Democrats in states that had already granted women the right to vote. The CU and the Woman's Party merged in early 1917. The name of new organization was the National Woman's Party. Ford, 131, 133; Dubois, 203. For a more detailed account, see Lunardini, *Equal Suffrage to Equal Rights;* Nancy F. Cott, *The Grounding of Modern Feminism* (New Haven, Conn.: Yale University Press, 1987), 53–81. For examples of Belmont's moral support, see "Attack on Wilson," *New York Times,* Sept. 12, 1917, p. 9; "Protest for Pickets Sent to President," ibid., Nov. 10, 1917, p. 3.

2. Paul Interview, 209, 346–47.

3. "New Suffrage Drive Planned by Women," *New York Times,* Nov. 7, 1917, p. 3; "Suffrage Fight Won in Cities," ibid., Nov. 8, 1917, pp. 1, 3.

4. "Serpent's Tooth Nothing to Her Suffrage Child," *New York World,* Nov. 13, 1917, p. 22.

5. It passed in January 1918. Geidel, 641.

6. Geidel, 673 note 95.

7. Geidel, 643–44.

8. "Mrs. Belmont Gives Her Suffrage Shop to Salvation Army," *New York Tribune,* Dec. 10, 1918, p. 9; "Office-Home for Soldiers," *New York Times,* Nov. 25, 1918, p. 8.

9. Geidel, 649.

10. "Her Pressure on Congress," *New York Times,* March 2, 1919, p. 71; "'Pressure' For Suffrage," ibid., May 25, 1919, p. 77.

11. Thomas R. Marshall, *Recollections of Thomas R. Marshall* (Indianapolis: Bobbs-Merrill, 1925), 234.

12. "Duchess Made Plea for Reconciliation," *New York Times,* March 24, 1920, p. 9; Balsan, 235–36.

13. "Divorce Given to Duchess of Marlborough," *New York Tribune*, Nov. 10, 1920, p. 3. In July 1921, Consuelo married Jacques Balsan, the heir to a French textile fortune. Balsan, 239.

14. Mary Beard to Alice Paul, Feb. 4, [1914], Reel 7, Frames 506–507, *NWP Papers.*

15. Field Interview, 257.

16. J. Stanley Lemons, *The Woman Citizen: Social Feminism in the 1920s* (Urbana: University of Illinois Press, 1973), 50–52, 55–56.

17. Stevens Deposition, pp. 66–67.

18. Lunardini, 152–53; Paul Interview, 261.

19. "Women's Party to Call a Convention," *New York Times*, Sept. 11, 1920, p. 2; Stevens Deposition, 66–67, 73–74.

20. Stevens Deposition, 67.

21. Stevens Deposition, 78–79; Cott, *Grounding of Modern Feminism,* 67–72; Dubois, 221.

22. "Declaration of Principles," in Alva E. Belmont, "What the Woman's Party Wants," *Colliers* 70 (Dec. 23, 1922): 6.

23. Waldo Emerson Waltz, *The Nationality of Married Women: A Study of Domestic Policies and International Legislation* (Urbana: University of Illinois Press, 1937), 19, 20, 23–25, 35, 37; Candice Lewis Bredbenner, *A Nationality of Her Own: Women, Marriage, and the Law of Citizenship* (Berkeley: University of California Press, 1998), 5–6, 9, 15; Nancy F. Cott, "Marriage and Women's Citizenship in the United States, 1830–1934," *American Historical Review* 103 (1998): 1456, 1459, 1461. In 1804 the Code Napoleon declared that women who married Frenchmen became citizens. Parliament passed a similar law in 1844. See Cott, "Marriage and Citizenship," 1458, and Virginia Sapiro, "Women, Citizenship, and Nationality: Immigration and Naturalization Policies in the United States," *Politics and Society* 13 (1984): 6–7. For a recent discussion of citizenship and statelessness, see Linda K. Kerber, "The Stateless as the Citizen's Other: A View from the United States," *American Historical Review* 112 (2007): 1–34.

24. The duchess entered the United States without incident in 1902, 1905, 1908, and 1914. Balsan, 191, 217; Stuart, 256, 264, 290, 341, 343.

25. Stevens Deposition, 73–74.

26. Paul Interview, 256; Lunardini, 154–55; Nancy F. Cott, "Feminist Politics in the 1920s: The National Woman's Party," *Journal of American History* 71 (1984): 55, says that the debt was $12,000.

27. Paul Interview, 429.

28. Stevens married Dudley Field Malone in 1921. Stevens Deposition, 82. For more information on transatlantic marriage among the very rich, see Brandon; Gail MacColl and Carol M. Wallace, *To Marry an English Lord* (New York: Workman, 1989); Montgomery, *"Gilded Prostitution."*

29. Amy E. Butler, *Two Paths to Equality: Alice Paul and Ethel M. Smith in the ERA Debate, 1921–1929* (Albany: State University of New York Press, 2000), p. 61, says the organization had only 400 members. According to Geidel, the

only salaried NWP employee in 1921 was a stenographer; Geidel, 686. According to Nancy Cott, in April 1921, the newly organized NWP had only 151 members; Cott, "Feminist Politics," 55.

30. In 1922 Congress passed the Cable Act, which provided some protection for American women. But the citizenship of any woman who married a foreigner and lived in her husband's country for two years or any other foreign nation for five years remained unprotected. Cott, "Marriage and Women's Citizenship," 1464.

31. Susan D. Becker, *Origins of the Equal Rights Amendment: American Feminism between the Wars* (Westport, Conn.: Greenwood Press, 1981), 23.

32. Geidel, 683–84; Paul Interview, 404, 409–410.

33. "Miss Alice Paul Retires," *New York Times,* Feb. 20, 1921, p. 3; Stevens Deposition, 77; Becker, 18; "Council Accepts Equal Rights Bill," *Washington Post,* Oct. 3, 1921, p. 2. Paul became vice president; Geidel, 684.

34. "Treasurer's Report at Baltimore, Conference, May 11, 1926," *Equal Rights,* May 22, 1926, p. 120; Paul Interview, 259–60, 262–63, 383; "New Woman's Party Headquarters," *Equal Rights,* July 27, 1929, p. 195; "'Watch Tower' of Women Open," *Washington Post,* Aug. 14, 1921, p. 10.

35. Mrs. O. H. P. Belmont, "Women as Dictators," *Ladies Home Journal* 39 (Sept. 1922): 7.

36. The house was in Eze-sur-Mer, France. Stuart, 403.

37. It was not until 1926 that the NWP finally clarified who was supposed to run the day-to day-affairs of the organization. At their convention, they agreed that whoever served as chair of the National Committee would ultimately be responsible for those matters. Geidel, 705; Becker 16. For a discussion of the national chairmen who served from 1921 to 1939, see Becker, 32–36.

38. Account of Alice Paul with Mrs. Oliver H. P. Belmont, March 10, 1927, Box 32, Folder 412, Paul Papers; Stevens Deposition, 119–22.

39. The introduction to the Doris Stevens Papers at the Schlesinger Library says that she was born in 1892. Leila Rupp claims that according to Stevens's passport, she was born in 1888. See Leila J. Rupp, "Feminism and the Sexual Revolution in the Early Twentieth Century: The Case of Doris Stevens," *Feminist Studies* 15 (1989): 290, 306, note 3.

40. Mary Trigg, "'To Work Together for Ends Larger Than Self': The Feminist Struggles of Mary Beard and Doris Stevens in the 1930s," *Journal of Women's History* 7 (1995): 54–55; Rupp, "Feminism and the Sexual Revolution," 290–91.

41. Doris Stevens, General Statement, [2] Box 9, Folder 292, Stevens Papers.

42. Stevens Deposition, p. 2.

43. Stevens Deposition, pp. 3–5, 8, 13–14, 22. Belmont was chairperson of the convention, gave its opening speech, and donated one-third of the money to run the affair. Geidel, 578–79; Doris Stevens, General Statement, [5].

44. Stevens, General Statement, [1].

45. Stevens Deposition, 9–10, 18, 31, 62, 68; Stevens, General Statement, [3, 4, 6, 9, 10, 14].

46. Stevens Deposition, 2.

47. Stevens, General Statement, [8]; Stevens Deposition, 54–55.

48. Stevens Deposition, 56.

49. Stevens Deposition, 181.

50. Stevens, General Statement,[ 2].

51. Stevens, General Statement, [4].

52. Stevens Deposition, 56; see also Stevens, General Statement, [8].

53. Stevens, General Statement, [9–10].

54. It is unclear when she stopped being paid by the NWP. In her deposition she says that her salary stopped in mid-June, 1919. Stevens Deposition, 60, 82. NWP Executive Committee minutes indicate that it raised Stevens's salary to $125 in 1918. In 1920, the committee raised it from $200 to $300. See Minutes of the National Executive Committee, National Woman's Party, March 5, 1917, Reel 87, Frame 378; April 12, 1918, Reel 87, Frame 426; and May 14, 1920, Reel 87, Frame 457, all in *NWP Papers.*

55. Stevens Deposition, 63.

56. The twenty-five-page manuscript is undated. However, on p. 18, Stevens writing for Belmont referred to having been forced to turn over her New York headquarters to the Salvation Army "last year." Belmont did this in December 1918. "Mrs. Belmont Gives Her Suffrage Shop to Salvation Army," *New York Tribune,* Dec. 10, 1918, p. 9. Indication that Belmont intended there to be a series of articles on her activities is suggested by the reference at the end of p. 25: "In my next article I shall tell you how we even gave the government practically three more years of peaceful persuasion without results, before resorting to American militancy."

57. Stevens-Belmont Memoir, Box 9, Folder 291, Stevens Papers.

58. Stevens Deposition, 67.

59. Stevens, *Jailed,* 158.

60. Dudley Field Malone, "The Protest of Dudley Field Malone," *Suffragist,* Sept. 15, 1917, pp. 7, 9.

61. "Some Men Who Helped," *Suffragist,* July 12, 1919, p. 9; Stevens, *Jailed,* 159.

62. Helen to Dear Mother, Nov. 13, 1917, Box 17, Folder 252, Paul Papers.

63. Geidel claims this was the case. See Geidel, 613.

64. Sara Bard Field to Charles Erskine Scott Wood, Aug. 27, [1917], Field Papers.

65. "Social Notes," *New York Times,* July 8, 1920, p. 10.

66. Belmont to Stevens [Dec. 1920], Box 8, Folder 269, Stevens Papers.

67. "Hardware Dealer Married Malone," *New York Times,* Dec. 11, 1921, p. 22; Stevens Deposition, 82–83, 121; Stevens, General Statement, [10].

68. "Commemorating Woman's Party," *New York Times,* July 15, 1923, p. X5; "Women Open Fight for Equal Rights," ibid., July 21, 1923, p. 8; "5,000 Pay Tribute to Susan B. Anthony," ibid., July 23, 1923, p. 13; Stevens Deposition, 83–84.

69. Stevens Deposition, 84.

70. Stevens Deposition, 84–87, 89, 95. 161; 1923, note card 4, Box 8, Folder 270, Stevens Papers; Paul Interview, 451.

71. "Proceedings of Congress and Committees in Brief," *Washington Post,* Dec. 11, 1923, p. 6.

72. Stevens Deposition, 90.

73. Stevens Deposition, 89–91.

74. Stevens Deposition, 91–92, 94–95, 97; "Flood Tide Slides Olympic from Pier," *New York Times,* Aug. 6, 1925, p. 12.

75. The International Woman Suffrage Alliance was organized in Berlin in 1904. NAWSA president Carrie Chapman Catt was its first president. Its purpose was "to secure the enfranchisement of the women of all nations, and to unite the friends of woman suffrage throughout the world in organizational cooperation and fraternal helpfulness." Mineke Bosch with Annemarie Kloosterman, *Politics and Friendship: Letters from the International Woman Suffrage Alliance, 1902–1942* (Columbus: Ohio State University Press, 1985), 8, 9; Leila J. Rupp, "Constructing Internationalism: The Case of Transnational Women's Organizations, 1888–1945," *American Historical Review* 99 (1994): 1575, 1576. Other international groups included the International Council of Women formed in 1888 and the International Committee of Women for Permanent Peace organized in 1915. Rupp, "Constructing Internationalism," 1574, 1575.

76. "World Suffragists Bar Woman's Party," *New York Times,* May 29, 1926, p. 4; "Equality Divides Women's Congress," ibid., May 30, 1926, p. XX8; "World Suffragists Bar American Group; British Party Quits," ibid., June 1, 1926, p. 1; Crystal Eastman, "The Great Rejection: Part I," *Equal Rights,* June 19, 1926, pp. 149–50; Crystal Eastman, "The Great Rejection: Part II," *Equal Rights,* June 26, 1926, pp. 157–59; "Mrs. Belmont Holds Mrs. Catt Is the Foe," *New York Times,* June 2, 1926, p. 23; Stevens Deposition, 104–105; Becker, 224–26; Paul Interview, 203–205, 360. Frustrated by her failure to gain membership for the NWP, Alva tried another tack. With Stevens's help, she tried to organize the French and British feminists into some sort of united front by promising to pay for a headquarters from which they could work together. That plan failed as well. Stevens Deposition, 109–110; Stevens, General Statement, [13]; Paul Interview, 206.

77. Alva E. Belmont to Miss Paul, July 3, 1926, Box 5, Folder 101, Smith Papers.

78. The Duke of Marlborough also wanted an annulment. Having converted to Catholicism, he wished to become a member of the church and could not do so because he was divorced. Stuart, 413.

79. Balsan, 242–43.

80. "Rutherford Named as Man Ex-Duchess Wanted to Marry," *New York Times,* November 25, 1926, pp. 1–2. Consuelo's governess also testified. See Balsan, 242. See also "Mrs. Belmont Used Threats, Vatican Reveals," *New York Herald Tribune,* Nov. 25, 1926, pp. 1, 2; "Vanderbilt Wedding Laid to Threats of Murder," *Los Angeles Times,* Nov. 25, 1926, p. 1; "Why Rome Freed Consuelo," *Chicago Daily Tribune,* Nov. 25, 1926, p. 1; "Mother Ordered Consuelo to Wed,"

*Boston Daily Globe,* Nov. 25, 1926, p. 1; "Mrs. Belmont Forced Wedding of Daughter," *Atlanta Constitution,* Nov. 25, 1926, p. 16.

81. "Mrs. Belmont Is Silent on Revelations of Rota," *New York Times,* Nov. 26, 1926, p. 1.

82. Balsan, 243.

83. Balsan 243–44. The Balsans were living on their estate in France when World War II began in 1939. When the Germans invaded the Netherlands, Belgium, and Luxemburg, they did what they could to help care for refugees and the wounded. In 1940, they decided to leave. Balsan, 299–326. Traveling through Spain and Portugal, they fled to the United States. Despite her American birth and the ratification of the Equal Nationality Treaty in 1934, Consuelo could not enter the country as a citizen. She and her husband had to apply for a naturalization certificate, which allowed them to remain in the country for the rest of their lives. Stuart, 470. Jacques Balsan died in November 1956. Stuart, 496. Consuelo died eight years later at her home, Garden Side, in Southampton, New York, at the age of eighty-seven. After a funeral in the same New York church where she had married the duke, she was flown to England and buried in the churchyard of St. Martin at Bladon in Oxfordshire. Stuart, 501–502.

84. Trigg, 54; Rupp, "Feminism and the Sexual Revolution," 291. They do not, however, provide convincing evidence that any of these things were true.

85. 1926, note card 8, Box 9, Folder 273, Stevens Papers.

86. Trigg, 54–55.

87. Belmont to Stevens, [Feb. 1927], Box 9, Folder 274, Stevens Papers. For reference to this letter, see Stevens Deposition, 115.

88. "Doris Stevens Sues Malone for Divorce," *New York Times,* July 22, 1927, p. 4; *New York Mirror* clipping, Sept. 1, 1935, Box 5, Folder 140, Stevens Papers.

89. Stevens Deposition, 116–117.

90. Stevens Deposition, 117–18; Stevens, General Statement, [14–15].

91. Stevens Deposition, 86.

92. Stevens Deposition, 125, 134; Stevens, General Statement, [16].

93. Stevens Deposition, 134.

94. Stevens Deposition, 140.

95. Stevens Deposition, 83–84, quotation on 140.

96. Stevens Deposition, 134.

97. Stevens, General Statement, pp. [16–17]; Stevens Deposition, 135–39. Paul was made chairman of the commission's nationality committee. Geidel, 711.

98. Stevens Deposition, 142.

99. 1928, note card 6, Box 9, folder 275, Stevens Papers.

100. Stevens Deposition, 147.

101. Stevens Deposition, 173.

102. Stevens Deposition, 171.

103. Stevens Deposition, 158.

104. Stevens Deposition, 142–43; Stevens, General Statement, [17].

105. Stevens Deposition, 172.

106. For Stevens version of this story, see Stevens Deposition, 144–52, 160; Stevens, General Statement, [18].

107. Stevens Deposition, 150–51.

108. Alva E. Belmont to Alice Paul, Aug. 29, 1928, Box 9, Folder 275, Stevens Papers.

109. Memorandum from Mrs. O. H. P. Belmont, Aug. 31, 1928, Box 5, Folder 101, Smith Papers.

110. NWP Motion, Box 5, Folder 101, Smith Papers.

111. Alva E. Belmont to Alice Paul, Oct. 23, 1928, Box 9, Folder 276, Stevens Papers; Stevens Deposition, 150–151.

112. Jane Norman Smith to Mrs. Belmont, Nov. 14, 1928, Box 5, Folder 101, Smith Papers.

113. Mary Gertrude Fendall to Mrs. Smith, Jan. 9, 1929, Box 8, Folder 153; Jane Norman Smith to Mary Gertrude Fendall, Jan. 11, 1929, Box 5, Folder 101; and Mary Gertrude Fendall to Mrs. Smith, Jan. 11, 1929, Box 8, Folder 153, Smith Papers.

114. Jane Norman Smith to Mrs. Belmont, Jan. 20, 1929, Box 5, Folder 102, Smith Papers.

115. Alva Belmont to the National Council of the National Woman's Party, Feb. 4, 1929, and Alva Belmont to Jane Norman Smith, Feb. 4, 1929, Box 5, Folder 102, Smith Papers.

116. Stevens Deposition, 152.

117. Stevens Deposition, 155–56.

118. Stevens Deposition, 157, 163, 167.

119. Stevens Deposition, 161, 164, 165; Stevens, General Statement, [20]. A number of noted British feminists, including Lady Rhondda and Emmeline Pethick-Lawrence, organized what they called the Open Door Council in Britain in May 1926. Its purpose was to ensure that female workers were treated the same way as men. They held an international conference to discuss this matter in Berlin in June 1929. From this meeting emerged a group called the Open Door International for the Economic Emancipation of the Woman Worker which lasted until 1965. Introduction to the Records of the Open Door Council, Women's Library, London Metropolitan University, London, England; Karen M. Offen, *European Feminisms, 1700–1950: A Political History* (Stanford, Calif.: Stanford University Press, 2000), 372.

120. Stevens Deposition, 166; Stevens, General Statement, [20].

121. Alva E. Belmont to Doris Stevens, April 5, 1929, Box 9, Folder 277, Stevens Papers.

122. Alva E. Belmont to Mrs. Smith, Feb. 23, 1929, Box 5, Folder 102, Smith Papers.

123. Jane Norman Smith to Mrs. Belmont, April 16, 1929, Box 5, Folder 102, Smith Papers.

124. Stevens Deposition, 174–75; Doris Stevens to George Gordon Battle, June 28, 1930, Box 9, Folder 278, Stevens Papers.

125. Stevens Deposition, 175–76; Stevens, General Statement, [22].

126. Stevens Deposition, 177–78; Paula F. Pfeffer, "'A Whisper in the Assembly of Nations': United States Participation in the International Movement for Women's Rights from the League of Nations to the United Nations," *Women's Studies International Forum* 8 (1985): 464.

127. Pfeffer, 464.

128. For expressions of concern about money, see Stevens Deposition, 160, 166, 175, 179, 180, 181, 188.

129. Alva E. Belmont to Doris Stevens, Jan. 20, 1927, Box 9, Folder 274, Stevens Papers.

130. Belmont to Stevens, Nov. 3, 1928, Box 9, Folder 276, Stevens Papers.

131. Alva E. Belmont to Emma Wold, Nov. 5, 1928, Box 9, Folder 276, Stevens Papers.

132. Belmont to Stevens, April 5, 1929, Box 9, Folder 277, Stevens Papers.

133. Stevens, General Statement, [23–24].

134. Stevens to Belmont, Jan. 20, 1931, Box 9, Folder 279, Stevens Papers.

135. She did not have her operation until 1932 after Belmont had suffered her first stroke. Stevens, General Statement, [22]; Stevens Deposition, 174.

136. Stevens Deposition, 182, 187; Stevens, General Statement, [23, 24].

137. Mrs. O. H. P. Belmont, "Are Women Really Citizens?" *Good Housekeeping* 93 (Spring 1931): 99, 132–33. Quotation on 133.

138. "New Woman's Party Headquarters," *Equal Rights*, July 27, 1929, p. 195.

139. Jane Norman Smith to Mrs. Belmont, Nov. 30, 1928, Box 5, Folder 101, Smith Papers.

140. "First Meeting of the Investment Fund, National Woman's Party, [Jan. 1929] and Memo," Box 8, Folder 153, Smith Papers; Summary of Receipts and Disbursements, Feb. 25, 1921–June 30, 1929, Box 7, Folder 138, Smith Papers; Original List Investment and Endowment Fund, Box 8, Folder 153, Smith Papers; Alva Belmont to Mrs. Wiley, March 30, 1932, Box 8, Folder 157, Smith Papers; typed note at the bottom of a partial copy of "Minutes of the Special Meeting of the National Council of the NWP, Dec. 7, 1927," Box 8, Folder 153, Smith Papers.

141. Jane Norman Smith to Mrs. Belmont, May 16, 1929, Box 5, Folder 102, and Alva E. Belmont to Mrs. Smith, May 27, 1929, Box 5, Folder 102, Smith Papers.

142. Alva E. Belmont to Alice Paul, Feb. 5, 1929, Box 5, Folder 102, Smith Papers.

143. Alva E. Belmont to Jane Norman Smith, March 28, 1929, Box 5, Folder 102, Smith Papers.

144. Alva E. Belmont to Maud Younger, June 4, 1929, Box 29, Folder 365, Paul Papers.

145. Alva E. Belmont to Mrs. Smith, May 3, 1929, Box 5, Folder 102, Smith Papers.

146. Radiogram from Alva E. Belmont to Mrs. Hilles, Oct. 9, 1929; quotation in Alva E. Belmont to Mrs. Hilles, [Oct. 1929]; Alva E. Belmont to Jane Norman Smith, Nov. 4, 1929; Jane Norman Smith to Alva E. Belmont, Nov. 7,

1929; and Alva E. Belmont to Mrs. Smith, Nov. 20, 1929, all in Box 5, Folder 102, Smith Papers.

147. Cable from Jane Norman Smith to Alva E. Belmont, [Nov. 24, 1929], and Jane Norman Smith to Mrs. Belmont, Dec. 10, 1929, Box 5, Folder 102, Smith Papers.

148. Alva E. Belmont to Mrs. Smith, Nov. 25, 1929, and Alva E. Belmont to Mrs. Smith, Dec. 21, 1929, Box 5, Folder 102, Smith Papers.

149. Alva E. Belmont to Mrs. Harvey Wiley, July 7, 1930, Box 9, Folder 278, Stevens Papers.

150. "Feminist Activities Intensified with New Year" and "Alva Belmont House," *Equal Rights,* Jan. 3, 1931, p. 379; "For an Equal Rights Auditorium," *Equal Rights,* Jan. 17, 1931, cover. The building is now called the Sewall-Belmont House.

151. Alice Paul to Doris Stevens, March 19, 1931, Box 9, Folder 279, Stevens Papers.

152. Stevens, General Statement, [26].

153. Stevens Deposition, 189–90; Stevens, General Statement, [27].

154. Doris Stevens, "The following memorandum refers to incidents during my visit to the chateau the latter part of July, 1931," Box 9, Folder 290, Stevens Papers, pp. 8, 13–14; Stevens, General Statement, [28]

155. Between October 15, 1921, and March 1927, Alva paid Alice Paul $30,000 to work for equal rights. Account of Alice Paul with Mrs. Oliver H. P. Belmont, March 10, 1927, Box 32, Folder 412, Paul Papers; "Treasurer's Report at Baltimore Conference May 11, 1926," *Equal Rights,* May 22, 1926, p. 120. The total income from all sources for this period, including income from royalties, rent receipts, ticket sales, and sale of *Equal Rights,* was $443,711.

156. Woman's Research Foundation, "Treasurer's Report for Aug. 6, 1923 to June 25, 1927," Box 71, Folder 968, Paul Papers. See inflation calculator.

157. Woman's Research Foundation, "Statement of Receipts and Disbursements for June 2, 1927 to Dec. 31, 1933," Box 71, Folder 968, Paul Papers.

158. National Woman's Party, "Contributions to the International Fund, 1928–29," Box 8, Folder 265, Stevens Papers.

159. Stevens Deposition, 187.

160. Stevens, Memorandum, 19–20.

161. Alva E. Belmont to Mrs. Harvey Wiley, Aug. 11, 1931, Box 9, Folder 279, Stevens Papers.

162. Mrs. Harvey Wiley to Mrs. O. H. P. Belmont, Aug. 20, 1931, Box 9, Folder 279, Stevens Papers.

163. Stevens, Memorandum, 13–16.

164. Stevens, Memorandum, 16; Stevens, General Statement, [27].

165. Stevens, Memorandum, 16, 19.

166. Stevens, General Statement, [28].

167. Surrogate Court Testimony, May 19 and 20, 1933, pp. 2–49, New York County Hall Records, Box 9, File 286, Stevens Papers; Geidel, 727. The witness-

es were Elsa Maxwell, one of Belmont's friends, Mary Young, Belmont's secretary, and Marcelle Alice Gay, a kindergarten teacher on the Belmont estate.

168. Quoted in Sapiro, 14–15.

169. Quoted in Sapiro, 17.

170. Quoted in Sapiro, 18.

171. "Lauds Nationality Bill," *New York Times,* July 3, 1930, 6.

172. Besides Belmont, the largest donors during this period were Mrs. Emile Berliner who gave $1250, Mrs. William Kent who gave $1100, Marion May who gave $1000, Alice Paul who gave $2670, and Mrs. Elizabeth S. Rogers who gave $1005. "International Fund of the National Woman's Party, Treasurer's Report for Sept. 6, 1930 to Oct. 28, 1933," Box 31, Folder 401, Paul Papers.

173. In months for which records are available for the years 1935 and 1937, donations from individuals ranged from $1.00 to $250. The total collected was less than $1500. National Woman's Party, "Contributions Received for International Work, August, September, October, 1935," Box 33, Folder 430, and National Woman's Party, "International Fund, June, July, August, September, 1937," Box 33, Folder 428, Paul Papers.

174. Bredbenner, 237–38.

175. "Hull Praises Miss Stevens on Her Victory over Him," *New York Times,* Dec. 25, 1933, p. 18. Despite her successful lobbying on behalf of the equal nationality rights treaty, she was replaced by Mary Winslow as the U.S. representative on the Inter-American Commission of Women at the 1938 Conference of American States in Lima. Bredbenner, 246–48.

176. "Equality in Nationality Becomes Law of the Land," *Equal Rights,* June 2, 1934, p. 139. These rights included the right of a woman to retain her citizenship when she married a foreigner and her right to transmit her nationality to her children.

177. Balsan, xiv.

178. Stevens Deposition, 139.

## 6. THE LAST WORD

1. Mary Young replaced Mary Gertrude Fendall in 1928 and worked for Belmont until Belmont's death in 1933. Stevens Deposition, 144–45. After Belmont died, Young began looking for a job with a consulate or embassy. There is no information on whether she successfully found employment. Mary Young to Dear Mama, March 31, 1933, Matilda Young Papers.

2. Mary Young left no notes, and the correspondence in her sister Matilda Young's papers gives little insight into her background or her attitude toward Belmont except that she apparently enjoyed her job and was good at it.

3. Young-Belmont Memoir, 96.

4. Young-Belmont Memoir, 154.

5. Young-Belmont Memoir, 151.

6. Young-Belmont Memoir, 152–53, 125–26.

7. As Teresa Odendahl has pointed out, "the philanthropy of the wealthy . . . assists in the social reproduction of the upper class. Private contributions by the elite support institutions that sustain their . . . interests." Teresa Odendahl, *Charity Begins at Home: Generosity and Self-Interest among the Philanthropic Elite* (New York: Basic, 1990), 232.

8. Young-Belmont Memoir, 99–101. Belmont also mentions building a hospital on Long Island for convalescing children (Young-Belmont Memoir, 94) and sending nurses abroad to help her daughter with hospital work during World War I (Young-Belmont Memoir, 61–62).

9. Sara Bard Field to Charles Erskine Scott Wood, July 31, 1917, Field Papers.

10. "There Are No Idle Rich, Declares Mrs. O. H. P. Belmont," *New York Times,* July 9, 1911, SM3.

11. Geidel, 728; Mary Young to Doris Stevens, May 27, 1932, Box 9, Folder 281, Stevens Papers.

12. Doris Stevens, General Statement, [31], Box 9, Folder 292, and Mary Young to Doris Stevens, May 27, 1932 and July 23, 1932, Box 9, Folder 281, Stevens Papers.

13. Matilda Young to Dearest Mother, Aug. 13, [1932], Young Papers.

14. Matilda Young to Dearest Mother, Aug. 28, 1932, Young Papers.

15. Matilda Young to Dearest Mother, Aug. 13, [1932], Young Papers.

16. Matilda Young to Dearest Mother, Aug. 27, 1932, Young Papers.

17. Matilda Young to Dearest, Dearest Mother, Aug. 21, [1932]; Matilda Young to Dearest Mother, Aug. 28, 1932, Young Papers.

18. Matilda Young to Dearest Mother, Sept. 12, 1932, Young Papers.

19. Maxwell, 110.

20. Mary Young to Doris Stevens, Nov. 19, 1932, Box 9, Folder 281, Stevens Papers.

21. "Mrs. O. H. P. Belmont Dies at Paris Home," *New York Times,* Jan. 26, 1933, p. 17; "Mrs. Belmont Dies at 80 in Paris Home," *Chicago Tribune,* Jan. 26, 1933, p. 1.

22. Paul Interview, 565.

23. "Belmont Funeral to Be Held Today," *New York Times,* Feb. 12, 1933, p. 35.

24. "Mrs. O. H. P. Belmont to Be Buried Here," *New York Times,* Jan. 27, 1933, p. 19.

25. "Women Meet Body of Mrs. Belmont," *New York Times,* Feb. 11, 1933, p. 15.

26. "Belmont Funeral to Be Held Today," *New York Times,* Feb. 12, 1933, p. 35; "Belmont Funeral a National Tribute," *New York Times,* Feb. 13, 1933, p. 17; "Party Renews Its Faith at Belmont Bier," *Equal Rights,* Feb. 18, 1933, pp. 19–21.

27. "Mrs. Belmont Dies at 80 in Paris Home," *Chicago Tribune,* Jan. 26, 1933, p. 1; "Mrs. O. H. P. Belmont Dies at Paris Home," *New York Times,* Jan. 26, 1933, p. 17.

28. "Mrs. Belmont Left Most to Daughter," *New York Times*, March 1, 1933, p. 15; Notice of Alva Belmont's bequest, Box 7, Folder 138, Smith Papers; "Mrs. Belmont's Estate," *New York Times*, March 24, 1934, p. 9. The value of her estate in 2008 would have been about $21,839,307. See inflation calculator (accessed Aug. 27, 2009).

29. Crocker, 305, 307, 309. The value of her estate as of 2008 would have been about $694,969,000. See inflation calculator (accessed Aug. 27, 2009).

30. Fields, 303–304. The value of her estate as of 2008 would have been about $223,314,600. See inflation calculator (accessed Aug. 27, 2009).

31. "To Honor Leaders for Women's Rights," *New York Times*, July 6, 1933, p. 24; "Ask Roosevelt Aid for Women's Jobs," ibid., July 9, 1933, N16; "Radio Dial Flashes," *Washington Post*, July 8, 1933, p. 16; "Women's Party Asks Equality in Employment," *Washington Post*, July 9, 1933, p. 10.

32. "Financial Report Submitted to the Alva E. Belmont Estate," Box 32, Folder 408, Paul Papers.

33. Doris Stevens, *Tribute to Alva Belmont: Late President of the National Woman's Party* (Washington, D.C.: Inter American Commission of Women, [1933]).

34. "Mrs. Belmont Left Most to Her Daughter," *New York Times*, March 1, 1933, p. 15.

35. Paul Interview, 560–61; Miscellaneous Memorandum—Chronicle of Events, Box 9, Folder 290, Stevens Papers.

36. Surrogate Court Testimony, May 19 and 20, 1933, New York County Hall of Records, New York, New York, Box 9, Folder 286, Stevens Papers.

37. Doris Stevens to Mary Young, Oct. 31, 1932, Box 9, Folder 281, Stevens Papers.

38. Doris Stevens, General Statement, Box 9, Folder 292, Stevens Papers.

39. Doris Stevens, "The following memorandum refers to incidents during my visit to the chateau the latter part of July, 1931," Box 9, Folder 290, Stevens Papers.

40. Vivian Pierce to Doris Stevens, July 5, 1933, Box 9, Folder 285, Stevens Papers.

41. Max Eastman to Doris Stevens, July 21, 1933, Box 9, Folder 285, Stevens Papers.

42. Stevens Deposition, 198; miscellaneous typescript, Box 9, Folder 287, Stevens Papers. Despite the fact that Stevens's deposition is self-serving, there is no reason to question Stevens's descriptions of the duties that she performed for Belmont. Her discussion of her attitude toward performing those duties is credible to the extent that any reasonable person was likely to feel the same way. Many of her statements about her activities can be verified by looking at surviving correspondence.

43. Stevens Deposition, 15–16.

44. Stevens Deposition, 16–17, 29, 33, 49, 130, 131; Stevens, General Statement, p. [14].

45. Stevens Deposition, 198.

46. Stevens Deposition, 20–21.

47. Stevens Deposition, 25–26.

48. Stevens Deposition, 23.

49. Stevens, General Statement, p. [6]; Stevens Deposition, 20–21.

50. Stevens, General Statement, pp. [3–4]; Stevens Deposition, 21.

51. Stevens Deposition, 21.

52. Stevens Deposition, 21, 49.

53. Stevens Deposition, 62.

54. Shirley M. Eoff, *Viscountess Rhondda: Equalitarian Feminist* (Columbus: Ohio State University Press, 1991), 93, 23–33, 54, 55, 64–99, 117–46.

55. Stevens Deposition, 106.

56. Stevens Deposition, 105–107, 113.

57. Stevens Deposition, 113.

58. Stevens Deposition, 120–21.

59. Stevens Deposition, 47.

60. Paul Interview, 564. Paul claims to have gotten this information from Belmont's lawyer. Stevens married Jonathan Mitchell, a writer for the *New Republic,* in late August 1935. "Doris Stevens, Noted Feminist, Marries Writer," *Washington Post,* Sept. 1, 1935, p. 8. She had no further dealings with the Vanderbilts and broke with the NWP in 1947, but she did not abandon her commitment to feminism. Through the Doris Stevens Foundation, she eventually endowed a chair in women's studies at Princeton University. Rupp, "Feminism and the Sexual Revolution," 292.

61. Paul Interview, 451; Stevens Deposition, 84–85, 161.

62. Stevens Deposition, 95.

63. Maxwell, 105.

64. Nancy Woloch, *Women and the American Experience,* 4th ed. (New York: McGraw-Hill, 2006), 507, 518, 526.

65. Judy Klemesrud, "Coming Wednesday: A Herstory Making Event," *New York Times,* Aug. 23, 1970, p. SM4; Linda Carlton, "Women Seeking Equality March on 5th Ave. Today," *New York Times,* Aug. 26, 1970, p. 44; Joe Nicholson Jr., "Lib Strike Activities Revealed," *Los Angeles Times,* Aug. 25, 1970, p. F3; "It's Women's Day—Watch It Bub!" *Los Angeles Times,* Aug. 26, 1970, p. 10; "Women on the March," *Time,* Sept. 7, 1970, http://www.time.com/time/magazine/article/0,9171,902696,00.html (accessed Feb. 12, 2009).

66. Woloch, 526; Flora Davis, *Moving the Mountain: The Women's Movement in America since 1960* (New York: Touchstone, 1991), 187–88.

67. Mary P. Ryan, *Mysteries of Sex: Tracing Women and Men through American History* (Chapel Hill: University of North Carolina Press, 2006), 262; Susan M. Hartmann, *From Margin to Mainstream: American Women and Politics since 1960* (New York: Knopf, 1989), 117–18; Davis, 360–61.

68. Nicholas D. Kristof and Sheryl WuDunn, "The Women's Crusade," *New York Times Magazine,* Aug. 23, 2009, pp. 29–39.

## POSTSCRIPT

1. Since the 1980s, feminist biographers have struggled to define their relationship with their subjects and have articulated feelings toward them ranging from admiration to ambivalence. As they worked to integrate their subjects into the canon of female worthies, they have expressed anxiety about being too close or not close enough to the women whose lives they were chronicling for fear of distorting their subjects' stories or undermining their authority. Bell Gale Chevigny, "Daughters Writing: Toward a Theory of Women's Biography," *Feminist Studies* 9 (1983): 79–82; Elizabeth Kamarck Minnich, "Friendship between Women: The Act of Feminist Biography," *Feminist Studies* 11 (1985): 287–305; Carol Ascher et al., eds., *Between Women: Biographers, Novelists, Critics, Teachers and Artists Write about Their Work on Women* (Boston: Beacon, 1984); Alpern et al., eds., *The Challenge of Feminist Biography.* For a discussion of this issue as it pertains to historians in general, see Jill Lepore, "Historians Who Love Too Much: Reflections of Microhistory and Biography," *Journal of American History* 88 (2001): 129–44.

2. Field Interview, 370, 371, 372.

3. Minnich, 287.

4. Michael Paul Rogin's *Fathers and Children: Andrew Jackson and the Subjugation of the American Indian* (New York: Vintage, 1975), and Fawn Brodie's *No Man Knows My History: The Life of Joseph Smith, the Mormon Prophet* (New York: Knopf, 1946) are examples.

5. Paul Miller, handwritten note, Gilmour Papers.

6. American Psychiatric Association, *Diagnostic and Statistical Manual of Mental Disorders,* 4th ed. (Washington, D.C.: American Psychiatric Association, 1994), 658–61.

## APPENDIX

1. Paul Interview, 382–84.

2. Paul Interview, 191–192.

3. "What Mrs. Belmont Has Done for Women," *New York Times,* March 9, 1910, pp. 1, 2.

4. Stevens-Belmont Memoir, 17; "Fair Miss Suffrage Waits on Strikers," *New York Times,* Nov. 26, 1911, p. 15.

5. *Suffragist,* Feb. 28, 1914, p. 2; Aug. 8, 1914, p. 3; Sept. 12, 1914, p. 8; Sept. 26, 1914, p. 8.

6. *Suffragist,* May 29, 1915, p. 8, June 26, 1915, p. 8; Sept. 18, 1915, p. 8; Nov. 13, 1915, p. 8; Dec. 11, 1915, p. 12; Dec. 25, 1915, p. 8.

7. *Suffragist,* Jan. 8, 1916, p. 8; Jan. 29, 1916, p. 8; March 18, 1916, p. 11; March 25, 1916, p. 11; April 8, 1916, p. 11; April 15, 1916, p. 11; June 10, 1916, p. 11; June 17, 1916, p. 11; Aug. 12, 1916, p. 11; Oct. 14, 1916, p. 11; Nov. 18, 1916, p. 11.

8. *Suffragist,* Jan. 31, 1917, p. 11; Feb. 24, 1917, p. 11; March 3, 1917, p. 15; May 5, 1917, p. 11; July 28, 1917, p. 11; Nov. 10, 1917, p. 11.

9. *Suffragist,* March 2, 1918, p. 15; Oct. 26, 1918, p. 10; Dec. 28, 1918, p. 11.

10. *Suffragist,* Feb. 1, 1919, p. 13; March 29, 1919, p. 11.

11. "Statement of Receipts and Disbursements," Feb. 25, 1921–Oct. 25, 1922, Box 31, Folder 397, Paul Papers.

12. Ibid.

13. "Statement for Oct. 26, 1922–Nov. 1, 1923," Box 31, Folder 397, Paul Papers.

14. Belmont Contributions to NWP July 1, 1921 to Jan. 25, 1923, Box 32, Folder 412, Paul Papers.

15. Itemized list of bills paid directly by Belmont from Oct. 1, 1921, to Jan. 15, 1923, and not passed through the NWP treasury, Box 32, Folder 412, Paul Papers. This included attorney fees, insurance premiums on NWP property, bank interest, property taxes, furniture, and maintenance expenses.

16. Belmont Contributions to NWP July 1, 1921 to Nov. 17, 1926, Box 32, Folder 412, Paul Papers.

17. Account of Alice Paul with Mrs. Oliver H. P. Belmont, Box 32, Folder 412, Paul Papers.

18. 1927 Monthly Statements, Box 32, Folder 407, Paul Papers.

19. Statement of Receipts and Disbursements for 1928, Box 31, Folder 398, Paul Papers.

20. Belmont Donations for 1929, Box 31, Folder 398, Paul Papers.

21. Gifts from Mrs. Belmont on three note cards, Box 32, Folder 412, Paul Papers.

22. The Woman's Research Fund began its work on July 1, 1923. [AP?] to P. Moir, July 11, 1925, Box 29, Folder 363, Paul Papers; a document in the Paul Papers states that between Aug. 6, 1923, and Dec. 8, 1926, Belmont gave the Woman's Research Foundation $27,500 for salaries and expenses. See note on Belmont's contributions, Box 31, Folder 398, Paul Papers. Belmont stopped contributing to the Woman's Research Fund in 1927. From June 2, 1927, to Dec. 31, 1933, the fund raised only $5769, including $2000 from the Carnegie Endowment and $1260 from Alice Paul = $3260. Statement of Receipts and Disbursements, Woman's Research Foundation, June 2, 1927–Dec. 31, 1933, Box 71, Folder 968, Paul Papers.

23. 1929, note card 11, Box 9, Folder 277, Stevens Papers; Contributions to the International Fund, 1928–29, Box 8, Folder 265, Stevens Papers.

24. International Fund Statement for Sept. 6, 1930, to Oct. 28, 1933, Box 31, Folder 401, Paul Papers; Financial Report of the NWP International Fund, Box 33, Folder 428, Paul Papers. After Belmont died, the NWP raised very little money for international work. Contributions Received for International Work, August through October 1935, Box 33, Folder 428, Paul Papers, indicates that during that period the fund raised a total of $910 in gifts of $1–$150. From June through September 1937, the fund raised a total of $522 in gifts of $1–$250. International Fund for June, July, August, September, 1937, Box 33, Folder 428, Paul Papers.

25. List of Contributions Given by Belmont to the Inter-American Commission on Women, Box 9, Folder 279, Stevens Papers.

26. Belmont's royalties donations, Box 32, Folder 407, Paul Papers.

27. Alva E. Belmont to Mrs. Wiley, Nov. 24, 1930, Box 8, Folder 155, Smith Papers; Anna Kelton Wiley to Alva E. Belmont, Dec. 11, 1930, Box 9, Folder 278, Stevens Papers.

28. Paul Interview, 566.

29. 1929, note card 11, Box 9, Folder 277, Stevens Papers.

30. Treasurer's Report, Administrative Department, Box 31, Folder 401, Paul Papers.

31. Treasurer's Report, Administrative Department, Box 31, Folder 401, Paul Papers.

32. Statement of Receipts and Disbursements, Box 31, Folder 400, Paul Papers.

33. Geidel, 461.

34. Alva E. Belmont to Alice Paul, March 20, 1914, Reel 8, Frame 753, *NWP Papers.*

35. "Newport Thé Dansant a Great Success," *Suffragist,* Aug. 7, 1915, p. 3.

36. "Suffrage Operetta Gives Cause $8000," *New York Times,* Feb. 20, 1916, p. 15.

37. Inventory of Belmont furnishings, Box 20, Folder 307, Paul Papers.

38. Stevens Deposition, 159–60.

39. Stevens Deposition, 166.

40. Stevens Deposition, 175.

41. Stevens Deposition, 188.

# BIBLIOGRAPHY


### MANUSCRIPTS

Huntington Library, San Marino, Calif.
Sara Bard Field Papers in the Charles Erskine Scott Wood Papers
Preservation Society of Newport County, Newport, R.I.
William Gilmour Papers
Rare Book, Manuscript and Special Collections Library, Duke University, Durham, N.C.
Matilda Young Papers
Schlesinger Library, Radcliffe Institute for Advanced Study, Harvard University, Cambridge, Mass.
Alice Paul Papers
Jane Norman Smith Papers
Doris Stevens Papers
United States Manuscript Census, Mobile, Ala., 1850
United States Manuscript Census, Mobile, Ala., 1860

### MICROFILM

*National Woman's Party Papers, Part II: The Suffrage Years, 1913–1920* (Bethesda, Md.: University Press of America, 1981).

### PERIODICALS

*Atlanta Constitution*
*Baltimore Sun*
*Boston Globe*
*Chicago Tribune*
*Equal Rights*
*Harper's Weekly*
*Los Angeles Times*

*New York Herald Tribune*
*New York Mirror*
*New York Press*
*New York Times*
*New York Tribune*
*New York World*
*St. Louis Post Dispatch*
*San Francisco Chronicle*
*The Suffragist*
*Time*
*Washington Post*

**BOOKS AND ARTICLES**

Adams, Bluford. *E. Pluribus Barnum: The Great Showman and the Making of U.S. Popular Culture.* Minneapolis: University of Minnesota Press, 1997.

Adams, Katherine H., and Michael L. Keene. *Alice Paul and the American Suffrage Campaign.* Urbana: University of Illinois Press, 2008.

Adams, Timothy Dow. *Telling Lies in Modern American Autobiography.* Chapel Hill: University of North Carolina Press, 1990.

Albion, Robert Greenhalgh. *The Rise of New York Port.* New York: Charles Scribner's Sons, 1939.

Alonso, Harriet Hyman. *Growing Up Abolitionist: The Story of the Garrison Children.* Amherst: University of Massachusetts Press, 2002.

Alpern, Sara, Joyce Antler, Elizabeth Isreals Perry, and Ingrid Winther Scobie, eds. *The Challenge of Feminist Biography: Writing the Lives of Modern American Women.* Urbana: University of Illinois Press, 1992.

American Psychiatric Association, *Diagnostic and Statistical Manual of Mental Disorders.* 4th ed., Washington, D.C.: American Psychiatric Association, 1994.

Amos, Harriet E. *Cotton City: Urban Development in Antebellum Mobile.* University, Ala.: University of Alabama Press, 1985.

Aron, Cindy Sondik. *Ladies and Gentlemen of the Civil Service: Middle-Class Workers in Victorian America.* New York: Oxford University Press, 1987.

Ascher, Carol, Louise DeSalvo, and Sara Ruddick, eds. *Between Women: Biographers, Novelists, Critics, Teachers, and Artists Write about Their Work on Women.* Boston: Beacon, 1984.

Baker, Thomas N. *Sentiment and Celebrity: Nathaniel Parker Willis and the Trials of Literary Fame.* New York: Oxford University Press, 1999.

Balleisen, Edward J. *Navigating Failure: Bankruptcy and Commercial Society in Antebellum America.* Chapel Hill: University of North Carolina Press, 2001.

Balsan, Consuelo Vanderbilt. *The Glitter and the Gold.* New York: Harper & Bros., 1952.

Barros, Carolyn A. *Autobiography: Narrative of Transformation.* Ann Arbor: University of Michigan Press, 1998.

Becker, Susan D. *Origins of the Equal Rights Amendment: American Feminism between the Wars.* Westport, Conn.: Greenwood Press, 1981.

Beckert, Sven. *The Monied Metropolis: New York City and the Consolidation of the American Bourgeoisie, 1850–1896.* New York: Cambridge University Press, 2001.

Belmont, Mrs. O. H. P. "Are Women Really Citizens?" *Good Housekeeping,* 93 (1931): 99, 132–33.

———. "Do Not Let Women Vote—Slogan of Political Bosses." *Chicago Sunday Tribune,* July 14, 1912, section 2, [p. 3].

———. "Equal Suffrage Not a National Question?" *Chicago Sunday Tribune,* Nov. 3, 1912, section 8, p. 5.

———. "A Girl? What A Pity It Was Not a Boy." *Chicago Sunday Tribune,* June 9, 1912, section 3, p. 1.

———. "How Can Women Get the Suffrage," *Independent* 68 (March 31, 1910): 686–89.

———. "How Shall the Market Basket of America's Poor Be Filled?" *Chicago Sunday Tribune,* Aug. 25, 1912, section 8, p. 1.

———. "How Suffrage Will Protect Women from Men Who 'Sow Wild Oats.'" *Chicago Sunday Tribune,* April 28, 1912, section 9, p. 1.

———. "How Votes For Women Will Improve Existing Conditions." *Chicago Sunday Tribune,* May 26, 1912, section 3, p. 1.

———. "In Non-Voting States Women Are Classed with Lunatics." *Chicago Sunday Tribune,* July 21, 1912, section 2, p. 3.

———. "In What Respect Do Women Differ From Slaves or Serfs?" *Chicago Sunday Tribune,* June 16, 1912, section 3, p. 1.

———. "The Liberation of Sex." *Hearst's Magazine* 23 (April 1913): 614–16.

———. "Man Has Failed to Care for Women and Children." *Chicago Sunday Tribune,* July, 28, 1912, section 2, p. 3.

———. "Men Will Forget the Rosenthal Murder, Women Will Remember It." *Chicago Sunday Tribune,* Aug. 11, 1912, section 2, p. 7.

———. "A Son Loses Respect for His Mother the Day He Votes." *Chicago Sunday Tribune,* June 2, 1912, section 3, p. 1.

———. "We Have Gone Back to the Worship of the Golden Calf." *Chicago Sunday Tribune,* Sept. 29, 1912, section 8, p. 1

———. "We Have to Take What We Can in the Company It Comes." *Chicago Sunday Tribune,* Sept. 22, 1912, section 8, p. 1.

———. "We Must Not Be Made the Laughing Stock of the Voters." *Chicago Sunday Tribune,* Oct. 27, 1912, section 8, p. 5.

———. "We Read Signposts along the Road that Leads to Votes for Women." *Chicago Sunday Tribune,* Sept. 8, 1912, section 8, p. 1.

———. "What the Woman's Party Wants." *Colliers* 70 (Dec. 23, 1922): p. 6.

———. "Why I Am a Suffragist." *World To-Day* 21 (Oct. 1911): 1173–74.

———. "Why Women Need the Ballot." *Chicago Sunday Tribune,* May 12, 1912, Section 3, p. 1.

———. "Woman Suffrage As It Looks To-day." *Forum,* 43 (March 1910): 264–68.

———. "Woman's Right to Govern Herself." *North American Review* 190 (Nov. 1909): 664–74.

———. "Woman's Suffrage Raises the Quality of the Electorate." *Chicago Sunday Tribune,* June 30, 1912, section 3, p. 1.

———. "Women as Dictators." *Ladies Home Journal* 39 (Sept. 1922): 7.

———. "Women Suffragists Ask for Progressive Constitution." *Chicago Sunday Tribune* July 7, 1912, section 3, p. 1.

Benstock, Shari, ed. *The Private Self: Theory and Practice of Women's Autobiographical Writings.* Chapel Hill: University of North Carolina Press, 1988.

Berger, Meyer. *The Story of the* New York Times, *1851–1951.* New York: Simon & Schuster, 1951.

Billson, Marcus. "The Memoir: New Perspectives on a Forgotten Genre." *Genre* 10 (1977): 359–82.

Bjelopera, Jerome P. *City of Clerks: Office and Sales Workers in Philadelphia, 1870–1920.* Urbana: University of Illinois Press, 2005.

Black, David. *The King of Fifth Avenue: The Fortunes of August Belmont.* New York: Dial, 1981.

Boorstin, Daniel J. "From Hero to Celebrity: The Human Pseudo-Event." In *The Image: A Guide to Pseudo-Events in America,* 45–76. New York: Harper and Row, 1961.

Bordin, Ruth. *Alice Freeman Palmer: The Evolution of a New Woman.* Ann Arbor: University of Michigan Press, 1993.

Bosch, Mineke, with Annemarie Kloosterman. *Politics and Friendship: Letters from the International Woman Suffrage Alliance, 1902–1942.* Columbus: Ohio State University Press, 1985.

Brandon, Ruth. *The Dollar Princesses: Sagas of Upward Mobility, 1870–1914.* New York: Alfred A. Knopf, 1980.

Braudy, Leo. *The Frenzy of Renown: Fame and Its History.* New York: Oxford University Press, 1986.

Bredbenner, Candice Lewis. *A Nationality of Her Own: Women, Marriage, and the Law of Citizenship.* Berkeley: University of California Press, 1998.

Brodie, Fawn. *No Man Knows My History: The Life of Joseph Smith, the Mormon Prophet.* New York: Knopf, 1946.

Brodzki, Bella, and Celeste Schenck, eds. *Life/Lines: Theorizing Women's Autobiography.* Ithaca, N.Y.: Cornell University Press, 1988.

Buell, Janet W. "Alva Belmont: From Socialite to Feminist." *Historian* 52 (1990): 219–41.

Burgess, Charles O. *Nettie Fowler McCormick: Profile of an American Philanthropist.* Madison: State Historical Society of Wisconsin, 1962.

Burrows, Edwin G., and Mike Wallace. *Gotham: A History of New York City to 1898.* New York: Oxford University Press, 1999.

Butler, Amy E. *Two Paths to Equality: Alice Paul and Ethel M. Smith in the ERA Debate, 1921–1929*. Albany: State University of New York Press, 2000.

Chervigny, Bell Gale, "Daughters Writing: Toward a Theory of Women's Biography." *Feminist Studies* 9 (1983): 79–102.

[Collins, Arthur]. *Collins's Peerage of England; Genealogical, Biographical, and Historical*. 9 vols., London: F. C. and J. Rivington et al., 1812.

Cott, Nancy F. "Feminist Politics in the 1920s: The National Woman's Party." *Journal of American History* 71 (1984): 43–68.

———. *The Grounding of Modern Feminism*. New Haven, Conn.: Yale University Press, 1987.

———. "Marriage and Women's Citizenship in the United States, 1830–1934." *American Historical Review* 103 (1998): 1440–74.

———, ed. *A Woman Making History: Mary Ritter Beard through Her Letters*. New Haven, Conn., Yale University Press, 1991.

Couser, G. Thomas. *Altered Egos: Authority in American Autobiography*. New York: Oxford University Press, 1989.

Crocker, Ruth. *Mrs. Russell Sage: Women's Activism and Philanthropy in Gilded Age and Progressive Era America*. Bloomington: Indiana University Press, 2006.

Culley, Margo, ed. *American Women's Autobiography: Fea(s)ts of Memory*. Madison: University of Wisconsin Press, 1992.

Davies, Margery W. *Woman's Place Is at the Typewriter: Office Work and Office Workers, 1870–1930*. Philadelphia: Temple University Press, 1982.

Davis, Flora. *Moving the Mountain: The Women's Movement in America since 1960*. New York: Touchstone, 1991.

DeLeon, T. C. *Belles, Beaux and Brains of the 60s*. New York: G. W. Dillingham, 1909.

DeVault, Ileen A. *Sons and Daughters of Labor: Class and Clerical Work in Turn-of-the-Century Pittsburgh*. Ithaca, N.Y.: Cornell University Press, 1990.

Dubois, Ellen Carol. *Harriot Stanton Blatch and the Winning of Woman Suffrage*. New Haven, Conn.: Yale University Press, 1997.

Dudden, Faye E. *Serving Women: Household Service in Nineteenth-Century America*. Middletown, Conn.: Wesleyan University Press, 1983.

Eakin, Paul John. *Fictions in Autobiography: Studies in the Art of Self-Invention*. Princeton, N.J.: Princeton University Press, 1985.

Eoff, Shirley M. *Viscountess Rhondda: Equalitarian Feminist*. Columbus: Ohio State University Press, 1991.

Fairfax, Beatrice (Marie Manning). *Ladies Now and Then*. New York: E. P. Dutton, 1944.

Fehrenbacker, Don Edward. *The Dred Scott Case: Its Significance in American Law and Politics*. New York: Oxford University Press, 1978.

Fields, Armond. *Katharine Dexter McCormick: Pioneer for Women's Rights*. Westport, Conn.: Praeger, 2003.

Finnegan, Margaret. *Selling Suffrage: Consumer Culture and Votes for Women.* New York: Columbia University Press, 1999.

Flexner, Eleanor. *Century of Struggle: The Woman's Rights Movement in the United States.* New York: Atheneum, 1972.

Foner, Philip S. *Women and the American Labor Movement.* New York: Free Press, 1979.

Ford, Linda G. *Iron-Jawed Angels: The Suffrage Militancy of the National Woman's Party, 1912–1919.* Lanham, Md.: University Press of America, 1991.

Friedl, Bettina, ed. *On To Victory: Propaganda Plays of the Woman Suffrage Movement.* Boston: Northeastern University Press, 1987.

Fuller, Hiram. *Belle Brittan on a Tour, at Newport, and Here and There.* New York: Derby and Jackson, 1858.

Fuller, Paul E. *Laura Clay and the Woman's Rights Movement.* Lexington: University of Kentucky Press, 1975.

Gamson, Joshua. *Claims to Fame: Celebrity in Contemporary America.* Berkeley: University of California Press, 1994.

Gerard, Jessica. "Lady Bountiful: Women of the Landed Classes and Rural Philanthropy." *Victorian Studies* 30 (1987): 183–210.

Gilman, Charlotte Perkins. *The Living of Charlotte Perkins Gilman: An Autobiography.* Madison: University of Wisconsin Press, 1990.

Gilmore, Inez Hayes [Irwin]. *The Story of Alice Paul and the National Woman's Party.* Fairfax, Va.: Denlinger's, 1977.

Ginzberg, Lori D. *Untidy Origins: A Story of Woman's Rights in Antebellum New York.* Chapel Hill: University of North Carolina Press, 2005.

Glenn, Susan A. *Female Spectacle: The Theatrical Roots of Modern Feminism.* Cambridge, Mass.: Harvard University Press, 2000.

Gould, Joan. *Spinning Straw into Gold: What Fairy Tales Reveal about the Transformations in a Woman's Life.* New York: Random House, 2005.

Harper, Ida Husted, ed. *The History of Woman Suffrage.* Vols. 5–6. New York: National American Woman Suffrage Association, 1922.

Harries, Elizabeth Wanning. "The Mirror Broken: Women's Autobiography and Fairy Tales." In *Fairy Tales and Feminism: New Approaches.* Edited by Donald Haase, 99–111. Detroit, Mich.: Wayne State University Press, 2004.

Harris, Neil. *Humbug: The Art of P. T. Barnum.* Boston: Little, Brown, [1973].

Hartmann, Susan M. *From Margin to Mainstream: American Women and Politics since 1960.* New York: Knopf, 1989.

Hoffert, Sylvia D. "Private Secretaries in Early Twentieth-Century America." *Labor: Studies in Working Class History in the Americas* 7 (2010): 45–65.

———. *When Hens Crow: The Woman's Rights Movement in Antebellum America.* Bloomington: Indiana University Press, 1995.

Homberger, Eric. *Mrs. Astor's New York: Money and Power in a Gilded Age.* New Haven, Conn.: Yale University Press, 2002.

Hoyt, Edwin Palmer. *The Vanderbilts and Their Fortunes.* London: Frederick Muller, 1926.

Hughes, Kathryn. *The Victorian Governess.* London: Hambledon Press, 1993.

Hunter, Jane H. *How Young Ladies Became Girls: The Victorian Origins of American Girlhood.* New Haven, Conn.: Yale University Press, 2002.

Jelinek, Estelle C. *The Tradition of Women's Autobiography: From Antiquity to the Present.* Boston: Twayne, 1986.

———, ed. *Women's Autobiography: Essays in Criticism.* Bloomington: Indiana University Press, 1980.

Jensen, Kimberly. *Mobilizing Minerva: American Women in the First World War.* Urbana: University of Illinois Press, 2008.

Juergens, George. *Joseph Pulitzer and the* New York World. Princeton, N.J.: Princeton University Press, 1966.

Kasson, Joy S. *Buffalo Bill's Wild West: Celebrity, Memory, and Popular History.* New York: Hill and Wang, 2000.

Katz, Irving. *August Belmont: A Political Biography.* New York: Columbia University Press, 1968.

Katzman, David M. *Seven Days a Week: Women and Domestic Service in Industrializing America.* New York: Oxford University Press, 1978.

Keeler, Rebecca T. "Alva Belmont: Exacting Benefactor for Women's Suffrage." *Alabama Review* 41 (1988): 132–45.

Kendall, Paul Murray. *The Art of Biography.* New York: W. W. Norton, 1965.

Kerber, Linda K. "The Stateless as the Citizen's Other: A View from the United States." *American Historical Review* 112 (2007): 1–34.

Kirkby Diane. *Alice Henry: The Power of Pen and Voice: The Life of an Australian-American Labor Reformer.* New York: Cambridge University Press, 1991.

Kraditor, Aileen. *The Ideas of the Woman Suffrage Movement.* Garden City, N.Y.: Anchor Books, 1971.

Kristof, Nicholas D., and Sheryl WuDunn. "The Women's Crusade." *New York Times Magazine,* Aug. 23, 2009, 29–39

Kroepel, Gail L. "Nettie Fowler McCormick: Her Philanthropy at Tusculum College." *American Educational History Journal* 30 (2003): 125–33.

Lears, Jackson. "The Managerial Revitalization of the Rich." In *Ruling America: A History of Wealth and Power in a Democracy.* Edited by Steve Fraser and Gary Gerstle, 181–214. Cambridge, Mass.: Harvard University Press, 2005.

Leary, Lewis Gaston. *The Book-Peddling Parson.* Chapel Hill: Algonquin Books, 1984.

Leff, Leonard J. *Hemingway and His Conspirators: Hollywood, Scribners and the Making of American Celebrity Culture.* Lantham, Md.: Rowman & Littlefield, 1997.

Lejeune, Philippe. *On Autobiography.* Edited by Paul John Eakin. Translated by Katherine Leary. Minneapolis: University of Minnesota Press, 1989.

Lemons, J. Stanley. *The Woman Citizen: Social Feminism in the 1920s.* Urbana: University of Illinois Press, 1973.

Lepore, Jill, "Historians Who Love Too Much: Reflections on Microhistory and Biography. *Journal of American History* 88 (2001): 129–44.

Leslie, Anita. *Lady Randolph Churchill: The Story of Jennie Jerome.* New York: Charles Scribner's, 1969.

Liddington, Jill, and Jill Norris. *One Hand Tied behind Us: The Rise of the Women's Suffrage Movement.* London: Rivers Oram Press, 2000.

Lubetkin, M. John. *Jay Cooke's Gamble: The Northern Pacific Railroad, the Sioux, and the Panic of 1873.* Norman: University of Oklahoma Press, 2006.

Lumsen, Linda J. *Inez: The Life and Times of Inez Milholland.* Bloomington: Indiana University Press, 2004.

Lunardini, Christine A. *From Equal Suffrage to Equal Rights: Alice Paul and the National Woman's Party, 1910–1928.* New York: New York University Press, 1986.

MacColl, Gail, and Carol M. Wallace. *To Marry an English Lord.* New York: Workman, 1989.

MacDowell, Dorothy Kelly. *Commodore Vanderbilt and His Family: A Biographical Account of the Descendants of Cornelius and Sophia Vanderbilt.* Hendersonville, N.C.: privately printed, 1989.

Mackenzie, Midge, ed. *Shoulder to Shoulder: A Documentary.* New York: Alfred Knopf, 1975.

Malone, Dudley Field. "The Protest of Dudley Field Malone," *Suffragist,* Sept. 15, 1917, pp. 7, 9.

Marchand, C. Roland. *The American Peace Movement and Social Reform, 1898–1918.* Princeton, N.J.: Princeton University Press, 1973.

Margadant, Jo Burr. *The New Biography: Performing Femininity in Nineteenth-Century France.* Berkeley: University of California Press, 2000.

Marks, Patricia. *Bicycles, Bangs, and Bloomers: The New Woman in the Popular Press.* Lexington: University Press of Kentucky, 1990.

Marshall, P. David. *Celebrity and Power: Fame in Contemporary Culture.* Minneapolis: University of Minnesota Press, 1997.

Marshall, Thomas R. *Recollections of Thomas R. Marshall.* Indianapolis: Bobbs-Merrill, 1925.

Marszalek, John F. *The Petticoat Affair: Manners, Mutiny, and Sex in Andrew Jackson's White House.* Baton Rouge: Louisiana State University Press, 1997.

Maxwell, Elsa. *R.S.V.P.: Elsa Maxwell's Own Story.* Boston: Little, Brown, 1954.

McArthur, Judith N. *Creating the New Woman: The Rise of Southern Women's Progressive Culture in Texas, 1893–1918.* Urbana: University of Illinois Press, 1998.

McBride, Teresa. "'As the Twig Is Bent': The Victorian Nanny." In *The Victorian Family: Structure and Stresses.* Edited by Anthony S. Wohl, 44–58. New York: St. Martin's Press, 1978.

McKay, Ernest A. *The Civil War and New York City.* Syracuse, N.Y.: Syracuse University Press, 1990.

McManus, Edgar J. *History of Negro Slavery in New York.* Syracuse, N.Y.: Syracuse University Press, 1966.

Minnich, Elizabeth Kamarck. "Friendship between Women: The Act of Feminist Biography." *Feminist Studies* 11 (1985): 287–305.

Moir, Phyllis. *I Was Winston Churchill's Private Secretary.* New York: Wilfred Funk, 1941.

Moore, Sarah J. "Making a Spectacle of Suffrage: The National Woman Suffrage Pageant, 1913." *Journal of American Culture* 20 (1997): 89–103.

Monaco, James. "Celebration." In *Celebrity: The Media as Image Makers,* 3–14. New York: Dell, 1978.

Montgomery, Maureen E. *Displaying Women: Spectacles of Leisure in Edith Wharton's New York.* New York: Routledge, 1998.

———. *"Gilded Prostitution": Status, Money, and Transatlantic Marriages, 1870–1914.* London: Routledge, 1989.

Odendahl, Teresa. *Charity Begins At Home: Generosity and Self-Interest among the Philanthropic Elite.* New York: Basic, 1990.

Offen, Karen M. *European Feminisms, 1700–1950: A Political History.* Stanford, Calif.: Stanford University Press, 2000.

Olney, James, ed. *Autobiography: Essays Theoretical and Critical.* Princeton, N.J.: Princeton University Press, 1980.

Pascal, Roy. *Design and Truth in Autobiography.* Cambridge, Mass.: Harvard University Press, 1960.

Patterson, Martha H. *Beyond the Gibson Girl: Reimagining the American New Woman, 1895–1915.* Urbana: University of Illinois Press, 2005.

Payne, Elizabeth. *Reform, Labor, and Feminism: Margaret Drier Robins and the Women's Trade Union League.* Urbana: University of Illinois Press, 1988.

Personal Narrative Group [Joy Webster Barbre et al.], eds. *Interpreting Women's Lives: Feminist Theory and Personal Narrative.* Bloomington: Indiana University Press, 1989.

Peterson, Linda H. "Audience and the Autobiographer's Art: An Approach to the Autobiography of Mrs. M. O. W. Oliphant." In *Approaches to Victorian Autobiography.* Edited by George P. Landow, 158–74. Athens: Ohio University Press, 1979.

Peterson, M. Jeanne. "The Victorian Governess: Status Incongruence in Family and Society." *Victorian Studies* 14 (1970): 7–26.

Pfeffer, Paula F. "'A Whisper in the Assembly of Nations': United States Participation in the International Movement for Women's Rights from the League of Nations to the United Nations," *Women's Studies International Forum* 8 (1985): 459–71.

Pinker, Steven. "My Genome, My Self." *New York Times Magazine,* Jan. 11, 2009, 24–31, 46, 50.

Ponce de Leon, Charles L. *Self-Exposure: Human Interest Journalism and the Emergence of Celebrity in America, 1890–1940.* Chapel Hill: University of North Carolina Press, 2002.

Poovey, Mary. "The Anathematized Race: The Governess and Jane Eyre." In *Uneven Developments: The Ideological Work of Gender in Mid-Victorian England,* 126–163. Chicago: University of Chicago Press, 1988.

Pugh Martin. *The March of the Women: A Revisionist Analysis of the Campaign for Women's Suffrage, 1866–1914.* New York: Oxford University Press, 2000.

Rector, Margaret Hayden. *Alva: That Vanderbilt-Belmont Woman: Her Story as She Might Have Told It.* N.p.: Dutch Island Press, 1992.

Renehan, Edward J., Jr. *Commodore: The Life of Cornelius Vanderbilt.* New York: Basic, 2007.

Riley, Glenda. "Sara Bard Field, Charles Erskine Scott Wood, and the Phenomenon of Migratory Divorce." *California History* 69 (1990): 251–59.

Rogin, Michael Paul. *Fathers and Children: Andrew Jackson and the Subjugation of the American Indian.* New York: Vintage, 1975.

Rollins, Judith. *Between Women: Domestics and Their Employers.* Philadelphia: Temple University Press, 1985.

Rosen, Andrew. *Rise Up Women! The Militant Campaign of the Women's Social and Political Union, 1903–1914.* London: Routledge & Kegan Paul, 1974.

Rosenzweig, Linda W. *The Anchor of My Life: Middle-American Mothers and Daughters, 1880–1920.* New York: New York University Press, 1993.

Ross, Ishbel. *Ladies of the Press.* New York: Arno Press, 1974. Originally published 1936.

Rudnick, Lois Palken. *Mabel Dodge Luhan: New Woman, New Worlds.* Albuquerque: University of New Mexico Press, 1984.

Rupp, Leila J. "Constructing Internationalism: The Case of Transnational Women's Organizations, 1888–1945, *American Historical Review* 99 (1994): 1571–1600.

———. "Feminism and the Sexual Revolution in the Early Twentieth Century: The Case of Doris Stevens." *Feminist Studies* 15 (1989): 289–309.

Ryan, Mary P. *Mysteries of Sex: Tracing Women and Men through American History.* Chapel Hill: University of North Carolina Press, 2006.

Sandage, Scott A. *Born Losers: A History of Failure in America.* Cambridge, Mass.: Harvard University Press, 2005.

Sander, Kathleen Waters. *Mary Elizabeth Garrett: Society and Philanthropy in the Gilded Age.* Baltimore, Md.: Johns Hopkins University Press, 2008.

Sapiro, Virginia. "Women, Citizenship, and Nationality: Immigration and Naturalization Policies in the United States." *Politics and Society* 13 (1984): 1–26.

Schickel, Richard. *Intimate Strangers: The Culture of Celebrity.* Garden City, N.Y.: Doubleday, 1985.

Schneiderman, Rose, with Lucy Goldthwaite. *All for One.* New York: Paul S. Eriksson, 1967.

Seward, Desmond. *Eugenie: The Empress and Her Empire.* Stroud, Gloucestershire: Sutton, 2004.

Shanley, Mary Lyndon. *Feminism, Marriage, and the Law in Victorian England, 1850–1895.* Princeton, N.J.: Princeton University Press, 1989.

Sledge, John. "Alva Smith Vanderbilt Belmont: Alabama's 'Bengal Tiger.'" *Alabama Heritage* 44 (1997): 6–17

Smith, Sidonie. *A Poetics of Women's Autobiography: Marginality and the Fictions of Self-Representation.* Bloomington, Indiana University Press, 1987.

Smith, Sidonie, and Julia Watson, eds. *De/Colonizing the Subject: The Politics of Gender in Women's Autobiography.* Minneapolis: University of Minnesota Press, 1992.

Smith-Rosenberg, Carroll. "The New Woman as Androgyne: Social Disorder and Gender Crisis, 1870–1936." In *Disorderly Conduct: Visions of Gender in Victorian America*, 245–96. New York: Oxford University Press, 1985.

Sochen, June. *The New Woman: Feminism in Greenwich Village, 1910–1920.* New York: Quadrangle Books, 1972.

Spinzia, Raymond E. "In Her Wake: The Story of Alva Smith Vanderbilt Belmont." *Long Island Historical Journal* 6 (1993): 96–105.

Stanton, Elizabeth Cady. *Eighty Years and More (1815–1897): Reminiscences of Elizabeth Cady Stanton.* London: T. Fisher Unwin, 1898.

Stern, Madeleine B. *Purple Passage: The Life of Mrs. Frank Leslie.* Norman: University of Oklahoma Press, 1953.

Stevens, Doris. *Jailed For Freedom.* New York: Boni & Liveright, 1920.

———. *Tribute to Alva Belmont: Late President of the National Woman's Party.* Washington, D.C.: Inter American Commission of Women, [1933].

Strom, Sharon Hartman. *Beyond the Typewriter: Gender, Class, and the Origins of Modern Office Work, 1900–1930.* Urbana: University of Illinois Press, 1992.

Stuart, Amanda Mackenzie. *Consuelo and Alva Vanderbilt: The Story of a Daughter and a Mother in the Gilded Age.* New York: HarperCollins, 2005.

Summerfield, Penny. "Dis/composing the Subject: Intersubjectivities in Oral History." In *Feminism and Autobiography: Texts, Theories, Methods.* Edited by Tess Cosslett, Celia Lury, and Penny Summerfield, 91–106. London: Routledge, 2000.

Susman, Warren. "Personality and the Making of Twentieth-Century Culture." In *Culture as History: The Transformation of American Society in the Twentieth Century,* 271–85. New York: Pantheon, 1984.

Tax, Meredith. *The Rising of the Women: Feminist Solidarity and Class Conflict, 1880–1917.* New York: Monthly Review Press, 1980.

Tetrault, Lisa. "The Incorporation of American Feminism: Suffragists and the Postbellum Lyceum." *Journal of American History* 96 (2010): 1027–1056.

Theriot, Nancy M. *Mothers and Daughters in Nineteenth-Century America: The Biosocial Construction of Femininity.* Lexington: University of Kentucky Press, 1996.

Trigg, Mary. "'To Work Together for Ends Larger than Self': The Feminist Struggles of Mary Beard and Doris Stevens in the 1930s." *Journal of Women's History* 7 (1995): 52–85.

Wallach, Jennifer Jensen. *"Closer to the Truth Than Any Fact": Memoir, Memory, and Jim Crow.* Athens: University of Georgia Press, 2008.

Walther, Luann. "The Invention of Childhood in Victorian Autobiography." In *Approaches to Victorian Autobiography.* Edited by George P. Landow, 64–83. Athens: Ohio University Press, 1979.

Waltz, Waldo Emerson. *The Nationality of Married Women: A Study of Domestic Policies and International Legislation.* Urbana: University of Illinois Press, 1937.

Ware, Susan, ed. *Notable American Women: A Biographical Dictionary Completing the Twentieth Century.* Cambridge, Mass.: Harvard University Press, 2004.

Wellman, Judith. *The Road to Seneca Falls: Elizabeth Cady Stanton and the First Woman's Rights Convention.* Urbana: University of Illinois Press, 2004.

White, Shane. *Somewhat More Independent: The End of Slavery in New York City, 1770–1810.* Athens: University of Georgia Press, 1991.

Woloch, Nancy. *Women and the American Experience,* 4th ed. New York: McGraw-Hill, 2006.

Zinsser, William, ed. *Inventing the Truth: The Art and Craft of Memoir.* Boston: Houghton, Mifflin, 1987.

### THESES AND DISSERTATIONS

Cappelluti, Kris Ann. "The Confines of Class: Alva Belmont and the Politics of Woman Suffrage." MA thesis, Sarah Lawrence College, 1995.

Fastenau, Maureen. "Alva Vanderbilt Belmont: Social Arbiter and Militant Feminist." MA thesis, San Jose State University, 1976.

Geidel, Peter. "Alva E. Belmont: A Forgotten Feminist." PhD diss., Columbia University, 1993.

Jaime, Ann H. "Alva Smith Vanderbilt Belmont: Radical Socialite Suffragist." MA thesis, Sonoma State University, 2002.

Keeler, Rebecca T. "Alva Belmont: Exacting Benefactor for Women's Rights." MA thesis, University of South Alabama, 1987.

### INTERNET SOURCES

*Biographical Dictionary of the United States Congress.* http://bioguide.congress.gov (accessed Sept. 18, 2009).

Genealogical information. www.familysearch.org (accessed Aug. 23, 2008).

Inflation calculations. http://westegg.com/inflation (accessed Aug. 27, 2009–Sept. 30, 2010).

Sklar, Kathryn Kish, Thomas Dublin, and Diedre Doherty. "How Did the Perceived Threat of Socialism Shape the Relationship between Workers and Their Allies in the New York City Shirtwaist Strike, 1909–1910?" In *Women and Social Movements in the United States, 1600–2000.* Edited by Kathryn Kish Sklar and Thomas Dublin. Database accessed through Evans Library, Texas A&M University (accessed Feb. 12, 2008).

Suffragist Interviews in the Regional Oral History Office, Bancroft Library, University of California—Berkeley, Berkeley, Calif. http://bancroft.berkeley.edu/ROHO/projects/suffragist/ (accessed April 24, 2008).

Amelia R. Fry. "Sara Bard Field: Poet and Suffragist: An Interview."

Amelia R. Fry. "Conversations with Alice Paul: Woman Suffrage and the Equal Rights Amendment."

Amelia R. Fry. "Speaker for Suffrage and Petitioner for Peace: An Interview by Amelia Fry."

# INDEX

SYLVIA D. HOFFERT is Professor Emerita of Women's History at Texas A&M University and author of *Private Matters: American Attitudes toward Childbearing and Infant Nurture in the Urban North, 1800–1860* (1989); *When Hens Crow: The Woman's Rights Movement in Antebellum America* (IUP, 1995); *A History of Gender in America* (2003); and *Jane Grey Swisshelm: An Unconventional Life* (2004). She has also published articles in the *Journal of Women's History, Labor,* the *Western Historical Quarterly, Frontiers, Journalism Quarterly,* and the *American Quarterly.*